JOHN DEWEY

and the Challenge of Classroom Practice

PRACTITIONER
INQUIRY
SERIES

Stephen M. Fishman
Lucille McCarthy

John Dewey and the Challenge of
Classroom Practice
STEPHEN M. FISHMAN & LUCILLE MCCARTHY

"Sometimes I Can Be Anything":
Power, Gender, and Identity
in a Primary Classroom
KAREN GALLAS

Learning in Small Moments:
Life in an Urban Classroom
DANIEL R. MEIER

Interpreting Teacher Practice:
Two Continuing Stories
RENATE SCHULZ

Creating Democratic Classrooms:
The Struggle to Integrate Theory and Practice
LANDON E. BEYER, EDITOR

Joeth Margulies.

JOHN DEWEY

and the Challenge
of Classroom Practice

❖

Stephen M. Fishman
Lucille McCarthy

Teachers College
Columbia University
New York & London

National Council of
Teachers of English
Urbana, Illinois

Published by Teachers College Press, 1234 Amsterdam Avenue, New York, NY 10027

Frontispiece and cover: Watercolor portrait of John Dewey by Joseph Margulies, reprinted by permission from the John Dewey Papers, Special Collections/Morris Library, Southern Illinois University at Carbondale.

Library of Congress Catalog-in-Publication Data

Fishman, Stephen M.
    John Dewey and the challenge of classroom practice / Stephen M. Fishman,
Lucille McCarthy.
        p. cm. — (the practitioner inquiry series)
    Includes bibliographical references and index.
    ISBN 0-8077-3727-5 (cloth : alk. paper). — ISBN 0-8077-3726-7 (pbk. : alk. paper)
    1. Dewey, John, 1859-1952. 2. Education—Philosophy. 3. Teaching.
    4. Education—Experimental methods.   I. McCarthy, Lucille Parkinson, 1944–.
    II. Title.   III. Series.
    LB875.D5F57 1998
    370'.1—dc21   98-5308

ISBN 0-8077-3727-5 (cloth)
ISBN 0-8077-3726-7 (paper)
NCTE Stock Number 25093

Printed on acid-free paper
Manufactured in the United States of America

05 04 03 02 01 00 99 98   8 7 6 5 4 3 2 1

for the children

✦

THE BEST WAY OF HONORING DEWEY is to work on Dewey's problems—to reconstruct his insights, to see, if need be, farther than Dewey saw. If it may be given to us to see farther, it will be largely because he pointed out to us where to look. In that way, you and I can be really working with Dewey, as he always wanted us to do, and sharing in that enjoyed meaning that was, and is, and will continue to be John Dewey.

— JOHN HERMAN RANDALL, JR., "JOHN DEWEY, 1859–1952" 1953: 13

Part Two
DEWEYAN CLASSROOM EXPERIMENTS

CONTENTS

THE GAP BETWEEN EDUCATIONAL THEORY and its execution in practice is always so wide that there naturally arises a doubt as to the value of any separate presentation of purely theoretical principles.

— JOHN DEWEY,
"The Theory of the Chicago Experiment" 1936: 463

INTRODUCTION

✦

WHY CARE ABOUT DEWEY NOW? *Steve Fishman*

Since the publication in 1983 of *A Nation at Risk*, by the National Commission on Excellence in Education, there has been an ongoing debate about the level of scholastic achievement in America's schools. Although the spectrum of commentators ranges from those who claim that the education system is a total failure to those who say it is one of the bright spots in our democracy, all would agree that our country's 3.1 million teachers are under greater scrutiny than ever before. In fact, current concern about quality instruction is so great that it has spread to include educational institutions previously immune to outside examination, namely, our nation's colleges and universities. Although research and publication remain the dominant criteria for college faculty retention, legislators and trustees, as well as the larger constituencies universities serve, have recently become insistent that even professors attend more carefully to their teaching. (For reviews of the debate about our nation's schools, see Berliner and Biddle; Davis; Stedman.)

Given this situation, the present study—an examination of Dewey's philosophy of education in the context of college teaching—is especially timely. This is because Dewey addresses two core questions currently facing all classroom practitioners. First, what is the proper ratio of student relevance to academic rigor in various school situations? And, second, having decided the proper student-curriculum ratio, what are the best means for achieving it?

Although Dewey's answers to these questions continue to generate controversy, his educational theory, nevertheless, merits our attention. I say this because of the broad philosophic foundations of his work. In other words, we should see Dewey's work not as a source of concrete teaching strategies, but as a set of lenses through which to view our classes. When we look to Dewey, we learn how our ideas about the student-curriculum relationship are rooted in our assumptions about experience, knowledge, and habits of good living. Thus, as we experiment with Dewey's educational ideas, their substantial theoretical footing allows us to make more considered decisions in the "laboratory" of our classrooms.

Dewey's recognition that teachers have to apply educational theories in their own ways leads him, happily, to supply us with principles rather than specific recommendations for resolving classroom difficulties. Although he held high hopes that his approach would promote a "New Education" in America, he viewed his work at the University of Chicago Laboratory School as merely demonstrating the "feasibility" of the "new movement" rather than providing procedures which could be "copied" for use elsewhere (*School* 7–8, 94; see also "Sources" 8).

Dewey's belief that there are various ways to put his educational theory into practice may seem frustrating initially, but the effect in the long run is to make us active inquirers into our teaching. And I take this as a positive result, for I agree with Dewey that techniques and attitudes cannot be adopted wholesale, without shaping by local context. In Dewey's words, they cannot be "hammered in" or "plastered on" (*Democracy* 11; "How the Mind" 216). Rather, if we are to advance our instructional effectiveness, we must struggle to our own resolutions. We must examine our pedagogical problems and be truly puzzled by them, with all the risks accompanying such perplexity. To study Dewey at the current time is helpful, therefore, not only because he addresses important contemporary pedagogical questions and offers theoretically well-founded answers, but also because he invites us to become students of our own teaching.

WHY THIS BOOK NOW?

Although there are many excellent volumes about John Dewey—several reflecting the current revival of Dewey scholarship—they tend, in the main, to be theoretical. These include the extensive historical accounts of Dewey's work (Rockefeller; Ryan; Westbrook), the outstanding philosophic ones (Bernstein; Hook, *Intellectual*; Rorty; Schilpp; Sleeper), the critical ones

(Hofstadter; Hutchins; Lasch; Mills; Mumford; Novack), as well as those focusing primarily on education (Frankena, *Historical*; Scheffler; Wirth). Although practical studies of Deweyan theory in actual classrooms were being done through the 1930s (e.g., De Lima; Mayhew and Edwards; Rugg and Shumaker), few have appeared since then.

Applying Deweyan Principles in a Core Curriculum, Regional State University Classroom

It is this lack of classroom-based studies in present Dewey scholarship that my coresearcher and I attempt to remedy. That is, our own work seeks to generate and study the concrete applications without which, Dewey says, philosophy remains "artificial" and mere "intellectual exercise" (*Democracy* 328). In particular, we explicate Deweyan theory by applying it to particular practice, our discussion of his educational philosophy never getting far from concrete school situations. Another way of distinguishing our work is to say it is integrated, generating what Dewey would have called an "art of educational engineering" ("Education As Engineering" 325). Lucille McCarthy and I apply Deweyan educational philosophy to my classroom, diagnose pedagogical problems, "engineer" changes in my strategies, and carry out a naturalistic study of these changes' effects. In this way, Dewey theory and practice intersect, allowing for an unusual illumination of both.

In bridging this gap between Dewey's educational philosophy and classroom practice, we intend to counteract criticisms of Deweyan pedagogy which have surfaced repeatedly since the founding of his Laboratory School 100 years ago. A persistent complaint has been that Deweyan pedagogy is too expensive and difficult to permit widespread application (Greene 83; Jackson xxvii–xxxiv; McCaul 70–71; Peters; Sarason 26–27; Wirth 71). In fact, one critic in the 1970s claimed there were not enough qualified students and teachers in the entire country to support a single Deweyan school (Perkinson 215). Undergirding these continuing criticisms is the assumption that Dewey intended the Laboratory School as a paradigm of rules and procedures for the new progressive education. However, for the most part, Dewey viewed his experimental school in quite a different light. He saw it functioning for his department of education in the same way that laboratories function for departments of physics and chemistry—promoting habits of theory-informed observation, invention, and judgment rather than a set of fixed answers to particular problems. Nevertheless, despite his claims that what teachers most need are intellectual tools for developing their own classroom techniques ("Sources" 14–15), the Lab School has frequently been seen as a utopian model of fixed pedagogical practices.

To be fair to Dewey's critics, his own ambiguities about the school may be partially responsible for their misconceptions. Although he repeatedly said he did not want the school's methods and materials to be "slavishly copied," at times he sounded more zealous than experimental, as if he hoped the school would produce missionaries, who, armed with progressive literature, would crisscross the country spreading the new word (see "University" [1900] 319). And on occasion he himself highlighted the school's unusual student body and student-faculty ratios, telling parents he only wanted students from homes imbued with cooperative spirit and noting that pupil attention at the Lab School was secured by "small groupings of children and a large number of teachers" (Mayhew and Edwards 27, 16–17). In fact, the Lab School was highly unusual in that it was radically interdisciplinary, attempting to introduce all subject matters as they were needed to complete concrete projects (Depencier 11–14). It was also lavishly staffed and expensively equipped. It had craft shops, kitchens, photo equipment, science labs, and planting fields, and, at its height during Dewey's years (1896–1904), it boasted 23 teachers and 10 part-time assistants for just 140 students (Mayhew and Edwards 8).

Given these circumstances, it is easy to understand why visiting teachers, without reminders that the Lab School's ultimate purpose was to promote enhanced instructor experimentation, observation, and judgment, would conclude, "This will never work back home" (see *School* 93; "University" [1900] 318). In addition, Dewey's efforts in later years to distance himself from other progressive educators may have helped exaggerate the difficulty of applying his theory in average classrooms. It certainly was not encouraging for potential experimenters to hear him say, in a 1930s lecture at the University of Vermont, that "no schools are currently employing instructional methods I can endorse" (Williams 26–27).

Of course, the failure of Dewey and other progressive educators to transform America's schools cannot be blamed solely on misinterpretations of the Lab School's significance. Some historians fault the bureaucracies of local school systems and the development of education "specialists," people making curriculum decisions with only a limited understanding of subject matter (Bestor 44). Dewey himself, in his last writing on education, claimed that authoritarianism was still widely prevalent in education, especially in the secondary schools and universities, and he accused the nation's teachers colleges of embracing his theories but giving them only lip service ("Introduction" 132). In particular, education professors, according to Dewey, continued to teach their own courses in the same old lecture style, presenting progressive education to their students as a "kit of tools," as "certain collections of fixed, immutable subject matter which they in turn are to transmit to the students under them" (133). And, finally, some theorists spotlight more general factors—the cold war climate of conservatism after World War II, post-Sputnik demands for upgraded science curricula, and the continuing sexist, racist, class-conscious nature of American culture—as reasons for our society's failure to embrace the radically democratic vision at the heart of Dewey's approach (see Zilversmit ch. 9).

Although I grant that many of these impediments to large-scale adoption of Dewey's approach are still in place, our study implements his notion that school reform rests upon practitioners capable of experimentation and change. In this light, our own work is very much a *feasibility* study, to borrow Dewey's term, an invitation, not to widespread, sudden revolution, but to patient classroom experimentation and the formation of communities of like-minded teacher-researchers. In other words, at a difficult time for American schools, we urge teachers to give Dewey another chance. That is, we believe that key Deweyan concepts can be experimented with in individual classrooms without schoolwide shifts to interdisciplinary programs, non-graded student groups, or open classrooms. In this way, individual teachers can contribute to the work of educational reform, work Dewey characterizes as "slow," "one step at a time," and "piecemeal" (*Democracy* 137).

To fill out for our readers the picture of such experimentation, our study goes beyond previous accounts of Deweyan classrooms which offer only teacher stories and descriptions of class routines (see Mayhew and Edwards; Rugg and Shumaker). By contrast, we present extensive evidence from student "informants," pupils whose perspectives we use to augment and crosscheck those of the teacher and outside observer. Furthermore, we outline our research methods in some detail and offer an intimate picture of a teacher doing the kind of observing, questioning, and judging for which Dewey argues. As a result, we believe our study can be helpful to teachers at all levels who want to conduct similar inquiries in their own classrooms.

In sum, an important goal of this volume—completed during the centennial year of the Laboratory School's opening—is to show that, contrary to the criticisms I have mentioned, Deweyan theory can be fruitfully applied in ordinary school situations. In particular, our study focuses on Deweyan experiments in my own Introduction to Philosophy course, a core curriculum offering at a regional branch of a state university where entering freshman SAT scores for 1995 averaged 931 and classrooms do not have advantageous pupil-staff ratios. In other words, we look upon our task as countering arguments that Dewey's theories are too impractical, demand wide-scale acceptance of fixed school procedures and goals, or require a broad change in American values.

Although we show that applying Deweyan theory in an ordinary school situation is possible, we also acknowledge that the task we undertake is not easy. First, Dewey presents his educational philosophy in such vague terms that it takes considerable effort to feel that one has captured the spirit of his work. In fact, Dewey's writing is elusive enough for pedagogists from sharply opposed camps, stressing different aspects of his theory, to claim him as their common ancestor (see Hlebowitsh, "Critical"), and for various school observers to make radically different assessments of the degree to which Deweyan pedagogy is currently in practice (for such a contrast, see, for example, Carroll; Kliebard).

Second, having faced the problem of interpreting Dewey fairly and comprehensively, one must then do the creative work of applying, shaping, and experimenting with his educational philosophy in one's own discipline and classroom. That this work of application is also difficult is suggested by Dewey himself. Although Dewey indicates that college underclassmen in his day probably needed better-planned instruction than they were receiving (*Way*), his own students testify that Dewey's teaching, paradoxically, was very un-Deweyan. They say he employed a monologue, thinking-aloud style, avoided eye contact, and rarely asked or solicited questions (Edman; Hook, *Out*; Lamont; Larrabee; Williams). Although there are features of this style, as I explain in Chapter 1 of this volume, which do reflect Dewey's own pedagogical principles, for the most part, as his students testify, he seems to have done little to make them the active learners his theory calls for. Further, as I discuss in Chapter 5, my own experience at Columbia University as student to Dewey's pupils was that they, as teachers, had only slightly more interest or success than Dewey himself in applying his theories in their classrooms.

However, I believe the present time is a propitious one—potentially, an unusually receptive one—for fresh experiments with Dewey's ideas. For alongside new attention to teaching by state legislators and boards of trustees, the last 20 years have also seen new teacher initiatives regarding instruction. One of the most notable came on the heels of public outcries in the 1970s that "Johnny can't read or write" (see Flesch, *Can't Read*; *Still Can't Read*; Sheils). Since that time, composition specialists, for example, have increasingly focused on ways in which both mature and inexperienced writers compose. And the results of such research have shifted instructional practices, not only of composition teachers, but also—through Writing Across the Curriculum programs (Walvoord et al.) and National Writing Project institutes (Freedman; Pritchard)—of instructors in every discipline and at every level. In addition, in the past 20 years, a small but growing teacher-researcher movement has developed in Great Britain and America, one which, without always explicitly acknowledging it, echoes Dewey's views on the importance of teacher classroom research for teacher development (see Brookfield; Cochran-Smith and Lytle; Goswami and Stillman; Hubbard and Power; Mohr and MacLean; Ray; Ruddock and Hopkins).

Organization and Approach of the Present Study

Lucille McCarthy, a composition specialist, and I, a philosopher, explore Dewey's educational principles by applying them in several ways. In Chapters 1 through 6, for which I have primary responsibility, I present these principles and then use them to analyze both my own university education as well as key pedagogical changes in my 30-year teaching career. In Chapters 7 through 11, for which Lucille McCarthy has first responsibility, she reports our naturalistic study of experiments with Dewey's principles in my fall, 1995, Introduction to Philosophy class at the University of North Carolina Charlotte. She gives special attention to my students' experiences as I struggle to reconcile the conflicting and interrelated classroom demands underlying the student-curriculum dichotomy which Dewey addressed long ago: individual and group, construction and criticism, continuity and interaction, interest and effort.

In addition to the integration of theory and practice, our book offers another sort of reconciliation, one which I believe Dewey would also have applauded, namely, a bringing together of the personal and professional. Although this study is an academic one, employing methods and language from both McCarthy's and my disciplines, it is also explicitly personal, risking the consequences of private exposure in order to heed Dewey's repeated warnings against "watertight compartments" (*Experience and Education* 48; *Human* 138; *Public* 191). For we take seriously his caution that academics, under the guise of being scientific and objective, often hide the values and traditions which permeate their work. In fact, it was this call for integration which most appealed to me as a young reader of Dewey, his sense that modern life is too specialized, too episodic, its stops and starts robbing our activities of meaning and energy. For Dewey, present-day recreation and labor, art and commerce, science and politics, school and home are too marked off, too discontinuous. So, although you will certainly hear our academic voices in this book, we give significant space to our personal ones as well.

A final note from me: In my opening chapters, I explicate Dewey's educational goals and principles with reference to his ideas of experience, knowledge, and moral living. As students of Dewey know, this is not a minor challenge. He wrote extensively about education for over half a century, and, as a result, his work, although consistent, is not systematic, no one piece representing his full discussion of an issue. For Dewey's expositor, this poses the problem of keeping in mind a great deal of material from many different sources at the same time. Although I organize this large corpus by highlighting key themes, my primary strategy is to explicate Dewey's work in terms of my own experience of it. Dewey himself seems to sanction this approach when, in both *Democracy and Education* and *How We Think*, he talks about the necessity of "wholeheartedness" for discovery, the need to be so obsessed by an overarching concern that it colors all we do (*Democracy* 173; *How* 31–32). In this sense, I honor Dewey's view that discovery is not a logical, orderly process, nor primarily a cognitive one, but is, in important ways, emotional: a unifying passion bringing together previously disparate experiences to yield personal reconstruction.

As an alternative to more formal or chronological presentations of Dewey's philosophy of education, therefore, I build my discussion around especially powerful moments, those phrases and turns in his writing where I best receive and interpret him. For I must be frank, I do not want to keep my distance from him. I cannot, because learning for me is indeed "wholehearted," an affair of both heart and mind. And for all I know, it is my heart to which Dewey first appeals. For, deep down, what draws me to him is his romanticism—not the sort which sees people through rose-colored glasses, the sort with which Dewey has sometimes been charged (Hofstadter 368), nor the romanticism which overestimates personal power and independence, the overblown individualism against which Dewey himself inveighs (*Experience and Nature* 199). Rather, the Deweyan romanticism which attracts me is his abiding faith in the possibilities of democratic culture, his commitment to a society which ties science and technology to communal and egalitarian values, which ties reason and thought to feeling and imagination. It is a populist vision of the worth of ordinary people, a faith in the common person's ability to participate in the disciplines of intelligent thought, a devotion to bringing about a world in which science, art, and technology are available to all, not just to the professional, powerful, and wealthy (*Common* 26; *Reconstruction* 209).

This faith in cooperative use of intelligence—this vision of egalitarian democracy buoyed by shared scientific method—shapes both Dewey's life and words. Although the criticisms of his writing style are legion, and although references to his New England reserve abound, at crucial moments, Dewey's democratic vision becomes poetry, his words fashioning that special angle where reader and writer meet. Our hope in these chapters is to find that angle, that place where the distance between our readers and Dewey vanishes, where you come face-to-face, where you and he recognize one another.

WHY CARE ABOUT STEVE FISHMAN'S INTRODUCTION TO PHILOSOPHY CLASS? *Lucille McCarthy*

In my naturalistic study of Steve Fishman's classroom experiments, I will, as he promises, pay special attention to Deweyan themes underlying the student-curriculum dualism. Following Fishman's explication of these theoretical concepts in the early chapters of this book, I will, in Chapters 8 through 11, show how these concepts play out in his fall, 1995, classroom. Yet our readers may wonder why they should care about the specific goings-on in a college philosophy course. I offer three reasons.

First, I spotlight Fishman and his students to show that, despite claims to the contrary, Deweyan principles can be implemented in an ordinary disciplinary classroom in ways that enhance teaching and learning. Fishman's experiments with Deweyan pedagogy are his effort to deal with two broad questions we characterize as central in today's climate of increased instructional scrutiny: What is the appropriate blend in various situations of student interest and academic subject matter? And how might we best achieve such integrations? Characteristically, Dewey's answers to these questions, ones he groups under the "child-curriculum dualism" problem, remain at the theoretical level. However, he repeatedly urges teachers not to emphasize one member of the dualism to the exclusion of the other. He claims we do not have to sacrifice student interest to achieve mastery of subject matter or sugar coat subject matter to excite student interest.

Trying to follow Dewey's advice, Fishman engages in a kind of high-wire act. We watch him struggle, on the one hand, to avoid swinging too far in the direction of his undergraduates' interests, that is, finding himself (as sometimes happens) leading class discussions which resemble dormitory bull sessions. On the other hand, Steve equally fears leaning too far toward the dualism's other pole, that is, finding himself (as also sometimes happens) asking students to learn philosophic subject matter which never touches their own lives, their ongoing moral dilemmas. Fishman's Introduction to Philosophy classroom, then, shows one teacher experimenting with Deweyan theory in response to some of the most troublesome challenges for today's teachers.

A second reason Fishman's story is of interest is that, in implementing Deweyan theory, he uses reading and writing extensively, as do many teachers along the academic and professional spectrums. Fishman is not a specialist in reading or writing but a disciplinary instructor who set out to do better at teaching both. In Chapter 6, he explains that he attended a Writing Across the Curriculum (WAC) workshop in 1983, and it "changed [his] life." Since that time he has developed his own writing, publishing short stories as well as academic work, but more important, he has never stopped experimenting with writing-to-learn in his classes. Fishman offers us, then, a rare portrait of a longtime WAC convert, and, from studying his classroom, we gain insight into the uses of writing for achieving Deweyan goals. (For more information about WAC programs and their effects, see Fulwiler and Young; Walvoord et al.)

Fishman's story is of interest for a third reason as well. In addition to facing head-on the student-curriculum challenge and taking the WAC message seriously, he has worked, over the years, to reflect on his own classroom practice. In fact, Steve seems to have been possessed by a desire to find out what is happening in his classroom, to understand the nature and consequences of his interactions with students. In this regard, he has probably been atypical among disciplinary teachers. By contrast, as he explains in Chapter 6, he was typical in being ill-equipped to explore and evaluate his techniques. Thus, when Steve and I first met at a WAC workshop in 1989, he questioned me eagerly about my classroom research methods, explaining that he was using WAC techniques and liking them, but he longed to find out more about how they were actually working. We eventually agreed to collaborate and have published a number of studies of his classroom. The methods and findings of our most recent inquiry constitute Part II of this book. As a result, for teachers who, like Steve, find themselves wanting to engage in reflective practice but lacking the requisite tools, our book offers help. We outline a model of reflective teaching, one that, as I explain in Chapter 7, Dewey would have approved.

So in this book we bring together Dewey's theory and Steve Fishman's practice, offering our readers information about one teacher's method of achieving student-curriculum integration. To do this, Fishman enacts Deweyan principles that we believe are potentially useful in a wide range of settings. We also show an instructor studying his own classroom, offering, thereby, a particular model for productive teacher inquiry.

THE AUTHORS' HISTORIES WITH JOHN DEWEY
Lucille McCarthy

Although in some sense this project began when Steve Fishman and I met in 1989, its sources are actually deeper. They go back to the period in each of our lives when we first encountered John Dewey. For me, it was at the University of Chicago in 1966, when I was a 22-year-old master in teaching (MAT) candidate studying under Dewey's portrait in the library and student-teaching in the Laboratory Schools he founded. Although Dewey headed the Department of Philosophy, Psychology, and Pedagogy at Chicago between 1894 and 1904, I was only dimly aware of him during my 2 years in the MAT program, never, so far as I recall, actually reading or discussing his work. Following World War II, in departments of education, interest in Dewey's writings and proposals for social and pedagogical change had declined severely. By the time I got to Chicago in the late 1960s, the education department which Dewey founded had abandoned him for theories in which learning was more easily quantified.

So when I left the University of Chicago in 1968, headed for 15 years of high school English teaching, I carried with me little that was explicitly Dewey. But, in retrospect, I heard his melodies, faint but insistent beneath the surface. I say this because I developed at the University of Chicago a deep interest, like Dewey's, in student experience, in student struggle and change. And I was offered tools for examining these. Dewey would have smiled, I believe, as my MAT director, an untenured assistant professor named Janet Emig—now considered by many a founder of modern composition studies—shared with us her in-progress dissertation research, transcripts of students composing which laid bare their struggles, their decisions about whom to write for and how, their satisfactions and frustrations with the process.

It was under Emig's direction nearly 30 years ago that I undertook my first naturalistic inquiry into student experience. In that 1968 master's project, I studied Chicago high school youth in a summer Upward Bound program. I listened carefully to individual students and observed their transactions within that community, mimicking the approach Emig had taken with her informants. I now see that my master's thesis—with its Deweyan concerns—was the primitive ancestor of the present study in both its methods and questions. For although we did not speak explicitly of Dewey in those MAT seminars, Janet Emig, far better than I in that era, understood that around that table, we were engaged in a Deweyan sort of inquiry. Now, years later, I can appreciate Emig's meaning when she asserts in her 1979 essay, "The Tacit Tradition," that "John Dewey is everywhere in our work" (150).

Just as I encountered Dewey early in my academic work, so did Steve Fishman. It was the summer when he was 17, and, as I have heard Steve tell students more than once, it was the beginning of a 40-year love affair. "I've been tempted by others," Steve explains, lowering his head, "but I've remained faithful to John Dewey."

Students laugh, but what Fishman says is true. In the summer of 1955, he had completed his freshman year at Columbia University, and he was, as he explains in Chapter 5, completely confused. In his introductory survey courses, he had tried to understand one philosopher after another, only to go to class and watch his teachers critique them, demonstrate their errors, and move on. By June, Steve recalls, he was skeptical of everything, unclear how to behave in this enigmatic university world, uncertain even of what philosophy was. Yet this academic community attracted him, and, in his quiet way, he determined to join. His teachers had inspired his admiration with their serious quest for understanding, their self-discipline, their commitment to the study of Plato and Spinoza and Hegel. In fact, Steve recalls as a freshman gazing up at the chiseled names of these philosopher elders on the frieze of Butler Library and realizing it was a tradition he longed to claim.

So Steve, eager to get on with what he knew would be a long initiation, signed up for summer school at Harvard after his freshman year. And there he was assigned Dewey's *Reconstruction in Philosophy*. In this volume, Steve glimpsed a framework for synthesizing philosophy and, at the same time, gained some insight into his personal conflicts. In Chapter 5, Steve describes this experience, his sense that, for a moment at least, he had, as he put it to a friend, "understood something."

Steve returned to the philosophy department at Columbia in the fall of 1955 and stayed until 1967, when he finished his doctorate, but never again at Columbia did he focus on Dewey. As Steve looks back, he shakes his head at the irony, because Dewey was associated with that department for 35 years (from 1904 until 1939), and many of Steve's teachers knew Dewey, having been Dewey's students and colleagues. Yet by the time Steve was at Columbia, in the 1950s and 1960s, forces within philosophy, as within education at Chicago, had swept Dewey out of vogue. However, despite his teachers' silence about Dewey, Steve "remained faithful."

In recent years, as Steve and I have conducted research in his Introductory Philosophy classroom, we have been able more fully to excavate the depth of Dewey's influence upon us both. At its heart, then, this book is an important stage in our journey toward Dewey, our developing appreciation of his educational philosophy and its significance for the challenges of classroom practice.

Deweyan Theory and Teacher Practice

---◆---

Part One

SUCH THINGS [KNOWLEDGE, BELIEFS, IDEAS] cannot be passed physically from one to another like bricks; they cannot be shared as persons would share a pie by dividing it into physical pieces.

— JOHN DEWEY,
Democracy and Education 1916: 4

Chapter One

DEWEY'S EDUCATIONAL PHILOSOPHY: RECONCILING NESTED DUALISMS

--- ❖ ---

Steve Fishman

Dewey's written work is vast—over 50 books, approximately 750 articles, and countless addresses, reviews, and encyclopedia entries—but through it all there is a recognizable signature: his attempt to reconcile what he considers dangerous or misleading dualisms. In his most autobiographical statement, Dewey names the mutually exclusive choices he found harmful as a youngster in Burlington, Vermont—self opposed to world, soul opposed to body, nature opposed to God ("From Absolutism" 153). This distrust of either-or choices, and Dewey's attempt to integrate apparently contradictory positions, is both a continuing theme and an organizing structure of his work.

RECONCILING NESTED DUALISMS: DEWEY'S PHILOSOPHY OF PROCESS

Although many have charged that Dewey's key terms are vague and his prose style impenetrable (cf. Featherstone; Hofstadter; Mumford), the motivating force of his writing is always clear: his unrelenting effort to reconcile false dualisms. For example, whereas from many traditional perspectives the self is viewed as opposed to world, a Deweyan analysis, although acknowledging their tension, would stress ways in which self and world condition one another and are necessary for one another.

This strategy of reconciling traditionally opposed forces by showing ways in which they cooperate and interact is central to Dewey's philosophic writing. For instance, concerning morality, he strives to demonstrate the mutual dependence of individual and group (*Public*); concerning art, he explores the interplay of creativity and appreciation (*Art*); concerning day-to-day practice, he emphasizes the joint conditioning of impulse and reflection (*How*); and with regard to education, he works to integrate the interests of both student and curriculum (*Democracy*). But just as Dewey believes that members of these four dualisms are not mutually exclusive or opposed, so equally he believes morality, art, day-to-day practice, and education are not mutually exclusive either. To describe, for example, a student's problem as "educational" is, according to Dewey, to emphasize only one aspect of the situation. From other angles, he would insist, that same problem can be seen as practical, aesthetic, or moral.

This recognition of the multiple and interpenetrating aspects of an activity means, according to Dewey, that situations can be investigated from a variety of angles. For Dewey, it turns out that the best perspective for understanding education's primary challenge—the reconciliation of the student-curriculum dualism—is achieved by going beneath the surface to locate and reconcile even more fundamental classroom forces. These underlying forces actually turn out to be present in all human situations. The ones I focus on in this study are, at the first level, *individual and group*, and, at an even more basic level, *continuity and interaction, construction and criticism*, and *interest and effort*.

As Dewey presents them, the educational dualisms he works to reconcile are *nested*. In other words, as we explore student and curriculum, we find beneath each dualism concentric circles of other dualisms. And, to make matters even more complicated for Dewey's expositors, when we study these more fundamental dualisms, we find ourselves amidst mirrors reflecting infinite regress. That is, to study these more basic dualisms is to find them reflected in the very process of studying them. For example, as Lucille McCarthy and I examine my classes for signs of continuity and interaction, construction and criticism, interest and effort, our examination itself—and, indeed, our writing of this book—displays tensions and transactions between continuity and interaction, construction and criticism, interest and effort.

Thus, as we approach Dewey, we should keep in mind that he is trying to describe a world of highly interactive processes, but he must do this in an English language based on strict subject-object distinctions, on the view that everything is what it is and not another thing. He must, that is, try to describe an Einsteinian world of relativity—a postmodern, Borgesian world—in a language tooled for fixed, unchanging truth and in a philosophic genre characterized by linear, logical argumentation (for a similar interpretation of Dewey's linguistic challenge, see Hook, *Out* 90). Put differently, Dewey's task is to speak of a reality which does not conform to the so-called law of excluded middle: that things are either A or not A. It is a reality in which past and future appear to be simultaneous in the present, where means are ends and ends are means, where education is intelligent practice, and intelligent practice is moral, and the moral is aesthetic, and— like the snake swallowing its tail—the aesthetic is educational. In short, it is a reality in which familiar distinctions are transformed.

This view of the world as interacting, reconcilable dualisms, nested within more fundamental dualisms, accounts, I believe, for the unsystematic quality of Dewey's discussions, the occasional sense that we, as readers, are going in circles. Just when we think we are talking about education, it turns out we are talking politics. Talk about knowledge turns out to be talk about social classes. But what Dewey's students may lose by way of classification, they gain in breadth of analysis. At his core, Dewey is a metaphysician attempting to fashion a language of process, a way of looking at the world; that is, he offers us, not a series of truths about reality, as did much classical metaphysics, but a method, a set of categories or questions with which to probe any perplexing situation. Faced with a problem—personal or professional, practical or theoretical, in the school or marketplace—Dewey's approach leads us to ask: What are the dichotomous activities at work in our situation? How might they be better integrated and balanced? In other words, Dewey's approach helps us attend to the conflicting activities within our dilemma and to approach our problem with the goal of reconciling its underlying forces.

Dewey's View of Philosophy: A Reconciliation of Dualisms

When I was a young student, one of my early satisfactions was that I could find in all of Dewey's writings his persistent effort to see life problems in terms of reconcilable dualisms. I saw it first in *Experience and Nature*—a volume Dewey's student and 20-year Columbia University colleague, John Herman Randall, Jr., calls Dewey's "most important" work ("Religion" 253)—each chapter of which can be read as a reconciliation of apparently mutually exclusive solutions to classic philosophic dilemmas. *Experience and Nature* is Dewey's edited version of his Carus Lectures at the University of Chicago in 1925. But 6 years earlier in *Reconstruction in Philosophy*, he displays the same impulse to look at problems historically and find ways to integrate opposing points of view, offering a social and historical view of philosophy. He sees it as ameliorating moral conflicts by developing methods to clarify and contextualize these conflicts (see also *Democracy* 323–31; *Nature* 326–27; "Philosophy and Civilization"; "Philosophy and Democracy"; for changes and developments in Dewey's conception of philosophy, see Ratner).

In Dewey's view, philosophy's mediating role emerges from clashes in ancient Greece between traditional, religious knowledge and matter-of-fact, practical knowledge, between separate class groups—aristocratic and plebian—which had different relations to these two funds of information about the world. To paraphrase him, tradition and religious story pulsated with the warm glow of values for which Greeks had always lived and fought, whereas matter-of-fact, scientific knowledge was dry and impersonal, laced with the humdrum know-how of daily life (*Reconstruction* 16). Again, typically, Dewey works toward middle ground. He argues that philosophy should "enlarg[e] . . . the meanings" of both types of knowledge, and it should do this by using each to question the other (*Nature* 332). Unless tradition is tested by science, its values petrify in a changing world, and unless science is prodded by religious ideals, its inquiries can become irresponsible and overspecialized.

As will become clear in Part II of this book, Dewey's view of philosophy undergirds my own Introduction to Philosophy class. My principal goal, as I have constructed it in that course, is encouraging students to clarify and "enlarge . . . the meanings" of personal problems by thinking philosophically about them, finding the competing values and points of view which lie behind them. In other words, drawing upon the history of ideas, students work to articulate the contrasting ways of understanding the world, human nature, knowledge, and the good life which generate and sustain their moral dilemmas.

STUDENTS' ACTIVE PARTICIPATION IN LEARNING

Just as philosophy, for Dewey, is never far from the flashpoints of cultural conflict, so learning is imbedded in the emotional moments when individual and environment clash. That is, learning in its broadest, nonschool sense, is a reconciliation of tensions between the self and its surroundings. It happens when desire is frustrated, attention is aroused, and we investigate our surroundings with purpose, learning new ways to achieve our sought-after ends (*How* 14–16; *Human* 181–92; *Interest* 51–54). As we shall later see, in the classroom this means teachers must encourage students to find genuine problems which excite their interest, problems which can be explored and ameliorated by engagement with the curriculum. Only in these circumstances, according to Dewey, will school learning have the emotional force of nonschool learning, and only in this way will students be motivated to investigate and remember course subject matter (*How* 278–79). When teachers succeed in setting these conditions, the resulting heightened student *interest and effort* leads to the student-curriculum integration that Dewey desires ("Attention;" *Interest*; "Interest").

One of the appealing features of Dewey's philosophy of education is that he shows learning to be natural, not a process confined, as it was for much traditional philosophy, to special schooling or a particular social class. It is not a product of leisure or wealth or divine inspiration. To the contrary, for Dewey, learning is rooted in biological life, not above the earth but embedded in it, emerging in the very process by which life evolves and is maintained (*Reconstruction* 87). We are always in motion, he says, seeking some goal, "intent on something urgent" (*Interest* 18; "Interest" 270). As our objectives are roadblocked, emotions like joy and fear, as well as dispositions like persistence and initiative, sustain the thinking which comes forward. And the result of this thinking—what Dewey calls our *constructions and criticisms*—is intelligent in that we employ information from the past and careful study of the present, reflecting upon and testing both (*How* 14–16).

It follows that learners, for Dewey, are never passive, neither disinterested spectators of ideas nor idle absorbers of sensations. They are always active, implicitly working to reconcile the ancient Greek epistemological conflict— outlined in *Reconstruction in Philosophy*—between tradition and practice, emotion and reason, doing and thinking. If learners are not always physically interrogating their environments, Dewey says, they are, at least, experimenting with the theories they use to analyze their environments. If they are not always engaged in controlled experiments, employing telescopes and prisms, they are, at least, squinting, rattling, and thumping (*Democracy* 270–71;

How 37; *Quest* 87). For Dewey, then, learning in natural settings requires interest, effort, and direction. Thus, by extrapolation, there can be no effective school learning—no student-curriculum integration—without the learner's active participation.

The Importance of Indirect Teaching: Helping Students *Use* The Curriculum

If I were asked to give an epigraph which captures Dewey's recognition of the importance of student interest and activity for learning, one phrase would stand out. At the opening of *Democracy and Education,* completed in 1916, Dewey tells teachers that we cannot hand ideas to students as if they were bricks (4). Although Dewey does not develop this image, I believe he would say we are tempted to try and pass out ideas because, like bricks, they are separable. They can be isolated and decontextualized. But, according to Dewey, to understand aims, beliefs, and ideas we must, to extend his metaphor, see bricks as part of the buildings they support, as connected purposefully to other bricks as well as to timber and steel. Further, to even care about bricks, we must have the need to use them. We must have the desire to live in a building, construct a new one, or demolish an old one. As we shall note throughout the remainder of these chapters, this view of Dewey's—that learning is tied to use, to the drama of doubt, need, and discovery—is central to his philosophy of education (see *How* 79–83, 154, 253–54).

The upshot of Dewey's metaphor is that education requires the attention and effort of the learner. It is not simply motion in one direction, from the curriculum via the teacher to the student. Rather, learning involves interacting processes, energy moving in a variety of directions: from student to the curriculum and vice versa, from teacher to student and vice versa, and from student to student as well. As a result, Dewey wants instructors, not to present already established truths via lecture, but to teach *indirectly,* to structure classes so that they and their pupils identify genuine problems, use the curriculum to investigate and discover solutions to these problems, and, as as result, establish connections with course subject matter. To borrow Deweyan terminology, he wants instructors to help students build their own *continuities and interactions* with the curriculum (*Experience and Education* ch. 3). Since we cannot hand over ideas like bricks, students will have to develop their ideas—and reconstruct themselves—through their own struggles with assigned material and one another. It is they, not only their teachers, who must supply the energy and care for their learning (*Democracy* 160; *How* 36, 147). (For my own efforts to teach indirectly, see Chapters 8, 9, and 10 of this volume.)

Dewey's Central Educational Strategy: Borrowing from Nonschool Learning

Before turning to Dewey's pedagogical principles and the goals he believes they promote, I pause to consider his overall educational strategy. This is his insistence that features of nonschool learning be used to "vitalize" the classroom (*Child* 201; *Democracy* 8–9; *How* 257–59, 277–79). Despite Dewey's appreciation of the need for formal schooling in technologically advanced societies, he worries that much is lost when knowledge is presented in abstract and highly symbolic ways. As I have indicated, Dewey recognizes that learning is dramatic and emotional as well as cognitive. In a noteworthy recollection, a student of Dewey's reports an exchange in a large evening class at Teachers College (Columbia University) in the mid-1930s. Responding to this student's question about the role of emotion in thinking, Dewey—after a silence lasting "for the better part of two minutes"—tells his student, "Knowledge is a small cup of water floating on a sea of emotion" (Williams 127).

This appreciation of the noncognitive side of learning—the attitudes, emotions, and moral dispositions which drive and shape it—is clear in many of Dewey's works. In *How We Think*, for example, Dewey distinguishes logical proofs which set forth what is already known from the more dramatic, inductive processes by which we arrive at knowledge (74; see also *Child* 197–201). He grants that formal proofs have value in education but is concerned that, if relied on too heavily, they will isolate the classroom.

> One reason why much of elementary schooling is so useless for the development of reflective attitudes is that, on entering school life, a break is suddenly made in the life of the child, a break with those of his experiences that are saturated with social values and qualities. Schooling is then technical because of its isolation, and the child's thinking cannot operate because school has nothing in common with his earlier experiences. (*How* 68)

In *Reconstruction in Philosophy*, as I have already explained, Dewey contrasts tradition, which "pulsates" with cultural values, and drier, more neutral, practical knowledge. But at the same time that he recognizes the shortcomings of tradition—that its stories are often held together only by emotional congruity—he also notes that elaborate formal proofs are also limited since they can hide an author's political and moral biases (20). Thus, he recommends that philosophy and tradition, science and story inform rather than ignore one another (26).

Dewey's desire to employ the power of abstract, symbolic knowledge in the classroom—while reducing the limitations of its decontextualized and emotion-evacuated forms—comes out most strongly in *Democracy and Education*. He tells us: "One of the weightiest problems with which the philosophy of education has to cope is the method of keeping a proper balance between the informal [nonschool] and the formal [school], the incidental and the intentional, modes of education" (9).

"Informal" and "incidental" learning in natural settings is crucial to Dewey because it offers clues about how we might minimize the shortcomings of "formal" and "intentional" instruction. Although nonschool learning is haphazard, its "vitality" and "urgency" according to Dewey, compensate for its narrowness (*Democracy* 8). His strategy is to emphasize continuities between school and nonschool life as a way of adding emotional intensity and relevance to formal instruction, promoting methods of discovery as opposed to mere training, use of knowledge as opposed to mere acquisition of it. When continuities between student and subject matter are established, pupils—as in informal instruction—have a stake in the educational situation. They are able to remember what they master of the curriculum because they use and care about it. In this way, formal learning starts to take on the vitality of real life discovery—doubts resolved, obstacles overcome, problems clarified. (For a contrast of Dewey's analysis of good thinking with current information-processing and problem-solving models, see Holder.)

Although in the previous chapter I label Dewey's own teaching "un-Deweyan" because of his failure to promote active learning—his neglect of opportunities for students to share with one another or develop conjoint projects—in at least one respect, his teaching was consistent with his own principles. For the most part, Dewey did not lecture to his students. He did not report on work already completed or present truths as conclusions of formal proofs. Instead, he employed, following his own suggestions, an indirect approach. In class, he thought out loud for his students, mulling and analyzing philosophic questions throughout the class period as if to put camera and microphone to his thinking (see Edman 141). I imagine that such an approach—to extend Dewey's own imagery—was intended to give students a better chance to feel the swells and turbulence of the emotional sea upon which his own thinking sailed. It was his invitation to students to share his false as well as his true steps, his persistence and wholeheartedness, his frustrations and excitements. Unfortunately, despite Dewey's intentions, the majority of his students suggest they had too little help finding continuities between their own concerns and Dewey's to profitably interact with the philosophic subject matter on which he was focusing.

INTEGRATING STUDENT AND CURRICULUM: FOCUS ON THE LEARNING PROCESS

Dewey's challenge to us to vitalize school learning is best answered, according to him, by teaching indirectly. In turn, teaching indirectly requires us to be sensitive to the interplay of student and curriculum. However, as Dewey sees it, educational theorists have neglected the codependence of student and curriculum in their desire to stress either one or the other (*Child* 182; *Experience and Education* 17). It is the educational dualism which Dewey works hardest to overcome, one with which we are still battling almost a half-century after Dewey's death.

I speculate that Dewey suffered from two sorts of educational nightmares, two sorts of failure to resolve this dualism. On the one hand, he had visions of progressive teachers who loved their students by letting them do what they wanted, avoiding the imposition of external authority, employing what he in another context calls a "sugar-coated pedagogy" (*Child* 208; "How Much" 325; *Interest* 4; "Interest" 263). Why call this situation nightmarish? Because, as Dewey would see it, such teaching leaves students unprepared for future life. It fails to challenge them, to help them build the character traits Dewey feels they need to expand their interests, make intelligent choices, and, ultimately, enrich their understanding of the significance of present experience (*Experience and Education* 73–80). Although classrooms which adopt a sugarcoated pedagogy may be pleasant, they lack sufficient opportunity for student development.

On the other hand, Dewey had dark visions of an opposite sort, of lectures with students sitting in rows answering their teachers' rote information questions—what Dewey elsewhere calls a "penitentiary pedagogy." He could see the less competitive students yielding to boredom, losing interest, deciding they had nothing to contribute which the teacher did not already know or which others could not more rapidly supply ("Ethical" 118–19). Perhaps my speculations about Dewey's thoughts are too symmetrical, but for me the second nightmare is the flip side of the first. Whereas the so-called permissive, student-centered teacher offers too chaotic a classroom, the more traditional, curriculum-centered teacher offers one that is too routine. Both lead to student callousness and reduce student chances for challenge and development (*Experience and Education* 26).

How does Dewey reconcile these apparently contradictory educational demands? As we might expect, he works hard to find middle ground. He believes education has both a reforming and a conserving function, a responsibility to develop each student's individual potential while "transmitting" the best thinking, doing, and feeling that the older generation can offer the younger (*Democracy*, chs. 1, 2, 7). Although the popular view is that Dewey emphasizes student-centered education, he, to the contrary, equally values mastery of traditional subject matter ("How Much Freedom"). In fact, he believes that what distinguishes us from other animals is memory, our ability to communicate traditional values and skills (*Democracy* 9; *Reconstruction* 1-2). A culture, he tells us, is shared stories (*Reconstruction* 8). A community, he tells us, is common history and objects of allegiance (*Democracy* 4). Yet, despite his appreciation of tradition, Dewey criticizes much curriculum-centered education, not because it values traditional knowledge and wisdom, but because of the way it tries to pass these on to students. He argues that too often proponents of curriculum-centered instruction attempt to transmit information directly. They view students as interchangeable receptacles, assuming they should be on the same page, at the same time, generating the same answers ("Ethical" 118). But, in fact, says Dewey, knowing how to build on individual student interests and their unique dispositions is the key to effective education.

So, if Dewey recognizes the importance of both student and curriculum, how does he reconcile this dualism without sacrificing either member? By changing the emphasis, by asking us to focus, not on the curriculum and not on the student, but on the learning process: situations in which the student needs the curriculum and, as a consequence, is prompted to intelligently explore, use, and remember it.

The Habit of Intelligent or Reflective Thinking

In emphasizing the learning process, Dewey makes clear that knowledge is not an ownable attribute or set of beliefs, but an emotionally charged activity, a process by which individuals shape new *continuities and interactions* with their surroundings. He thus pays less attention to students' end products and more to the habits they are developing, the sorts of persons they are becoming. More precisely, he wants to encourage students' "innate disposition" to infer, experiment, and test (*How* 83). He wants them to develop the habits of what he calls *reflection* or *intelligence* (terms he, by and large, uses interchangeably; see *Democracy* 163).

Cognitive Components of Intelligence

What Dewey has in mind is helping students develop the ability to examine their beliefs, to understand and test their grounds and consequences, their reliability. He argues that encouraging such habits is an important educational goal because it permits action with foresight. Although the form of intelligent or reflective thinking may vary from one discipline to another (*How* 67), it generally offers increased control of behavior and gives our experience of things and events enriched, deepened meaning (*Democracy* 341). Dewey sees this careful sort of thinking as directly opposed to the kind which accepts beliefs blindly, on the basis of authority, tradition, fancy, or superstition (*How* 17). When making choices, Dewey wants students to employ the following approach:

> [Take into account] observation of the detailed makeup of the situation; analysis into its diverse factors; clarification of what is obscure; discounting of the more insistent and vivid traits; tracing the consequences of the various modes of action that suggest themselves; regarding the decision reached as hypothetical and tentative until the anticipated or supposed consequences which led to its adoption have been squared with actual consequences. This inquiry is intelligence. (*Reconstruction* 164)

Moral Components of Intelligence

So far, Dewey's view of intelligent thinking appears to focus exclusively on cognitive skills—things we do dispassionately with our heads—a set of procedures students could mechanically invoke to change themselves from "received," passive knowers into "separate," critical knowers (see Belenky et al.). But Dewey, especially in *Democracy and Education* and in the revised edition of *How We Think*, quickly gives the lie to that impression, warning that no amount of exercise in "correct thinking" makes a good thinker. He tells us we can only take advantage of the principles of reflective thinking when they are driven by appropriate traits of character, for example, "open-mindedness," "wholeheartedness," and "responsibility" (*Democracy* 173–79; *How* 30–33; see also "Theory of Emotion" 157). In fact, he says, regarding their importance for intelligence, if he had to choose between technical skill in logical processes and moral traits of character, he would choose the latter (*How* 34).

To illustrate, Dewey refers to the lives of new-world explorers, the "courage" they display in their willingness to challenge accepted belief (*How* 8, 73). These examples help him show the moral and psychological conditions of intelligent thinking. They help him emphasize that careful, orderly, open reflection rides upon character, the will to scrutinize accepted language, practice, and belief (see *Nature* 200–01). Thus, for Dewey, intelligence is both cognitive and moral, something one does as well as something one strives to perfect. That is, intelligence is both one of the means as well as one of the ends of education.

Integrating the Means and Ends of the Learning Process

A pedagogical consequence of seeing intelligent activity as having both immediate as well as ultimate value is that Dewey raises daily schoolroom activities to unusual importance. Although we tend to subordinate classroom experience to final transcripts and end products such as essays or research papers, Dewey criticizes this approach as part of a static worldview, a flawed inclination to see means as distinct and less important than the objectives they appear to serve. To the contrary, Dewey says, when means and ends are seen as interactive, school routines become, in important ways, ends, for they determine student personality and moral character. That is, the "deposit," or residue, from classroom activities, supposedly *mere* means, remains long after the so-called *more important* end products have been forgotten (*How* 153, 268). Similarly, for Dewey, ends operate more like means than static philosophies would suggest. Ends, he claims, are neither remote nor above the hurly-burly of daily activity. Rather, they shape the present, determining what we do today, the priorities we set ("Some" 339). Just as means do not disappear when we achieve our goals, so ends are not way off in the future. They function right now, shaping present experience (see *Theory* 40–50).

Dewey also points out that narrow use of the means-ends distinction can result in too-easy dismissal of large segments of our lives in the name of efficiency. He has in mind "Fordism," the cost-saving work of factories and assembly lines, efficient in the rapid production of commercial goods but inefficient in generating quality worker experience (*Democracy* 120–22;

Reconstruction 170–71). Dewey also has the classroom in mind. His nightmares, which I described earlier, are about neglect of the consequences of our educational practices, neglect of what he calls students' "collateral learning" (*Experience and Education* 48) or what is today referred to as the hidden curriculum. He argues that by teaching skills like reading and writing out of context, in assembly line fashion, we overlook the impact of these skills on students' habits and dispositions. And ignoring the ways in which classroom practices influence dispositions like self-esteem, initiative, and openness toward learning, according to Dewey, diminishes student chances at a good life. (For contemporary debates between progressives and radicals about the hidden curriculum, see Hlebowitsh "Forgotten.")

In sum, Dewey takes students seriously enough to worry, not about year end exams, but about the sorts of character they are developing. He also takes curriculum seriously enough to want students to be able to intelligently access, evaluate, and make it their own. In other words, if we really care about curriculum, we should help students use it, test it, and preserve what is best in it for a developing world. And if we really care about students, we need to study curriculum to understand how it can best promote the methods and traits of character students require for informed, fulfilling lives.

Dewey's General Educational Goal: Growth

What Dewey wants from student-curriculum integration, in the most general terms, is "growth" (*Democracy* 51–3; *Experience and Education* 36, 48; "Need for Philosophy" 4). And, reflecting his view of the interconnectedness of all life activities, this goal of growth should also be the object, not just of schooling, but of every human association (*Reconstruction* 186). However, unlike more static views of human development, growth, for Dewey, is not ascending a clearly marked stairway; it is something more open ended:

> The process of growth, of improvement and progress, rather than the static outcome and result, becomes the significant thing.... Not perfection as a final goal, but the ever-enduring process of perfecting, maturing, refining is the aim in living. Honesty, industry, temperance, justice, like health, wealth and learning, are not goods to be possessed as they would be if they expressed fixed ends to be attained. They are directions of change in the quality of experience. (*Reconstruction* 177)

Schooling, for Dewey, therefore, should be a rich experience that leaves students with the capacity for even richer, "larger," and "deeper" experience (*Experience and Education* 27–8, 74; see also *Human* 294). Speaking in this apparently circular way—saying that the purpose of growth is more growth—is an example of Dewey's attempt, as I have already noted, to describe processes which are both means and ends, simultaneous and recursive, in a language better suited for linear, cause-effect relations and clear-cut distinctions. Dewey's worry with regard to education is that we will treat classroom means and ends as discontinuous—for instance, attempting to teach swimming by rehearsing the Australian crawl out of water or teach moral behavior by preaching it rather than by letting students experience and practice it in the school situation ("Ethical" 116; *Moral* 13–14; "Social Aspects" 241). That is, for Dewey, any educational goal we name is an objective for both now and the future. Thus, the best preparation for growth—extraction of the most meaning from present experience—is growth itself (*Experience and Education* 49).

Although Dewey's language may make his goal of growth seem circular (a charge made by many of his critics), he tells us more than enough to figure the direction in which he wants teachers to go. He is, as we have seen, concerned that students practice intelligent or reflective thinking. As we have also seen, despite Dewey's use of the word *intelligence*, this practice is not primarily cognitive. His ideal of careful, deliberate reflection also depends on certain dispositions and moral traits of character. How, as teachers, do we encourage these methods and attitudes? He tells us we must teach indirectly, as I have said, that we must set the conditions in which it is likely that students will be motivated to use the curriculum and, as a consequence, develop habits of reflection, expand their interests, and "grow" (*Interest and Effort* 39–40). To better understand these conditions, it is important to analyze more fully the fundamental processes or nested dualisms—all of which I have already introduced—underlying the student-curriculum dichotomy. For Dewey, these are continuity and interaction, construction and criticism, interest and effort. Analysis of these three dualisms is the focus of the following chapter.

Chapter Two

Nested Dualisms Underlying Dewey's Student-Curriculum Integration

————— ✤ —————

Steve Fishman

I n this chapter, I describe the dualisms underlying Dewey's view of student-curriculum tensions: continuity and interaction, construction and criticism, interest and effort. I then relate them in a cause-effect way for the purposes of clarification. In doing so, I find myself on a slippery path, violating Dewey's view of these activities as nested, interactive, and mutually conditioning. However, after outlining these distinctions in a means-external-to-ends, linear fashion, I will discuss their pedagogical implications in a way more faithful to their interactive nature.

CONTINUITY AND INTERACTION

As soon as we scratch the surface of student-curriculum tensions, we encounter one of Dewey's most important distinctions for teacher practice: continuity and interaction. These dual concepts are the probes, according to Dewey, through which we determine the quality of a student's experience (or anyone else's, for that matter). And since quality student experience is paramount in Dewey's vision of educational success, he gives their determinants considerable attention (*Experience and Education* 25–50).

With regard to the first half of the dualism, Dewey uses the term *continuity* to indicate that experiences are complex *temporally*, penetrating one another, earlier ones leaving deposits or residues which influence later ones. By contrast, *interaction*, for Dewey, indicates that each individual's experience is complex *spatially*, the result of an exchange between an organism and its environment—*environment* used in the broad sense to include subjects talked about, books read, or experiments carried out. Dewey characterizes continuity and interaction as "the longitudinal and lateral aspects of experience" (*Experience and Education* 44).

As already noted, these concepts—as determinants of the quality of our experience—have, in Dewey's scheme, extraordinary significance for teachers. This is so because student experience in school and the classroom's impact on student experience outside school are his litmus test for education. Granted, he wants schooling to help students achieve control over their lives (*Experience and Education* 64; *How* 17, 86), discover their "calling" (*Democracy* 308), explore the customs, values, and knowledge of their culture (*Democracy* 10–22), "expand" their world (*Experience and Education* 74), and find freedom through cooperation with others ("Need for Philosophy" 13). But his justification for all these objectives boils down to increased chances for enriched experience. In fact, as an indication of the ultimate importance of the quality of experience for Dewey, he tells us that although democracy is valued for its promotion of individual freedom and respect for diverse communities, its most fundamental defense is its capacity to enrich the experience of its citizens. He asks:

> Can we find any reason [for preferring democracy] that does not ultimately come down to the belief that democratic social arrangements promote a better quality of human experience, one which is more widely accessible and enjoyed, than do non-democratic and anti-democratic forms of social life?" (*Experience and Education* 34)

Before looking more closely at continuity and interaction, I offer a brief word about Dewey's idea of "enriched experience." Among his discussions of experience in numerous texts, one of his fullest occurs in *Art As Experience*. And it turns out that, for Dewey, a rich experience is highly creative and aesthetically pleasing. It has development, yet unity. It is immediately powerful and fulfilling, yet sums the past and expands the future. In short, enriched experience is marked by a meaning which grows, one which accumulates, reaches out, and builds toward an emotionally satisfying end (*Art* 38–9).

Given that enriched experience is Dewey's ultimate educational goal, his notions of continuity and interaction are crucial, since they help us explore how enriched experience develops, the ways in which it constructs its connections, meaning, and significance. In understanding these two dimensions of experience, I am helped by thinking of individuals as trains trying to fashion a purposeful course by choosing from alternative tracks (continuity) while, at the same time, readjusting their direction as they learn from new passengers (interaction) who board along the way.

As with most analogies, mine breaks down when taken too literally. If individuals are trains, they are certainly unusual ones. They have neither fixed destinations nor timetables. Further, the sound of their travel is not a monotonous clickety-clack but, ideally, the complex rhythm of successful adventures: purposes achieved, old habits redone, new vistas opened. In addition, these trains' passengers—events, people, judgments, books, discussions—have no clear itinerary. Some stay on, becoming major voices in the engineer's cabin, while others disappear, leaving only a modest trace. And with regard to the classroom, I envision it as a many-platformed station, to continue my analogy, where student trains exchange passengers and load fuel for their ongoing journeys.

If Dewey were to graph the quality of student experience, I believe he would trace a changing value with continuity and interaction as its coordinates. He would chart students' moment-to-moment progress as, with greater or lesser success, they reach both backward and forward in time as well as out into their present surroundings. However, we need to keep in mind that, for Dewey, *every* experience has continuity: it is permeable, taking something from the past and leaving tracks which shape the future. Likewise, every experience has interaction: it involves exchanges between an organism and its world or environment. Whether a particular experience is educative, however, depends on the *quality* of its continuities and interactions, on students taking a residue of greater rather than lesser curiosity and initiative, sensitivity and responsiveness, desire and purpose from their classrooms (*Experience and Education* 25–6, 38).

What are the marks of quality student continuities and interactions? For Dewey, *continuity* is educationally effective when a sequence of experiences, despite occasional cul de sacs and detours, is so driven by deeply held purposes that it coheres, develops, and finds fulfillment; for example, a problem is solved, a discussion is played out, a piece of writing reaches consummation rather than mere cessation (*Art* 35–51). By contrast, *interaction* is educationally worthy when classroom conditions and student interests are synchronized so that students maximally explore—get the fullest meaning they can from—their school environment (*Experience and Education* 45, 49).

It should be clear that, although I have separated them for purposes of clarification, continuity and interaction work together when experience is fulfilling and meaningful. As students and their classroom intersect—as pupils both take from and give to each other, their teacher, and the curriculum—successful pupils enrich their experience by extending their horizons and reconstructing themselves. That is, their classroom *interactions* promote the construction of fresh *continuities* between school and their important life concerns. Of course, how to go about recognizing and measuring enriched experience or student growth is not self-evident, and, unfortunately, Dewey provides little help in this regard. In Chapter 9 of this volume, Lucille McCarthy undertakes the difficult task of operationalizing these Deweyan concepts, of describing particular students' continuities and interactions in my Introduction to Philosophy class. In Chapters 10 and 11, she attempts to evaluate their reconstruction and growth as we put into practice Dewey's claim that quality student experience is the measure of classroom success (*Experience and Education* 74).

CONSTRUCTION AND CRITICISM

As I have just said, the first of these two dualisms, continuity and interaction, refers to characteristics of every experience, whether or not these experiences are educational. By contrast, the second dichotomy, construction and criticism—also referred to by Dewey as synthesis and analysis—seems narrower in scope, applying specifically to human judgment or production. At this point, however, I feel myself on the slippery ground I warned about earlier, losing my footing as I use linear language to describe recursive processes. For despite the fact that in important ways the continuity-interaction dualism is broader than the construction-criticism dualism, in certain other and equally important ways they are similar. Insofar as construction brings together previously separated materials, it is a form of continuity, and insofar as criticism breaks down previously joined materials, it relies on the narrowing focus of interaction. In other words, both distinctions—continuity and interaction, construction and criticism—point to what Dewey saw as a double-motion in all thought (*How* 104–05). It is a forest-and-trees phenomenon, a back-and-forth between enlarging and narrowing lenses, between putting together and taking apart. However, setting such similarities aside for the moment, I proceed with my cause-effect, linear discussion of construction and criticism, hoping to better distinguish and relate the dualisms beneath the student-curriculum dichotomy.

Dewey uses the construction-criticism dualism in two ways. First, in their more general senses, he employs construction and criticism as if they were mutually exclusive. Construction refers to all productive human activities, the result of any situation in which we are allowed to "give out," to "contribute," or to do ("How the Mind" 219). They are the expression of impulses which find fulfillment in appropriate organizations of material. In school, this requires classroom practices which put student voice, initiative, and creativity above memorization and repetition. By contrast, when Dewey uses criticism in this first, general sense, he refers to negative judgments in general, the sort of spirit-sapping, constant correction he finds totally opposed to construction. Dewey employs criticism in this way when he claims that teaching focused on what students should *not* do destroys pupils' constructive abilities. One of his examples is composition instruction geared to correcting grammar instead of promoting student motives for using and improving writing ("Period" 289–90).

Whereas in Dewey's first, general use of construction and criticism, they are mutually exclusive, in his second, more restrictive use, they are mutually dependent. In this second usage, they are the "synthetic" and "analytic" aspects of our creations and productions. *Construction* refers to our ability to synthesize new connections, to place things previously unrelated in an "inclusive situation" or context—Dewey's example is Newton's connecting the fall of an apple with the motion of the moon—and *criticism* refers to our ability to identify things by focusing on their distinctive traits, marking off important attributes previously left vague or submerged in the larger whole—Dewey's example is a child's distinguishing a dog from other four-legged animals by the way it wags its tail (*How* 157–59, also 128–30, 197–202; "Period" 291–93). In short, whereas the more general meanings of construction and criticism make them seem totally opposed—the former encouraging and the latter discouraging original work—in their narrower meanings they are mutually dependent. There can be no genuine construction without criticism, and there can be no genuine criticism without construction.

To further illustrate the restricted meaning, that is, the use of construction and criticism as the synthetic and analytic phases of thought, I apply them to Dewey himself. When we analyze Dewey by bringing forward the reformist, Darwinian, or Hegelian qualities in his thinking, we are being critical, attempting to better understand Dewey by separating important from trivial characteristics of his philosophy. Alternatively, when we connect Dewey with a reform movement like British Liberalism, we are engaged in synthesis, using a quality we have analyzed out of Dewey's work to link him to other theorists. And, as Dewey suggests, we experience the double-motion, or restlessness, in thought as we move back and forth between synthesis and analysis, between applying freshly identified characteristics to new cases and reexamining these characteristics for additional refinement. To continue this example, after constructing a connection between Dewey and British Liberalism, our synthesis might lead us to further analysis or refinement of Deweyan traits, asking, perhaps, how Dewey's reformist inclinations contrast with those of the British liberal, John Locke. As Lucille McCarthy details in Chapter 10, once students in my Introduction to Philosophy class identify philosophic attributes of an individual text or position, they are inclined, in the way Dewey leads us to expect, to synthesize, applying these attributes to additional, and previously unrelated, texts and positions.

Throughout the ensuing discussion, I will try to be faithful to Dewey's second, or narrower, use of construction and criticism, seeing both synthesis and analysis as necessary for successful work. This is Dewey's approach in the essay in which he most fully discusses these concepts, "Construction and Criticism":

> Creation and criticism cannot be separated because they are the rhythm of output and intake, of expiration and inspiration, in our mental breath and spirit. To produce and then to see and judge what we and others have done in order that we may create again is the law of all natural activity.... Production that is not followed by criticism becomes a mere gush of impulse; criticism that is not a step to further creation deadens impulse and ends in sterility. (139–40)

Student constructions and criticisms come in for special treatment by Dewey because he sees American society struggling to maintain the vitality of its judgments, in particular, its citizens' independence and intelligence, both crucial for democracy ("Some" 341). In his view, what erodes independent and original work is our society's reliance on mass production, a tendency that leads us to accept predigested, off-the-rack ideas.

In suggesting ways to encourage originality, Dewey shows his individualistic side, his sense that, despite our porousness to social forces, each of us has an opaque edge of uniqueness (see *Nature* 198). If our constructions and criticisms are to be worthy, he tells us, we must put something of ourselves, of our own "spontaneity," into them ("How the Mind" 220). We must transcend borrowed standards to find the idiosyncratic reactions where genuine taste and inclination begin. Quoting from Emerson, Dewey speaks of "the gleams of light that flash from within," the internal rustlings when some idea "truly our own" stirs toward birth ("Construction" 139). These gleams, however, are just the beginning of worthy constructions, for, untempered by criticism, our constructions are undisciplined venting, and, in parallel fashion, criticisms without construction are roads to dead-end inactivity. Intelligent, original judgment only develops, Dewey claims, when construction and criticism, synthesis and analysis, work hand in hand.

INTEREST AND EFFORT

Dewey's discussion of the third dualism underlying the student-curriculum dichotomy—interest and effort—is crucial for his project of pupil-curriculum reconciliation. It is shaped by a pedagogical debate which was especially vigorous in his University of Chicago years around the turn of the 20th century, a debate that gives insight into the sources of the educational nightmares I attribute to Dewey in the previous chapter. On the one hand, certain educational theorists (usually identified with Johann Herbart) emphasized student interest, arguing that students' native inclinations and tastes were central to successful schooling. On the other side were theorists (usually identified with Wendell T. Harris) who emphasized effort. They claimed student discipline and responsibility could only be developed if pupils learned to complete tasks which sometimes seemed distasteful and irrelevant. (For Dewey's discussion of this debate, see *Child* 185–88; *Democracy*, chs. 6, 10; *Interest*, ch. 1; "Interest"; for secondary accounts, see Ryan 138–42; Wirth, ch. 7; for an analysis of ambiguities in Dewey's use of the term *interest*, see White.)

Dewey's own position emerged, typically, from his acknowledgement of strengths and weaknesses in both the Herbart and Harris alternatives. Although he championed the value of student interest and attention, he worried that much "progressive" education took students' interests as they were, indulging pupils by demanding no more than what was "easy and amusing" ("Attention" 280). In response, Dewey argued that student interests could only be maintained if they were deepened and expanded through challenge, and he also claimed that student interests were educationally important but, primarily, as seeds of eventual understanding, criticism, and use of subject matter in its most developed forms.

With regard to the other side of the debate, Dewey accepted that student effort was essential, and he granted that it could be stimulated by threats of punishment and poor grades. But he distinguished forced from voluntary effort (*School* 148–49), insisting that the latter was crucial for effective education.

Dewey's overall position rested on his view that interest connects two things that are otherwise apart. Drawing on the etymology of interest as "to be between" (inter*esse*), Dewey saw interest as a sign of union between "the person and the materials and results of his [sic] action" (*Interest* 17; see also "Attention" 290; *Democracy* 172; "Interest" 269). This interpretation allowed Dewey to identify interest with self (*Democracy* 352; *Interest* 90; "Interest" 265; *Psychology* 216). To be genuinely interested in something, he claimed, is to identify with it, and when students have such voluntary interest or identification, they throw themselves fully into their work, generating passions which sustain their effort despite significant obstacles. By contrast, when effort is demanded from without, schoolwork becomes a necessary evil, something to be gotten through, and students are forced to pretend interest, their attention divided, their selves split (*How* 31). Instead of experiencing "intellectual integrity," they learn to "serve two masters" and to "deceive" (*Democracy* 176; "Interest" 267).

In short, Dewey was critical of both Herbart and Harris followers for seeing interest and school effort as opposed. The Herbartians, whom he described as advocates of a "sugar-coating" or "soft" pedagogy, attempted to make school effort pleasant and sensorially satisfying in order to motivate students. Followers of Harris, whom he described as advocates of a "penitentiary" or "hard" pedagogy, attempted to "hammer" in school effort with threats of punishment.

Despite their different approaches, Dewey takes the classroom results of both soft and hard pedagogy to be identical: divided student attention and "mental truancy" (*Experience and Education* 46). The problem, according to Dewey, is both sides' failure to recognize that students already have deep interests which can find development in school subject matter. In other words, contrary to assumptions by both Herbart and Harris supporters, students' native interests are rich enough to support the special effort and commitment that learning requires. (This same line of thinking helps Dewey argue—against Kantians—that interest and moral duty, like interest and effort, are compatible; see *Democracy* 350–54.) However, although Dewey does not believe interest and effort are opposed, he does not claim they are an easy partnership. Instead, he maintains that when they are successfully related, there is a delicate balance between the two. That is, if interest is too easily satisfied, we experience pleasure initially, but in time our interests fail to expand, and so they dissipate. On the other hand, if efforts to gratify our interests are mounted but too quickly frustrated, our interests also dissipate. It follows that for interest and effort to work productively, satisfaction of the former must come about in appropriate ways. For example, interest must be gratified slowly enough and with sufficient challenge that it has an opportunity to grow, so that our efforts can turn up fresh, related materials to maintain and expand it. Ideally, for Dewey, education should sufficiently deepen students' interests so they may experience the curriculum or subject matter in its "richest," most "maturely organized" forms (see *Experience and Education* 73–74, 79–83; *Interest* 55–58; "Interest" 275).

Although Dewey never compares or rank orders these first two sets of dualisms—continuity and interaction, construction and criticism—I believe, as I noted earlier, that continuity and interaction are more fundamental. I say this because I believe the quality of our experiences (that is, our continuities and interactions with our environment) determines the quality of our productions (that is, our constructions and criticisms). Had Dewey carefully related these first two sets of distinctions, he would, I believe, have used the third set, interest and effort, to establish their connection. Without interest and effort, our response to the environment is apathetic, and any resulting productions are likely to be sterile. To the contrary, when interest and effort are keen, our continuities and interactions with our surroundings are deep, and any resulting productions are likely to be original and audience grabbing. Therefore, because interest and effort are necessary conditions of meaningful experience and successful work, Dewey pays special attention to them in his applied pedagogy.

The Mechanics of Interest and Effort in the Classroom

Dewey details the mechanics of interest and effort in an attempt to help set the conditions for student growth through student-curriculum integration. He sees interest and effort as having three principal components:

• *"For-what(s)," or Goals.* For pupils to be interested in their school environment, an assigned text, for example, they need to have what Dewey calls "for-whats," or goals ("Attention" 272–74). Without significant for-whats—such as problems students want to solve, causes they want to forward, things they want to say—pupils cannot build continuities between their school assignments and their futures.

• *"To-what(s)," or Objects of Focus.* But simply having future goals is not enough to maintain interest and determined effort. Students also need what Dewey labels "to-whats," or objects of focus ("Attention" 272–74). They must be able to figure out to-what they should attend in their environments in order to achieve their goals. For instance, if a female student's for-what is to convince a male classmate to reconsider his misogynist views, she must decide to-what in the assigned reading they are discussing she might point him. Ideally, and this is crucial for teaching, course subject matter becomes an important to-what which students need to attend to and master in order to reach their goal, or for-what. If their goal is one in which they have genuine, personal interest, then the course material becomes the means to a valued end (*Interest* 34).

• *"With-which(s)," or Bridges.* It is at this point that students are in a place similar to Vygotsky's "zone of proximal development" (Vygotsky 84–91). To deal successfully with the important to-whats in their environment, students must work from the familiar to the unfamiliar. And these must be in proper relation, because if the to-whats that students need to master are either too puzzling or too familiar, interest will be squelched (*School* 143–44). Dewey calls experiences from the past which students use to understand unfamiliar elements in the classroom environment their "with-which(s)," or bridges ("Attention" 276).

This means that sustained interest and effort require that students build continuities of two sorts: to their future in the form of goals, or for-whats, and to their past in the form of with-whichs, or familiar experiences with which to unlock the unfamiliar. In fact, according to Dewey, the heart of successful assignments is the incorporation of challenges which provoke students but do not require unreasonable extension beyond their present skills. He writes,

The secret of instruction is very largely that kind of judgment which enables the teacher to present new points in material in such a way that while they seem to be new and thus stir up the mind and arouse it to put forth new energy, [they] are not felt to be so new... that the pupil, hunting over his [sic] present store of knowledge, can[not] hit upon something that shall enable him to deal with them. ("Attention" 276; see also *Interest* 56)

Having genuine for-whats (goals), identifiable to-whats (objects of focus), and appropriate with-whichs (bridges) increases student chances for fulfilling interactions with the curriculum and meaningful continuities between the curriculum and their past and future. For instance, pupils, instead of seeing the curriculum—let us say, addition and subtraction—as a mere means to achieving a desirable end (figuring the total cost of videos they want to buy) begin to see the curriculum as something more compelling than the original end they had in view. They begin to be interested in and enjoy the practice of addition and subtraction for the general ability it gives them, their increased power to use math in a wide range of situations. When this happens, students find that what they once considered a mere to-what becomes a new and important for-what. Put differently, what Dewey on occasion calls "the indirect interest"—in this case learning to add in order to figure video costs—becomes a "direct interest"—learning to add for the general ability it provides (*Interest* 38–41; "Interest" 274–75).

Let me return to my earlier example, the case in which a female student's initial for-what is to influence her male classmate's attitudes toward women. Let us say that in the process of trying to influence him, she reads several feminist authors (her to-whats), and, as a result, her interest expands from wishing to influence her classmate to wanting to learn the history and methods of the feminist movement. Thus, this student's original interest (or self) develops, because, as she works toward her initial goal, she adds a new one, one which not only calls forward increased effort but also ultimately increases her power to deal with future discriminatory situations (see "Period" 292–93). In this way, Dewey hopes the integration of student and curriculum will not necessarily transfer focus from practical problems to academic ones but, rather, promote more thorough transactions between the two.

To summarize the mechanics of interest and effort in the classroom: For students to be interested in and make persistent effort with, for example, an assigned reading, is for them to get the most they can from it, to interact with it richly and fully. And to interact fully, they need to build continuities from the text to their future as well as from the text to their past. The first step in bringing this about is for teachers to help students identify goals they care about that are best reached through mastery of the assigned subject matter. When teachers succeed, students are motivated to explore the assigned material and make the effort to overcome its unfamiliar or challenging parts in order to achieve their goals. As students interact with subject matter in this way, their constructions and criticisms—for instance, interpretive essays to be exchanged with partners—become more original, displaying something of the authors themselves. In other words, such essays reflect the keenness with which students carried forward their projects. The result is that, under a Deweyan analysis, when certain student works draw our sustained attention, they do so because high levels of interest and effort, as well as rich continuities and interactions, accompanied their production.

Emphasizing Interest and Effort in the Classroom

Given that Dewey points to the primacy of interest and effort in generating quality student experience and, therefore, quality student work, it follows that teachers should focus on the conditions which stimulate successful work rather than on its formal properties. Dewey's remarks in other contexts, specifically regarding artistic creativity, provide additional support for this approach. In talking about the appreciation of art, he emphasizes that the viewer cannot get out of an object something that was not put into it. In several places, he says that an audience goes through an ordering and thinking process comparable to the one the producer underwent, and that aesthetic appreciators must "retrace the course of the [artist's] creative process" ("Qualitative" 262; see also *Art* 54). In other words, the thinking and feeling that goes into a work is what an audience gets out of it, sensitive viewers responding with emotions and processes akin to the artist's.

Dewey thus focuses on the generating conditions rather than the formal properties of successful works. It is not that he dismisses formal properties. In *Art As Experience*, for example, he talks about the organic unity of successful art, the necessity with which its elements cohere, the foreshadowing of the whole in each part. But Dewey insists that these formal elements can all be present, yet still be ineffective if produced mechanically. This is so because creative work manifests the process of enrichment and development of a "line of action" or thought as it moves forward to its "appropriate termination" (*Interest* 34). Such a process is successful, according to Dewey, when the line of action moving toward fulfillment is controlled by a felt quality, not some mathematical formula. That is, to reduce originality and discovery to properties related by precise mathematical ratios misses creativity's core. He writes,

> Upon subsequent analysis, we term the properties of a work of art by such names as symmetry, harmony, rhythm, measure, and proportion. These may, in some cases at least, be formulated mathematically. But the *apprehension of these formal relationships is not primary* for either the artist or the appreciative spectator. [This is because the work of art] . . . is primarily qualitative, and is apprehended qualitatively. Without an independent qualitative apprehension, the character-istics of a work of art can be translated into explicit harmonies, symmetries, etc., *only* in a way which substitutes mechanical formulae for esthetic quality. ("Qualitative" 251, emphases mine).

For Dewey, then, more important than the separable, analyzable elements of the creative object is the interest and effort which brought them together, the impulse which shaped them into an integrated whole. His focus is on the governing force deciding which materials best feed, clarify, and deepen the "underlying quality" seeking expression (*Art* 37).

Regardless of what we think about Dewey's claim that only attentive and keenly interested artists can create attention-grabbing work, I believe it is appropriate, at least in the classroom, to stress the interest and effort that goes into successful productions rather than their material features. I believe this, although I grant that interest and effort are no guarantee that student productions will be successful. And certainly, as teachers, many of us have reluctantly, and with some pain, assigned average grades to work from sincere, conscientious students (for discussion of the tensions between process and product, teacher as coach and teacher as judge, see Elbow "Embracing"). However, Dewey—anticipating the "process" theories of composition researchers like Elbow, Murray, and Graves—might reply that developing the context for successful work is more important than close analysis of student texts or, for that matter, close analysis of exemplary classic models (see *How* 65, 283). When teachers help students generate valued for-whats, he might continue, pupils will be much more attentive to-what teachers say about the formal qualities of effective texts because they have a need to know these ("Period" 297).

Although I am correct, I believe, about the implications of Dewey's thinking, he offers no empirical evidence to support the view that focus on interest and effort will generate better constructions and criticisms than will attention to formal properties. In Part II of this book, however, Lucille McCarthy offers data which show the positive results of emphasis upon interest and effort for my own students.

SETTING THE CONDITIONS FOR QUALITY STUDENT EXPERIENCE AND WORK

I now develop further classroom applications of Dewey's pedagogical principles. In doing so, I try to soften the cause-effect line I have pursued while analyzing the nested dualisms underlying student-curriculum tensions. In readopting Dewey's interactive view, I cannot say which comes first—interest and effort, continuity and interaction, or construction and criticism. In my desire to present them clearly, I imposed an artificial ordering with the first determining the second and the second the third, thus making interest and effort the linchpin or, apparently, the most significant of the three nested dualisms. As Dewey would be eager to point out, however, each of these dimensions of thought and work is recursive and mutually conditioning. For example, although both continuity and interaction and interest and effort appear more basic than construction and criticism, it is nonetheless clear that the quality of our constructions and criticisms dramatically affects the quality of our continuities and interactions as well as the levels of our interest and effort. In other words, had I chosen to tell the story somewhat differently, either construction and criticism or continuity and interaction might have appeared as the central linchpin.

Thus, as teachers, we should not just encourage student interest and effort as if this in itself were sufficient for effective instruction. After all, there is no way students can sustain interest and effort without both a high degree of continuity and interaction in their experiences as well as attractive opportunities to build their own constructions and criticisms. Therefore, in addition to helping students identify significant for-whats, to-whats, and with-whichs, we need to structure highly continuous and interactive classes. And we must also orchestrate an effective balance of constructive and critical thinking. In other words, we should proceed simultaneously in a variety of ways if we want to promote quality classroom experience and work. This way, success in any one area encourages and conditions success in the others.

Attending to Continuity and Interaction

In setting the conditions for classes rich in interaction—what Dewey calls their "lateral" aspects—teachers should promote not just transactions between individual students and the curriculum, but also exchanges among readings, class discussions and homework, and pupils themselves. For example, teachers should establish structures so students are able to exchange their homework and classwork and thus develop appreciation of the different ways to engage and interpret assignments and subject matter. Without such structuring, students remain, although in the same room, walled off from one another, without the benefits better interactions might provide. By contrast, when classwork and homework are exchanged—rather than simply taken up by the instructor to be returned at a later date—pupil cooperation for a common goal is likely to generate heightened interest in the curriculum as well as productive classmate interactions.

As teachers, we should also be more sensitive to the importance of continuity or the "longitudinal" aspects of the classroom. We should encourage continuities, not just between individual students' nonschool lives and course subject matter, but also between class sessions themselves, so these develop coherence over time. This means attending to the flow and momentum of classroom events, planting the seeds of ongoing themes, nourishing them, and anticipating their impact upon future student learning (*How* 54). It means knowing, for example, when student curiosity is ripe for direct instruction and when answers would only be a burden, retarding further development of pupil initiative and questioning (*How* 40). In other words, we should be aware of the narrative aspects of the classroom and design class sequences so challenges complexify and habits of reflection deepen over the length of the course.

Ideally, when we as teachers make the depth of class interaction and the flow of course continuity one of our important goals, our own interest, as well as students', will not be static but will expand with fresh attention to the to-whats of syllabus, reading materials, assignments, and projects. When we attempt the difficult job during class discussion, for example, of directing student recitations toward deeper transactions with the subject matter, toward clearer continuities with previously unrelated materials—what Dewey calls "harmonizing it all" ("Attention" 283)—our own daily class efforts will be sparked by the joys of conflicts resolved, interests and self extended. Under these conditions, our teaching is more likely to display intellectual integrity and coherence, qualities sensitive students can recognize and from which they can learn.

For Dewey, the promotion of the sort of interactions and continuities I have just named increases student chances for quality school experience and work. In other words, according to him, successful classrooms, as well as all other processes, are characterized by integration of their present, past, and future, that is, their means and ends. In *Art As Experience*, he tells us:

> The most elaborate philosophic and scientific inquiry and the most ambitious industrial or political enterprise has, when its different ingredients constitute an integral experience, esthetic quality. For then its varied parts are linked to one another, and do not merely succeed one another. And the parts through their experienced linkage move toward a consummation and close, not merely to cessation in time. This consummation...is anticipated throughout and is recurrently savored with special intensity. (55)

It follows that when learning is at its best, it too is highly integrated. We experience our inquiry as resolving conflicts, moving forward toward our for-whats, gathering momentum, uniting previously disparate materials as unfamiliar to-whats take on new meaning. Put alternatively, our best learning yields enriched experience, meaning-ladened moments of fulfillment. We feel our inquiry in our arms, legs, and stomachs, our bodies registering the drama of our struggle for expression and clarification. True to Dewey's idea that all processes are ultimately relatable, we are, on these occasions, not just thinkers. We are also feelers and doers: all our faculties—mental and physical, intellectual and emotional, sensory and motor—fully alive and integrated. In other words, for a learner's curiosity to run its course to ful-fillment in original work, there must be deep integration of the classroom's underlying dualisms.

Attending to Construction and Criticism

In setting the conditions for an effective balance of constructive and critical thinking, it is tempting to ask about their proper ratio and order. Is it advisable to have equal amounts of both? Should one precede the other or should they occur simultaneously? Dewey's insistence that all productions are context bound, that we must always attend to their particular situations, suggests he would strongly resist offering an ideal construction-to-criticism ratio or sequence. And the fact, for example, that equally original and successful artists seem to work very differently supports such a cautious approach. I have in mind the poet Richard Wilbur, who once said (at a reading I attended) that he never rewrote a line of his work. This indicates that Wilbur had so perfected his craft that he did not have to engage in explicit criticism at all or that lots of criticism and rehearsal went on in his head before he went to pencil and paper. In sharp contrast, James Mitchener claims he is terrible at first drafts but superior at rewriting. So I suspect that Mitchener, unlike Wilbur, does lots of constructing, perhaps what Dewey might call "gushing" (*Art* 62; "Construction" 140), before he begins the process of critical review. (For additional discussion of such contrasts, see Elbow, "Uses"; *Writing* 12–47; Fishman; Jones).

In sum, because Dewey believes the classroom's dualisms are interactive and mutually shaping, he suggests they must all be attended to if we are to dispel his educational nightmares. I believe he would say there must be quality interaction, criticism, and effort if, on the one hand, we are to avoid the educational dangers of chaotic, too-permissive, student-centered instruction. And, on the other hand, there must be quality continuity, construction, and interest if we are to avoid the dangers of deadening, overly curriculum-centered routine ("Ethical" 135; "How the Mind" 219). Since the optimal interplay of these forces varies with each learning situation, this translates into significant teacherly responsibility. In the absence of any one-directional, cause-effect relation among these nested dualisms, we must try to be sensitive to all of them, balancing multiple forces as we design and monitor our classrooms, shaping these dualisms to promote student-curriculum integration.

Chapter Three

MORAL TRAITS OF CHARACTER AND DEWEY'S STUDENT-CURRICULUM INTEGRATION

❖

Steve Fishman

I n chapters 1 and 2, I spotlighted Dewey's efforts to reconcile dualisms underlying student–curriculum tensions. These efforts appear at first blush to center on individual development, namely, helping students use personal goals to learn classroom subject matter and generate enriched, meaningful experience. However, Dewey insists that—given the social, practical, and emotional aspects of intelligent thought—education also has an abiding responsibility to develop moral traits of character, including the will to cooperate with others. These moral traits are my focus in the present chapter.

That Dewey can talk about the morality of education at all—much less write articles and books with such titles as "The Democratic Faith and

Education," "The Ethical Principles Underlying Education," and *Moral Principles in Education*—may seem overly bold to us, living as we do in an era nervous about the prospect of linking morality and public education. One of the reasons he can connect the two is that Dewey believes moral and democratic communities are identical, and he presupposes a widespread agreement among Americans that classrooms should foster a democratic spirit. Another and equally important reason is that Dewey's process philosophy, as I have explained, makes it difficult for him to separate activities like intelligent thinking from ethical thinking. That is, for Dewey, if intelligence is to be effective, it must be moral: Its need for openness requires respect for others, and its need for originality requires respect for self.

SETTING THE CONDITIONS FOR DEVELOPING MORAL TRAITS OF CHARACTER

Promoting Student Integrity

Dewey's reconciliation of tensions between concern for self and concern for others depends upon his belief that when students use their genuine interests to engage with school subject matter, they not only master and find meaning in the curriculum, but also develop habits of integrity, honesty, and wholeheartedness. How? When our assignments allow pupils to generate their own goals—and see the curriculum as continuous with these goals—they learn something about integrity of action as well as integration of activity. For when they act with full attention and effort, each task enroute to their ends takes on significance. That is, every means is loaded with the value of the ends and lives on in the ends (see "Interest" 273–75), and students feel focused, wholehearted, and honest about what they do (*Democracy* 176–78; *How* 32–33). Their lives "add up" and take on meaning. No step along the way is performed grudgingly, and no task or person along the way is treated insincerely.

In bringing themselves fully to each of their actions, students also learn something about the freedom of self-direction. They learn about honest choice and sustained commitment. And this sort of taking responsibility for oneself is central, as Dewey sees it, to morality. It is the type of opportunity for which classical liberals have fought for almost 400 years: the chance to make choices for oneself. Dewey notes,

> This [connecting the student and the curriculum] can be done only through
> the medium of the child himself [sic]; the teacher cannot really make the
> connection. He can only form the conditions in such a way that the child may
> make it for himself. Moreover, even if the teacher could make the connection,
> the result would not be ethical. The moral life is lived only as the individual
> appreciates for himself the ends for which he is working, and does his work in
> a personal spirit of interest and devotion to these ends. ("Ethical" 131)

In other words, as we enable students to take possession of themselves and
their learning—to work with full attention and persistent effort—we also
enable them to experience integrity, sincerity, and the moral exercise of will.

However, for Dewey, helping students take charge of themselves is only
part of education's ethical responsibility. The moral dimension of education
fails unless we also prepare students to participate cooperatively in social
life and advance "community welfare" ("Ethical" 118; *Moral* 17). Dewey
claims, "it behooves the school to make ceaseless and intelligently organized
effort to develop above all else the will for co-operation and the spirit
which sees in every other individual one who has an equal right to share in
the cultural and material fruits of collective human invention . . ."("Need
for Philosophy" 13; see also *Public* 201; "Social Aspects" 231; "Social
Value" 322).

Promoting Cooperative Living

For Dewey, if personal growth is to be moral, it must also bring happiness to
others. And, for Dewey, as I have already observed, these two sorts of
growth, personal and social—although conceivably contradictory—actually
coincide. Indeed, he believes educators can so promote students' interest in
the common good "that they will find their own happiness realized in what
they can do to improve the conditions of others" (*Ethics* 243).

But how do we structure our courses to accomplish this double objective? How do we integrate or reconcile the needs of individual and group?
Once again, Dewey's analysis leads to the fundamental and underlying
dualisms of the classroom. I say this because in our earlier discussion of the
importance of interest and effort for quality work, we have the beginnings of
our answer.

As we have seen, when students are helped to identify compelling goals
and to see mastery of curriculum as an important means to these goals, they
can approach their work with single-minded attention and wholehearted
effort. As we have also seen, this approach promotes integrity of student

thought and action. Ideally, this kind of wholeheartedness also helps students develop their capacities for openness and cooperation. Why? Because if interest is to be maintained, it cannot remain fixed or static. To the contrary, it must be on the move, hunting new materials, or to-whats to forward expression of the self's developing impulse ("Attention" 281; *Democracy* 13–32; "Interest" 271). Through this process, pupils begin to develop commitment to perfecting the practices in which they are engaged as well as to the people and communities sustaining these practices. Their deepest personal interests expand to identify with profoundly social ones. Lucille McCarthy finds evidence that at least a few of my own pupils expanded their interests in this way (see Chapters 8 and 9). What begins as a for-what aimed primarily at getting high grades transfers, for some, to interest in the assignment itself, to perfecting the practices and cooperating with the people needed to successfully complete it. (For more on communities of shared practice, see MacIntyre, ch. 14.)

How does this need to promote student openness and willingness to cooperate with others translate into concrete school terms? In the classroom setting, this means better attention to pupil-to-pupil exchanges, that is, to promoting shared homework and classwork—in-class and out-of-class projects—in order to encourage group collaboration. Such promotion of conjoint projects is crucial for Dewey, because, in the context of group work, attention and effort do not appear arbitrary or dictated from without. Rather, when class members commit to completing shared goals, group discipline feels self-imposed, and the division of tasks seems freely undertaken.

Because of Dewey's view that morality is tied to group cooperation he is especially critical of competitive individualism. He denigrates classes which promote academic "sharps," students who use their skills for display or personal advantage (*Democracy* 9; see also "Educational" 420; "Need for a Philosophy" 11–12). In this same spirit Dewey chastises students who work simply for grades. Desire for high marks, he believes, only takes students so far. Grades deflect from the process of learning and encourage pretended interest or the "hypocrisy" of divided attention ("Interest" 279). For these reasons, Dewey stresses the vitalizing consequences of interest in subject matter and contribution to cooperative practice ("Ethical" 119–120).

The Project Method

Dewey provides few specific details about how to achieve his goal of cooperative classrooms; one specific technique he does discuss, however, is "the project method" (for controversies surrounding progressive educators' different approaches to the project method, see Cremin 216–20; Ravitch 48–52). Considering what Dewey and two of his instructional staff, Mayhew and Edwards, say about his Laboratory School at the University of Chicago, it seems Dewey had success with an "occupational" or "project" pedagogy in the lower grades, especially with students between 4 and 8 years of age ("Psychology" 227–29; "Social Value" 314–15). This approach emphasizes direct production of things, and it organizes the curriculum around careers familiar to elementary school students, for example, farming, building, and retailing ("Three"). This allows students to learn about the values associated with familar vocations while working cooperatively on related projects. Faced, for instance, with the task of constructing a sand-table farm, students would ideally experience self-motivation and self-discipline, working with classmates and teachers to learn the math, carpentry, geography, and so on required to complete their project.

Although Dewey sees the project method as a way of helping students be more active and responsible learners, he also worries that this approach might become too student centered or haphazard, failing to prepare students to engage with subject matter in its more mature forms. In *The Way Out of Educational Confusion*, his 1931 Inglis Lecture at Harvard, Dewey warned, "Many so-called projects are of such a short-time span and are entered upon for such casual reasons, that extension of acquaintance with facts and principles is at a minimum" (31). In other words, as he says in *The Child and The Curriculum*, the point of tapping into students' interests is not simply to provide pleasurable experiences, but to identify and nurture in them those particular interests and skills fulfilled by mastering academic disciplines and methods (*Child* 189–93; see also *How* 217–29).

Interestingly, despite Dewey's concern to distance himself from what he saw as overly student-centered uses of the project or problem method, he points to it, at the close of his Inglis Lecture, as a technique worth testing at the high school and university levels. He says, "I do not urge it [the project method] as the sole way out of educational confusion, not even in the elementary school, though I think experimentation with it is desirable in college and secondary school" (36).

This remark holds my attention because it is as close as Dewey comes to a specific prescription for secondary and postsecondary teaching. And his willingness to shed his usual reluctance to prescribe for the classroom in this case makes sense. His work to reconcile student and curriculum, as well as his emphasis upon the importance for learning of wholeheartedness, responsibility, and group cooperation, seems especially compatible with the project approach. Given current institutional constraints, the obvious sort of "project" in science courses is the lab experiment and in humanities, the research essay or paper.

However, embracing Dewey's educational goals and believing that the project approach is a good bet for achieving them only gets us to the threshold of the classroom problem. Certainly countless lab reports and research papers have not yielded the "inquiry into fresh fields of subject matter" or the "extension of acquaintance with facts and principles" which Dewey wanted (*Way* 31; see also *How* 218). It is not clear how to keep projects from forcing students to undertake tasks in which they have little interest or for which the teacher does not already have answers. Nor is it clear how to prepare college students to access subject matter relevant to projects they *do* wholeheartedly undertake. As we shall see in following chapters, just because students have an interest or need to engage with a mature discipline does not mean they have the skills to do so. In Chapter 10, Lucille McCarthy focuses specifically on my own use of term project essays in my Introduction to Philosophy class, on my attempts, that is, to integrate student and curriculum within a context of cooperation among pupils and teacher.

THREE SOURCES OF DEWEY'S EMPHASIS ON COOPERATIVE CLASSROOMS

Dewey's emphasis upon cooperative classrooms and projects draws, first, upon his belief that the will to cooperate, like our potential to think intelligently, is "engrained in human nature" ("Does" 184). Humans have, according to Dewey, an inborn need for companionship and mutual aid. Children, especially, have a natural impetus to contribute in their unique ways to conjoint projects, "to give out, to do, to serve" ("Ethical" 119; *Moral* 22; see also *Democracy* 24; *Experience and Education* 56).

Second, Dewey's prescription for cooperative classrooms also draws upon his understanding of the sciences. Although he appreciates the critical aspects of scientific method, he equally admires its cooperative elements ("Authority" 142; *Experience and Nature* 28). No individual researcher can make proprietory claims, he says, since to be scientific is to make one's work public, to display its underside for examination and evaluation (*Individualism* 154–55). The scientific milieu minimizes self-concern: Senior scholars collaborate, mentor their juniors, and allow experience to be the final arbiter of dispute. As Dewey sees them, scientific communities, more than literary, artistic, or philosophic ones, show that intelligence is, at its best, sincere, courageous, and democratic. That is, full colleageship permits intelligent thinking to honor its initial impulse while opening to as many diverse views and as much data as possible.

Finally, Dewey's understanding of the moral dimension of education reflects his identification of democracy with cooperative activity. In *The Public and Its Problems*, Dewey argues that community is simply another name for democracy, an opportunity to join with others, to find common projects and concerns (148). In other words, for Dewey, there is nothing incompatible about pursuing individual development while fostering social cooperation.

The problem, in Dewey's view, is that modern nation-states have maintained a frontier conception of individualism, a self-centeredness which, given present social and material conditions, is no longer appropriate. This entails, for Dewey, redesigning our idea of individuality, fashioning a conception which, while recognizing the need for developing each person's utmost potential, promotes communal structures which encourage everyone to contribute to the enrichment of others (*Individualism* 32–34). He claims our most pressing current challenge is not nature, the wilderness frontier, but human relations, the social frontier ("Creative" 221).

The depth of Dewey's commitment to his ideal of community can be heard in the way he speaks about the power of communication. In *Experience and Nature* he declares,

> Of all affairs, communication is the most wonderful. That things should be able to pass from the plane of external pushing and pulling to that of revealing themselves to man [sic], and thereby to themselves; and that the fruit of communication should be participation, sharing, is a wonder by the side of which transubstantiation pales. (138)

He writes with similar hopes for communication at the close of *Reconstruction in Philosophy*:

> And when the emotional force, the mystic force one might say, of communication, of the miracle of shared life and shared experience is spontaneously felt, the hardness and crudeness of contemporary life will be bathed in the light that never was on land or sea. (211)

Such romantic, Wordsworthian talk leads some to dismiss Dewey's view of morality in education as nostalgia for 19th-century America and a desire to withdraw from our technologically driven age (see Robertson). But I do not read Dewey this way. Because, for all the virtues of small-town living—its face-to-face exchanges, family businesses, and first-hand contacts with the ingredients of social life—Dewey is all too aware, from his own boyhood, of its dangerous provincialisms. And, despite the human cost of present industrial cities, he recognizes urban society's potential for "increase in toleration, in breadth of social judgment, [in] larger acquaintance with human-nature..." (*School* 12). Rather, as I see it, by "the hardness of contemporary life" Dewey means primarily, not the radical changes in household economy and neighborhood systems created by industrial society, but the deep-seated habits and conceptions keeping us from achieving and equitably distributing such a society's vast technological promise. In particular, he means our inability to give up our notions of scarcity, the idea that we as individuals are caught in death-clutch struggles with nature and one another, and to accept that we are in an age of material plenty, an era in which outmoded notions of individuality need to be reconstructed.

In Dewey's emphasis upon cooperative classrooms—his view of communication as a way of achieving communion—he envisions a post-Darwinian world of evolving mutual enrichment rather than survival of the fittest. However vulnerable Dewey's vision is to charges of naivety, I prefer to praise him for pointing to the roots in human nature of what can be cultivated and is potentially best in modern, industrial life—free, classless, cooperative living—rather than to criticize him for underestimating obstacles to its achievement. I prefer to praise his foresight. Although he knows that society can promote indifference and cruelty, he is nevertheless devoted to helping us better secure its moments of communion, friendship, and love. Before turning, in the following chapter, to the ideology behind Dewey's pedagogical aims and approach, I summarize my discussion of them thus far.

SUMMARY OF DEWEY'S PEDAGOGICAL AIMS AND APPROACH

Although Dewey has often been criticized for being overly permissive with students and indifferent to traditional subject matter, this is, as I have pointed out, far from the truth. To the contrary, he both expects a great deal from pupils and appreciates the importance of such subject matter. In fact, his educational aims are twofold: (1) enriched experience through intelligent student use of new subject matter and (2) development of moral traits of character, especially those sustaining intelligent, cooperative thinking.

In addition to presenting these primary educational objectives, Dewey also offers ideas about how we might achieve them. He says their realization depends upon close attention to transactions between student and curriculum in the classroom. Behind this approach is Dewey's view that ideas are learned through use, not passive reception. Ideas cannot be handed over like bricks; pupils must be active and supply the energy for their own learning.

To underline the need for this approach, Dewey offers his estimate of prevailing teaching practice. When he looks at classrooms, he tells us, he finds too many pupils with divided interest, and he believes their mental truancy is the result of overemphasis on direct instruction and formal presentation. By contrast, when he looks at learning outside the classroom, he finds *indirect* instruction, work laced with the drama and tension of discovery: desires aroused, problems clarified, and hurdles cooperatively overcome. Dewey thus asks teachers to incorporate features of nonschool learning to vitalize their classrooms.

The task Dewey presents teachers is not an easy one. It forces us to focus more on student thinking than on pupil end products such as final exams or papers. We have to study emerging habits. We have to be alert for signs of pupils' growth and expanded interest, for indications they are being challenged to use what they know to make sense of what they do not know. And this brings student experience—the nested dualisms of continuity and interaction, construction and criticism, interest and effort—to center stage.

Such focus on student experience, according to Dewey, begins with examination of the continuities students build to the classroom. This type of investigation is crucial because the connections students build from home life to school life determine their interest in the curriculum, the way they interact with it, and the extent of their effort to understand and use it. Interest and effort are, thus, for Dewey, the linchpins of quality student experience and work. When pupils find reasons for using the curriculum, it takes on meaning. It becomes a *means* to valued ends. Just as important, when students find goals they can reach by using the curriculum, they experience drama in the classroom, the sort of enriched experience crucial to remembering and making the curriculum their own.

So far, despite all his insightful pedagogical footwork, Dewey is still on fairly orthodox ground. He wants students to learn subject matter, to master the knowledge they need to lead meaning-filled lives, to participate, criticize, and reform their culture. True, his views about the importance of students' experience, their continuities and interactions, their interest and effort, present large tasks for teachers. Nevertheless, his educational objective—

student mastery, criticism, and use of curriculum—however progressive, seems quite familiar.

Yet as I have indicated, because Dewey believes that mastery of subject matter requires more than just intelligent, reflective thinking, he introduces the controversial issue of moral education in the classroom. He does this because he believes students cannot succeed with reflective thinking— cannot test their accepted beliefs in intelligent fashion—unless their thinking is driven by moral traits of character, traits like courage, open-mindedness, and wholeheartedness. This additional Deweyan objective increases the responsibility placed on teachers, adding significant weight to our need to focus on student experience. It also brings us to Dewey's central educational strategy.

Dewey believes that if we teach indirectly—borrow a page from non-school learning—and structure our courses to arouse student interest, our pupils have a chance to defeat mental truancy and work with full attention. When this happens, students are encouraged to care about their work, feel responsible for it, and experience moral integrity. Further, under these conditions, student responsibility may expand to the school community itself, to the people who help sustain and perfect the practices schoolwork requires. In other words, when we promote wholehearted, sincere student effort, we help pupils develop the will to act cooperatively with others. And this is what Dewey's fuss with education is all about: fostering individual growth or enriched experience through cooperative, democratic inquiry, the type which courageously scrutinizes accepted belief in the service of an uncertain but shared future.

Chapter Four

DEWEY'S IDEOLOGY AND HIS CLASSROOM CRITICS

❖

Steve Fishman

Key aspects of Dewey's approach to education—for example, the importance of student activity, ownership of work, and collaborative learning—have become, at least on the surface, so familiar that it can be difficult to see the ideology behind his positions. However, by looking at some general criticisms his educational views have provoked, we can gain further insight into the social theory behind them. We can begin to understand the political as well as philosophic sources of Dewey's educational strategies.

DEWEY AS BOTH INDIVIDUALISTIC AND COMMUNITARIAN

A markedly unfair but common broadside is that Dewey is responsible for moral permissiveness, materialism, and lowered standards in American

education (see Adler 22–23; Kirk 365–66; for responses by Dewey supporters to such broadsides, see Brubacher; Burnett; Hook, "John Dewey";
Newkirk). A couple of semesters ago, when I checked the bookstore to make
sure *Reconstruction in Philosophy* had been ordered for my Intro class, the
student working at the counter asked, "Is that the same Dewey who said a
lot about education?" When I answered yes, she went on, "I'm surprised
you're ordering that. My sociology professor says he's responsible for all that's
wrong in America."

Although I cannot be sure, I suppose this young woman's professor was
referring to the more liberal aspects of Dewey's approach. For example, in
political works, such as *Individualism Old and New, Liberalism and Social
Action*, and *The Public and Its Problems*, Dewey makes clear his willingness
to experiment with industrial or guild socialism. He believes industrialized
countries have exchanged political dictatorships for economic ones
(*Liberalism* 9, 28). What he means is that all facets of contemporary life,
government, school, family, and church, are dominated by commercial
interests. Although we have exchanged autocratic control of political matters
for representative government, industry remains in the hands of the few,
workers having little say about decisions affecting them (*Individualism* 46;
Public 129–30). Dewey urges us to ameliorate these conditions by experimenting with democratic, worker-run industries (*Individualism* 98). And
this is the same experimental spirit he wants to develop in pupils. For, as we
have seen, although Dewey cares a great deal about student mastery of
subject matter—insisting that to be part of a community is to share common
language, values, and practices—he is equally concerned that students
develop critical methods or habits of thought so that communal traditions
can be tested and revitalized (*Democracy* 4; 151).

This Deweyan emphasis on reflective thinking rather than on doctrinaire
truth has historically raised negative responses from conservatives. Robert
Hutchins, for example, argues that without inculcation of the values
dominant in Western culture, pedagogies like Dewey's would be unable to
develop students' moral judgment. That is, Hutchins saw Dewey's methods
as legitimate tools for reaching the good life, but they could not take us far
since, in Hutchins' view, they were unable to tell us anything about the
nature of the good life (53; for a similar criticism of Dewey, see Mumford).

To argue, as Hutchins did, that Dewey's pedagogical goals are without
moral content is correct in a narrow sense. When Dewey says, for instance,
that the purpose of education is growth, and that the purpose of growth is
more growth, he struggles to avoid presenting education as wedded to a

particular ideology or set of values. However, as we have also seen, Dewey understands growth or expanded student interest in a complex way. Although he views it as a process with important cognitive aspects, such as critical mastery of the curriculum, he believes it also has important creative and moral aspects. In other words, intelligence, for Dewey, as we have observed, is not focused on IQ scores. Rather, it involves patience, tolerance for doubt, and sincerity. It is open and collegial, and, to flourish, it requires diverse points of view, with everyone having equal access to cultural resources and the spheres of public discourse. Alternatively put, scientific or intelligent thinking, according to Dewey, can only prosper in democratic contexts. As a pedagogical goal, therefore, student growth and enriched experience are hardly morally neutral. Although they rely on cognitive traits like careful observation and patient weighing of facts, they also demand social environments which promote moral integrity, wholeheartedness, and cooperative interaction.

Dewey's insistence that the classroom be designed to foster enriched student experience and expanded interest reflects his individualistic, classically liberal side. And it was with this Dewey that I believe the bookstore clerk's professor was most likely upset. However, I cannot be sure, since Dewey has another side, a more communitarian one that certain types of liberals, as opposed to conservatives, find disturbing. If that professor were liberal in the sense that he stressed individual rights and autonomy above all else, then he might find Dewey's liberalism too republican, too focused on the good of the community. In other words, the professor's criticism could represent either the conservative reaction that Dewey's goal of growth is too open ended, not tied enough to established curricula, or the laissez-faire, individualistic, liberal reaction that Dewey's goal is too controlling. That is, liberals, for whom individual rights are sacrosanct, might argue that the goals of education should be left to each student. Schools should put forward various courses of study, but students should decide what they want to do with them. If students want to resist becoming more sincere, critical, and cooperative, that's fine, say these liberals, that's their right. The school's primary responsibility is to make sure each child receives equal attention and opportunity, the greatest liberty consistent with equal liberty for others. Put another way, these liberals doubt that in a multicultural society like ours, we can find educational goals upon which everyone can agree. For instance, some might claim that schools should prepare students to be employees: loyal, obedient citizens striving to preserve the nation just as it is. On the other side would be those who hold that schools should turn out revolutionaries to correct the injustices embedded in our national institutions. For Dewey or anyone else to decide who is correct, say these liberals, is to push public education from its appropriate, neutral stance.

Criticism from the liberal Left, in its boldest form, sees Dewey as a subtle manipulator. It views him as flirting with trouble when he asks more from society than simply freedom from political oppression and from invasion of the private sphere. Indeed freedom for Dewey is not just a don't-tread-on-me situation but an opportunity to cooperatively plan, revise, and carry out carefully considered purposes (*Experience and Education* 61–65). However, from the liberal Left, it looks as if Dewey has crossed a dangerous line, going beyond what political theorists call negative liberties to champion certain positive ones, like cooperation, social intelligence, and integrity (for more on these two types of liberty, see Berlin). A critical commentator like Christopher Lasch, for example, argues that Dewey, in the name of scientific or enlightened education, engages in a form of "I-know-better-than-you-what-is-good-for-you" approach, attempting to use public schools to force middle-class and professional values on immigrant and lower-class children (Lasch, ch. 5; for similar criticisms, see Feinberg; Itzkoff; Wissot; for the Marxist charge that Dewey fails to understand how cooperative group work "reproduces" a repressive ideology, see Myers).

Dewey As Welfare Liberal

These criticisms from the conservative Right and the liberal Left reveal Dewey's approach, once again, as an effort to integrate opposing forces: in this case, to preserve pupil autonomy while structuring the classroom to encourage cooperative student work. (For criticisms from both Right and Left by a single author, someone who seems to view Dewey as both too individualistic and not individualistic enough, see Hofstadter 377–84.) These criticisms from right and left also point to the hybrid quality of Dewey's ideology. Although he calls himself a liberal, he is a liberal in a very different way than a laissez-faire one like John Locke. Dewey would hardly say, as Locke does, that we are entitled to the fruits of our labor, the products we have shaped from natural materials through personal effort (*Two* 134–35). Dewey is too much the communitarian or social constructionist for that. In other words, he recognizes that people do not own their talents, because, for good or bad, we are all heavily molded by our social conditions. For instance, Henry Ford can say he invented the car, but, in doing so, he appropriates for himself at least 200 years of cooperative, technological work by others. (For background on the liberal-communitarian debate see Mulhall and Swift; Frazer and Lacey.)

What makes Dewey a liberal is not, as it is for Locke, respect for individual property, but respect for individual initiative and uniqueness, for equal opportunity, and not just in the formal sense of equal rights, but in the material sense of equal resources. He does not see much benefit in granting people equal political and civil rights when many do not have the jobs, schooling, or resources to take advantage of such rights. If I were to put a label on him, I would call Dewey a welfare liberal. For unlike many other liberals, Dewey is willing to recognize differences in people's needs. The requirements of the disadvantaged—the young, the disabled, the aged, the poor—must be taken into account, for Dewey, if equality is to be achieved (*Liberalism* 38–39; *Public* 149–50).

In worrying about people's actual abilities to compete, Dewey goes a lot further toward interfering in people's lives than many liberals would condone. And this is reflected in his attitude toward the classroom. Dewey is not content to let the gifted do their own thing for their own advantage. He wants classes to be cooperative, built around tasks which require student give-and-take. Although he aligns himself with liberalism, he also says surprisingly communitarian things about liberty and equality. For Dewey, liberty is being able to join groups and work with others. Equality is giving to conjoint projects according to our ability and taking according to our need (*Public* 149–55). It is true that he treasures difference and eccentricity, that he sees these as necessary for successfully enacting and responding to change. But, as much as Dewey supports liberalism's stress on individuals and their critical abilities, he also values conjoint activity and community. And his most frequent metaphors for well-functioning groups have a pronounced communitarian flavor.

Dewey's Organic Images for Community

Societies are ideally, for Dewey, organic wholes. They mirror close-knit families or animal bodies whose different and unique parts contribute essentially and vitally to shared goals. However, stress should be on the word *ideally*, because Dewey recognizes that *community* is used in honorific (normative) as well as descriptive ways. He recognizes that society, in fact, is composed of a plurality of groups, some more open than others (*Democracy* 82). This is an important reason why he argues democratic education must emphasize open-minded and cooperative thinking, must allow students "to come into contact with a broader environment" than the ones into which they are born (20). For Dewey believes democracy at its best is dynamic, allowing for diverse groups and promoting open interaction among them (83).

Dewey's view that democracy is full interaction among diverse communities is consistent with his claim that difference is not just to be tolerated, allowed to sit there occupying its own space or occasionally touring adjoining spaces before quickly returning home. Rather, Dewey sees difference as functional, as a valuable opportunity for interaction, criticism, and new construction. So the idea of agreeing to disagree in order to withdraw or find safety in an "inner" life seems undemocratic and immoral to him (*Democracy* 122). What is controversial, or what commentators like Hofstadter (383) fear about Dewey's view of well-functioning community, is that in the name of the group, individuals, including students, who do not share majority values can be suppressed or treated as means to others' ends, forced to participate or reveal themselves against their will. Although I do not fully agree with these criticisms, I do acknowledge that it is difficult, in a culture often driven by group-think, to be sanguine about reconciling social solidarity and respect for individual uniqueness. I also admit that Dewey does not confront head-on the enormous difficulties we face in developing groups—and relationships—in which we can realize our best potential and to which we can make our best contribution.

Related to the school, Dewey's organic view of community means that student tasks, classroom rules, and course curricula should be organized around shared purposes. In opposition, laissez-faire liberals might worry, as I have indicated, that, despite Dewey's optimism, we probably cannot agree on the nature of such common purposes. At most, such liberals would continue, we might be able to agree on the nature of what we want to avoid, and, for these theorists, what we want to avoid is disrespect for students' needs to decide for themselves. They would conclude that in more autonomously minded and less communitarian classrooms than Dewey's, everyone may not get what they most want—the realization of their utopian visions—but at least everyone can avoid what they most fear: the loss of individual choice (for concerns about the "consensus" ethos underlying classroom group work, see Trimbur).

Understanding Dewey's welfare liberalism as an effort to reconcile individual and community goals, to honor both individual and group demands, may help us see our own classes in fresh ways. Excavating his ideology, his view of the ideal class as composed of diverse, open, and fully interacting subgroups, is, I believe, worthwhile even if it only helps us realize that as we teach, we rely on practices and languages whose ideology may be hidden. Alerted, we may see, for example, that defending the rights of individual students, even their right to be silent and left alone, may sometimes contradict the communitarian value of having classmates work cooperatively with one another. We may see our classrooms as, in fact, ideologically complex rather than simple, as mixed visions combining aspects of various ideals such as selfless family life, civic-minded parliaments of equals, and perfectly competitive marketplaces.

LIBERALIZING STUDENTS: DEWEYAN POLITICS AND PUPIL CHANGE

What is the relevance for contemporary teachers of Dewey's classroom ideology? In addressing the sorts of change he wants for students, Dewey sheds light on current debates about education's potential for social reform. Although many of us may agree that a more inclusive society, one which encourages individual growth in accord with the betterment of the least advantaged, is desirable, deciding which classroom structures best help us achieve this goal is not easy. For example, it is unclear how we can avoid the type of school politeness which condones an unjust status quo while, at the same time, sidestepping the pitfalls of indoctrination, the inclination to make all students "p.l.u."s (people like us). Dewey's outline of classrooms likely to promote democracy contributes to our discussion of what can reasonably be expected from an education which tries to optimize individual potential while striving for improved collective life.

Although Dewey says over and over again that he wants schools to be agents of reform (*Democracy* 20, 79, 98; "Education and Social" 692; *Quest* 252), I believe he would be unhappy with teachers' simply urging their own favored positions on students. As he puts it:

> Education means the creation of a discriminating mind, a mind that prefers not to dupe itself or to be the dupe of others.... [It means] the habit of suspended judgment, of skepticism, of desire for evidence, of appeal to observation rather than sentiment, discussion rather than bias, inquiry rather than conventionalized idealizations. ("Education as Politics" 334)

In short, the important thing, for Dewey, as I have noted, is not what students can say or their particular position at the close of a course. It is, rather, the habits for future learning and cooperative activity they take with them, their ability to "inquire, judge, and act" for themselves ("Are" 464; "Some" 337–38). Having students adopt the instructor's line on, say, affirmative action, abortion, or the possibility of a "just" war would not be Dewey's goal. This would put too much stress on only one product of the educational experience and, for Dewey, not the most important. Two students could say the same lines about abortion and have those lines mean very different things depending upon the struggles, or lack thereof, behind those words. Dewey would argue that to simply attend to what students are saying, to believe that they have changed for the better because they have moved to views teachers find acceptable, is to separate *means* from *ends* in a shortsighted way, to overlook the most important residue of the learning process. He complains, "Too large a part of our citizens has left our schools without power of critical discrimination, at the mercy of special propaganda, and drifting from one plan and scheme to another according to the loudest clamor of the moment" ("Need for Orientation" 91). In other words, under the wrong conditions, students who, for example, surrender racist talk for civil justice talk—if left with only the tools of passive, received knowing—may be in no better position for further education, for deepened and enlarged experience, than they were at the beginning of their schooling.

Dewey's approach to classroom politics and student transformation reveals both his commitment to democratic society and his recognition of the changing nature of our world. Life is a gamble, he once wrote. "The world is a scene of risk: it is uncertain, unstable, uncannily unstable" (*Experience and Nature* 38). With this in mind, Dewey wants students to develop the habit of intelligent, cooperative inquiry, the disposition to work with others to understand and shape their changing environment (*How* 270–71). In other words, given the nature of the world and our society, he does not want students leaving our classes clinging to rehearsed lines. That just will not do in a world as fluid and uncertain as ours.

LIBERALIZING THE CURRICULUM: REFORM OF ACADEMIC AND VOCATIONAL SCHOOLING

Dewey's liberalism not only leads him to focus on the habits or residues that students take from our courses, it also shapes his attitude toward the school curriculum. As chair of the Department of Pedagogy at the University of

Chicago (1894–1904), he directed several primary and secondary schools, including a high school of manual training. Beginning in this period and throughout his career, Dewey consistently worked to "liberalize" the school curriculum at all levels.

Overall, when he viewed the American school scene, Dewey saw as the major impediment to liberalized education the tension between educating for labor and educating for leisure. College and preparatory institutions, he claimed, were designed to develop student taste, aesthetic sensibility, and intellectual independence. Lower grades and vocational schools, by contrast, were directed toward labor, toward occupational skills learned through repetition and routine. Dewey saw both types of education—for leisure and for labor—as poorly conceived and ineptly carried out. Vocational training, he argued, is often impractical. Skills taught, allegedly central for adult occupations, are frequently presented as detached from real-life applications. This makes such training, in his view, narrow and nontransferable. On the other hand, the so-called liberal arts, according to Dewey, are frequently not at all liberating, promoting ostentatious display rather than intellectual courage and cooperation.

Dewey's effort to liberalize education—to integrate teaching for leisure and teaching for labor—is a consistent theme throughout his educational writing. We find it in 1893 in "Teaching Ethics in the High Schools"; we see it in middle works such as "The Educational Situation" (1902), "Significance of the School of Education" (1904), and *Democracy and Education* (1916); and we hear its final development in late pieces such as *The Way out of Educational Confusion* (1931) and *Experience and Education* (1938). The language changes, but the theme remains the same. In "Teaching Ethics in the High Schools" the tension between leisure and labor education is discussed as the conflict between abstract ethical precepts and concrete human relations; in "The Educational Situation" it is aristocratic versus democratic culture; in "Significance of the School of Education," it is theory versus practice; and in *Democracy and Education* it is explicitly leisure versus labor. But the impediment to liberalization of the curriculum is always the same: the separation of social classes and types of knowledge he elaborated in *Reconstruction in Philosophy*.

What is Dewey's solution? He urges teaching occupational skills to provoke student curiosity and intelligence, offering enough theoretical foundation so that in the workplace students can adjust to rapidly changing political and marketplace conditions. Conversely, he urges teaching traditional academic subjects, not as isolated ends in themselves, but as interdependent tools for addressing pressing social problems. He praises the introduction of "commercial and social studies" into the college curriculum and the maintenance of technological schools at major universities ("Educational" 413). He supports the growing tendency to use the first 2 years of college for survey courses and the last 2 for professional training or preparation for each student's "particular calling in life" ("Are" 473). And in his early article on teaching ethics in the high schools, he argues that history and literature are important, not in themselves, but for what they teach about daily life. Where there is one reason, he writes, for average students to study geometry, physics, Latin, or Greek, "there are twenty" for them to study human interaction ("Teachings" 60).

The result, in short, of Dewey's curriculum-liberalization strategy is, on the one hand, to teach what is useful—productive and socially serviceable occupations—in an enriching and intellectually provocative way and, on the other, to teach what is enriching—studies which develop refinement of taste and appreciation of the free play of ideas—in a way which bears upon everyday practice (*Democracy* 258–60; "Social Value" 315–16). In his words,

> If the cultural work of schools became too remote and abstract and dead, because of isolation from the more immediately practical moving force of society [like business], so also manual and commercial education easily becomes cramped, servile, and hard when apart from the illuminating and expanding elements of a cultural education. ("Significance" 446; see also "Educational" 411 and *Way* 26–27)

I note in passing that it is easy to see why this sort of Deweyan work to balance polar forces often makes him a target of people, like the bookstore clerk's professor, who are unsympathetic with his integrative efforts. Regarding his push for a liberalized curriculum, conservative critics see Dewey's celebration of the practical or vocational as a dangerous devaluation of the classics. By contrast, left-leaning critics observe the same emphasis and charge Dewey with promoting vocational schooling to boost narrow capitalist interests.

DEWEY'S CHALLENGE TO TEACHERS

I have presented Dewey's educational philosophy as a reconciliation of powerful and sometimes conflicting activities: the nested dualisms of student and curriculum, individual and group, continuity and interaction, construction and criticism, interest and effort. He gives us a large canvas of educational guidelines rather than a hardened tablet of teaching techniques and rules. This is wise strategy, I believe, for he challenges us as teachers to be "inventive pioneers," reflective and experimental ("Education As Engineering" 328). He encourages us to establish interplay between his principles and our own classroom practices, a dialogue in which both are modified and adjusted. Although, as I have said, current calls for improved teaching at all levels make Dewey's educational philosophy worthy of special attention, his principles leave us with a tall order. That is, he wants us to structure our classes so they promote (1) enriched experience through mastery of new subject matter and (2) development of moral character, especially habits of cooperative, intelligent thinking.

Although this is a tall order, it is not an impossible one. The deep conceptual roots of Dewey's pedagogical ideas provide a powerful framework within which to critically examine our classrooms. I offer evidence for this claim in the following two chapters as I explore Dewey's pedagogical principles from two new angles: first, from the perspective of my own education and, second, from the standpoint of my own teaching.

THE MORAL LIFE IS LIVED ONLY AS the individual appreciates for himself [sic] the ends for which he is working, and does his work in a personal spirit of interest and devotion to these ends.

— JOHN DEWEY,
"Ethical Principles Underlying Education" 1897: 131

Chapter Five

MY OWN SCHOOLING WITHOUT STUDENT-CURRICULUM INTEGRATION

Steve Fishman

I n this chapter, I analyze my own university experience to illustrate the negative consequences of inadequate student-curriculum integration. In particular, I use my university schooling to make vivid Dewey's cautions against neglect of moral traits of character and constructive work. Without fully understanding it, throughout my university years I hungered for integration of two types. On the one hand, I blindly searched for continuities between the curriculum and myself, that is, for ways to do schooling with more integrity and wholeheartedness. On the other hand, I also sought ways to balance the critical, analytic thinking in my courses with synthetic or constructive work.

I offer an account of my education, in other words, to provide further perspective on the Deweyan theory I have discussed in Chapters 1 through 4. The fruitfulness of Dewey's conceptual lenses—especially his ideas on integrity and wholeheartedness, construction and criticism—is illustrated as they gradually clarify the frustrations which baffled me as a student and from which I could not easily step clear.

MY UNIVERSITY EDUCATION: A DIVIDED SELF SEEKING DIRECTION

My education at Columbia University, as I look back on it, is marked by three transformative moments, all connected to problems I experienced adjusting to the change from secondary school to college. Although it has taken a long time for me to clarify and link these moments, Dewey's emphasis on integrating student and curriculum has been central to that eventual understanding. From an almost 30 year distance—and using Deweyan language—it looks as if, during college and graduate days, I could not organize an integrated self. My old high school habits were wanting, but I had too few tools to develop satisfying new ones.

Actually, it was not so much the change from high school to college that unglued me as it was the change from freshman to upperclass college life. Whereas I enjoyed my contacts during my first year with my assistant professors, in subsequent semesters my tenured professors appeared indifferent and remote, their courses in my major—philosophy—seemingly discontinuous with the rest of my life. I managed to survive the last 3 undergraduate years and then 7 more in graduate school, but with divided attention. I labored, like a character in Dewey's educational nightmares, confused, unable to integrate my activities—my efforts "half-hearted," my work alternately chaotic or boring. So why did I stick it out? And why did I go into teaching? Because I thought, crazy as it sounds, that I could make things easier for my students than it had been for me.

So I did not join the academy expecting to write books or become chairperson or dean. I really wanted to teach, of all things. I was puzzled about what happened to me between freshman and later university years, about my inability to be wholehearted about my schooling, to find continuities between myself and my professors, my courses and my life. And I stuck to my career choice because of the somewhat naive idea that as a teacher I could eventually change things so later students would not hurt so much or be so puzzled.

But why Dewey? Why is he at the center of all this? Well, without my knowing it, as my academic life and teaching career moved forward, I was somehow moving backward to Dewey. Unwittingly, I was filling out and working to better understand my initial, adolescent encounter with his work.

DEWEY'S UNIVERSITY WITHOUT DEWEY

I came as a freshman to Columbia University in 1954, 24 years after Dewey had retired from its philosophy department, 2 years after his death (see Randall "Department"). And although John Herman Randall, Jr., and Ernest Nagel and Justus Buchler, all of whom had known Dewey well, would later be my teachers, they never discussed him. They never even asked me to read Dewey, although a couple of his books—*Art As Experience* and *Experience and Nature*—were on the lengthy reading list for my graduate school comprehensives. But that was it. At most, Dewey was the thinnest of aromas on the seventh floor of Philosophy Hall, only a photo on Randall's desk, a slim, dark-suited figure in front of a summer cottage beside a Model T Ford. The recent history of American philosophy explains this oddity.

After World War II, by the time I was a Columbia undergraduate, language analysis had taken over Anglo-American philosophy departments. The key figures were Wittgenstein, Russell, Moore, and Ayer, plus selected members of the Vienna Circle like Schlick and Reichenbach. Language analysis was a reformist movement tracing its origins to Hume and seeing traditional philosophy as an embarrassingly endless, futile discussion. The movement's explanation was that philosophers had been linguistically naive, misled by language itself to ask meaningless questions like, What is the essence of self? What is the first cause of things? What is the nature of goodness? They argued that traditional philosophy, especially in the realm of morals or anything having to do with evaluation, like aesthetics, had been extremely foolish, assuming there could be justifiable criteria for deciding between competing value judgments. For example, claims about good and bad when examined closely were, for Bertrand Russell, only thinly disguised promotions of one's own wishes. They were written in declarative sentences and sounded like empirical observations but were actually, under scrutiny of linguistic analysis, merely reports about a writer's preferences. Ethics, said Russell, is in the end a matter of propaganda and rhetoric, a situation in which, without any facts to go on, writers and speakers use assorted strategies to get others to adopt the positions that they themselves favor (*Religion* ch. 10). Other ordinary-language philosophers, like A. J. Ayer, went further, claiming that *X is good* did not necessarily mean that the author liked X, since someone could speak this way without liking X at all. In fact, Ayer said, *X is good* is totally meaningless, sort of like a grunt or noise (Ayer ch. 6). As a result, language analysts set the task of future philosophy as marking more clearly the limits of knowledge, making us sensitive enough to the misleading structure of language so we would stop asking meaningless questions and use our time more productively.

Dewey was pushed aside by this movement because his orientation was quite different. He had been doing philosophy in what language analysts saw as an old-fashioned way, trying to understand the human condition, the dynamics of art, morality, and education in an effort to ameliorate contemporary social problems. Analyzing the word *philosophy* in a 1950 letter, Dewey acknowledged the minority position in which he found himself. He noted: "['Wisdom,' 'sophia'] is a 'practical' or moral term; 'love,' 'philo' is emotive. [But] practical philosophy today is largely in academic doldrums— its 'professors' rarely even attempting to use it in its application to life's issues" (qtd. in Williams 88). In fact, Dewey went so far as to argue that scientific method, in a broad sense, could be applied to moral and social questions (*Human* 295; *Ethics* 282). He attacked Russell's moral subjectivism and denied that to desire X meant the same as *X is desirable* ("Religion" 462). For Dewey, preferences were important, but they were only the start; they had to go through the crucible of reflection, discussion, and experimentation before we could label them worthy. Moral judgments, like all judgments, even those in the physical sciences, are subject to reappraisal, but for Dewey that did not mean we could not or should not distinguish judgments which had been openly discussed and evaluated from those which had not (*Ethics* 262–68).

This post–World War II turn of events created serious shifts of power in American philosophy departments. Intellectual historians and existentialists, aestheticians and phenomenologists, as well as anyone believing philosophy should be relevant to practical problems, as Dewey believed, were looked upon as misguided, pursuing questions for which, as the history of philosophy had allegedly shown, there would never be answers.

I wish I could say that as a graduate student I stood up in seminars and protested that ordinary-language analysis was a bigger waste of time than the philosophy it attacked. I wish I could say I tried defending Dewey or other alternative movements in philosophy. But I did not. Although I remained muddled and dispirited, I played along and did what everyone else in philosophy seemed to be doing. In fact, I actually did well on the philosophy of science, epistemology, and logic sections of my comprehensives and very poorly on aesthetics, metaphysics, and ethics. You see, compared to other approaches, and given the overall confusion in which I rowed, the language analysts seemed relatively specific and concrete, and I guess I learned to imitate their way of multiplying and analyzing ordinary uses of devilish words like *see* and *know* and *good* well enough to sound as though I was beginning to master their dialect. So, again, you ask, if no one spoke about Dewey at Columbia, where did he come in?

MEETING JOHN DEWEY THROUGH A BACK DOOR

Dewey came to me in a course I took in the summer between my freshman and sophomore college years. And it was not at Columbia, and it was not from a Columbia professor. I had gotten an afternoon job in Boston for July and August but spent mornings in an Introduction to Philosophy course offered by someone from the University of Michigan, William Frankena. His name meant nothing to me then, but later, in graduate school, I learned Frankena was internationally respected, that Dewey had himself taught at Michigan before the turn of the century, and that Frankena had written a famous and frequently anthologized article defending the ethical approach Dewey favored (Frankena "Naturalistic"). In his Intro course, Frankena assigned books by four different philosophers—Ayer, Cassirer, James, and Dewey. I struggled with all four, and Frankena, in a large lecture hall, seemed quite distant. But I did bring Dewey back to Columbia with me when I returned from Boston at the end of that summer.

Dewey's Continuities Enter My Fragmented World

The book by Dewey which Frankena asked us to read was *Reconstruction in Philosophy*, lectures Dewey gave on a visit to Japan in 1919. For me, it was important because, in these lectures, Dewey outlined significant themes in the history of philosophy. During my freshman year at Columbia, before I read Dewey, I had experienced the famous Humanities and Contemporary Civilization courses, classes which are still in place, required of all freshmen, and which meet four times a week the entire first year. Daniel Bell offers an historical account of the development of these general education courses (see also Buchler "Reconstruction"), but my own sense was that they were remedial, a lot of authors thrown at freshmen as if to regain lost time. For instance, in the Civilization course, we began with Thales and read excerpts from other authors running to over a thousand pages of small print. The course included philosophers and theologians, psychologists and economists—the academic elite, I suppose. I can remember snippets of Ricardo and Freud and Adam Smith and Durkheim. But I had little idea how to organize them or explore their relevance to my life.

In Dewey's language, there was a lot of interaction with the curriculum, but it did not go deep, because I had none of the appropriate tools, the to-whats and for-whats, necessary to guide my reading (see Chapter 2). As a consequence, I was unable to fashion either significant continuities between my readings and personal concerns or meaningful syntheses of the readings themselves. Before every Civilization class, I would try to make sense of an author, perhaps Descartes or Hegel, and attempt to connect the truth I thought that author had discovered with truths I had salvaged from previous readings. However, like clockwork, in class, my instructor would explode my connections, pointing out the by now legendary mistakes the author had made.

My teacher's daily displays of analytic work eventually left me in a cul de sac because they shattered the small meanings I had squeezed from each author the night before. Erasmus and Epictetus and Calvin were all famous, I thought. If I can just understand and relate them, I will get a handle on the truth. But now my instructor is breaking their arguments apart, showing how inadequate they really are, so what I am to do? So far, when it comes to putting the readings together or understanding their significance, I am chalking up a zero.

When I took the final exam for freshman Civilization that spring, despite the fact that we had focused on criticism, I attempted to build my own connections. I wrote furiously in my blue book, putting down all I could remember of all the authors I could recall, and I concluded that the last person we read—I think it was Santayana—had learned so much from the previous authors that he had finally gotten it right. The feeble narrative I managed at the end of my Civilization course was a Grand March of Human Thought theory: The last one to write is correct because the last one has the advantage of learning from all the others. Although I hoped my instructor would not notice, I was actually confused and dispirited. I had not the slightest idea what to do with all the material tossed my way. That summer, when Frankena threw four more authors at me, Dewey happened to say some of the right things at the right time to the right person. He offered someone desperate for connections a moment of unifying direction.

You see, in *Reconstruction in Philosophy*, a work I refer to frequently in Chapter 1 of this volume, Dewey does not offer a set of characteristics as a way of defining philosophy. He does not say it is a series of definite questions or a list of canonic texts. Instead, he tells how philosophy functions in a culture, its origins and social results, describing it as a cultural debate over competing values, with succeeding generations answering earlier ones. This way of seeing philosophy—as reflection on broad and continuing cultural movements—gave me a narrative with which to begin connecting figures I had read during freshman Civilization (see *Reconstruction* 1–27).

After Frankena's summer course, in 1955, I returned to New York feeling a little relieved and a little more confident, but it was short lived. That fall, when I tried in class to explain what I had read in Dewey, it was a muddle both to myself and others. Yet I felt a spark because, although I could not quite articulate what Dewey was saying, I had a sense I had gotten something of what he had put there for readers to find.

THREE TRANSORMATIVE MOMENTS

As I mentioned earlier, my affinity for Dewey did not come straight away but grew gradually. Looking back, it seems I was storing up moments which were important to me, which kept returning, but which I did not quite understand. And I was storing up Dewey as well, as if waiting for the time when he and these moments would come together, when he would provide a narrative both uniting them and pulling me further into his thought.

Philosophy As Serious Business: Moment Number One

The first moment has to do with my freshman Civilization course. As I have already indicated, my instructor (Sid Morgenbesser, then an assistant professor and later to succeed Ernest Nagel as John Dewey Professor of Philosophy), took a critical stance toward most of our course readings. He inspired me to try my best, and I very much admired his understanding of the material and his analytic skills. On occasion, I even tried battling him, attempting, I suppose, to salvage something of the meaning I had wrestled from our assignments. I believe we were discussing Georges Sorel, and I went to Morgenbesser after class—this was some time in the spring—and told him there were things I did not understand about the reading. He kept his eyes on his papers and, without glancing at me, asked, "Did you have dinner last night?" I answered yes. He then looked up to catch my eyes, "Next time, don't eat dinner until you understand the material." I was taken aback, but it made perfect sense. Of course, he was correct. Philosophy was serious business, and I respected that. I too wanted to be serious. The following week I signed up to become a philosophy major.

Philosophy as Mysterious Business: Moment Number Two

Having thus decided my life course, I took, as a sophomore, three year-long philosophy courses: American Philosophy with Joseph Blau; Introduction with Charles Frankel; and a seminar on Santayana with Justus Buchler, my college advisor and future dissertation director. American Philosophy seemed like history, and Frankel, well, he was a handsome man, and the premeds thought he was great, but, sorry to say, I did not think he took us seriously. I concluded he was performing in his three-piece suits for an audience which did not include me.

As for the Buchler seminar, only four other students registered, all seniors. Some of them had already received graduate fellowships at important schools, and so I respected them. I also believed I could learn from Buchler. But, I swear, in that small, quiet seminar room, the words I heard from the other five men—it was an all-male college—made sense singly but not in the aggregate. The few times I tried to participate, I got stares, confirming my sense that the discussion was over my head. My last attempt to speak was a comment about Santayana's *Scepticism and Animal Faith*. When I finished, Buchler remarked that what I had contributed did not sound anything like Santayana to him.

My disorientation and dissatisfaction built during my sophomore year, and the second transformative moment which Dewey later helped me understand came on a clear, spring, Friday afternoon. I was desperate. I ran from my dorm to Hamilton Hall and found Joseph Blau in his second-floor office. "I just don't know how to do it," I said. "How do I know when I'm writing philosophy?" He was a solid, square man with narrow feet. He had wonderful curly white hair and eyebrows, appearing like a philosopher should, even to the smell of his pipe. He sucked a breath and smiled as though I were a 6-year-old interrupting his reading. "Fishman," he said, "the nature of philosophy is the last question you ask, not the first." Then he sighed and got to his feet. "I've got to go now and teach Civ to the kiddies," he whispered conspiratorially. "Got to give them the truth." He winked, and I smiled back, but inside I felt brushed off. I also wanted to defend the freshmen. I still do.

Leaving Blau, I ran the Hamilton Hall stairs to the fourth floor to look for Buchler and, to my relief, found him in. He had the odd habit of sitting in his office with the lights off. I never saw him smile, and he always spoke in abstract terms, even when discussing apparently mundane things. A nail in the street was a "vehicular hazard," and city road jams were "vicissitudes of metropolitan traffic." Nevertheless, I felt he knew what was important to know. I was positive of it, and I also attributed deep suffering to him, a noble sort, which made me want to learn all about him.

On Buchler's door was a handwritten note which read Enter without knocking. I did. He was alone and looked over at me. "I want to ask you something," I said. "Well," he answered, "I'm your advisor, so I guess I have to listen." Taking that as encouragement, I walked to the chair near his desk and sat down. He was looking out his office window toward Amsterdam Avenue. I asked, "How do you know when you're doing philosophy? I'm trying to write these papers, and I don't know if I'm being philosophic." He turned and gazed straight ahead. "It's a level of sophistication. You'll reach a level of sophistication." And then he nodded at me as if he were satisfied and had said all he could. I did not feel patronized, and I still wanted to learn all about him, but I left more uneasy than when I entered. Great advice, I thought. Like a high jumper, I will just urge my thoughts to another level. I rushed to the stairs again, wondering just how I was going to get more sophisticated.

Morgenbesser shared a small office on the top floor of Hamilton, but he was not there. And then I remembered he had a carrel in Butler Library, so I hurried across campus hoping to catch him. I did. His carrel was even smaller than his office, and he did not invite me in. I had never seen him in shirtsleeves before, and he was wearing glasses, for reading, I guessed. As I stood in the corridor, air from his carrel seemed warm, as if Morgenbesser had been working and reading a long time. I hoped my bothering him would not anger him. "I'm really discouraged," I said. "I have no idea what philosophy is." He laughed a full laugh. "Aha, Fishman, that's a good sign. You're making progress. The first step in understanding philosophy is to be confused." I did not know what to make of that. I did not know if he was laughing because I had asked such a dumb question, or if he was serious. "You think this is good?" I asked. "Yeah," he replied, "you're making progress." To push Morgenbesser further, I felt, would be an imposition. I said thanks and left.

Walking back to my dorm, the contrast between my high school enthusiasm for college and its depressing reality was obvious. At the close of my first year, I had felt pretty good about committing to philosophy. It seemed the most serious challenge, the noblest cause. And, now, toward the close of my second year, I could not put things together or figure out how philosophy might be valuable to me. I was not far from the high school shore, yet I was unable to turn back, caught in what seemed to be meaningless drifting.

My Philosophic Confusion Deepens: Moment Number Three

My final transformative moment occurred during graduate school. I was enrolled in another seminar with Buchler, this time on Wittgenstein and process philosophy. It was a group of more than 20, and Buchler lectured. I thought the point of the course was that Wittgenstein was not quite the innovator everyone said he was, but I was not sure. Midway through the semester, I was still having trouble choosing a term paper topic, and I went to see Buchler. He was now serving as department chair, had become Samuel Johnson Professor of Philosophy, and had moved his office to Philosophy Hall. I caught him at 5 in the afternoon by the seventh floor elevator. "I'm having trouble finding a topic," I began, "and time is running short. Have you any suggestions?" He shook his head no while pressing the button for the lift. "You'll have to do that on your own," he said quietly. "But how do I do that? Where do you find good topics?" Before getting on the elevator, Buchler pointed to his stomach with his index finger and pushed. "From in here," he said.

It took me by surprise, someone reserved and articulate, pointing to his stomach like that. As I watched the elevator close behind him, I felt he was being honest, yet I still felt unhelped. Okay, I thought, topics have to come from inside. But what do I do if there is nothing there? Can't he look at me and see I'm empty? In my heart of hearts, I longed to observe him at work, to quietly sit at the corner of his desk as he wrote through the night. It was my persistent daydream. I saw myself watching his words form on the page, gradually understanding how he chose his topics, how he moved from thinking like everyone else to thinking like a philosopher.

I ended up writing about Spinoza, of all people, and when I got the paper back, Buchler had written, next to the grade at the top, "Good as far as you go." I took it as a considerate way of saying my efforts were still clumsy. I had managed to learn a little about Spinoza. There were small sections of his *Ethics* which I understood. But I had no idea what to do with the little I knew, or why it might be important.

DEWEYAN INSIGHTS ABOUT MY TRANSFORMATIVE MOMENTS

The three moments I have outlined seemed, for a long time, like dots in a child's coloring book I could not connect or, when connected, formed figures I could not recognize. But Dewey eventually helped.

Deweyan Insight Number One: The Need to Be An Active Learner

Basic to my story, I now believe, is an effort to transform what Dewey would call passive habits of learning into more active ones. That is, I see myself leaving high school with the view that, as Dewey would put it, I could be given ideas as if they were bricks. In college, I encountered professors for whom, generally, I had respect and for whom I did the required work. Yet something was wrong. I kept assuming philosophy was a skill I could learn by memorizing rules and procedures others could hand me.

On reflection, I had a correct diagnosis of my problem: I had too little sense of the characteristics distinguishing philosophic work from, for example, history or psychology. But I was wrong about the prescription. My frustration with my professors was misdirected since they could not do for me what I wanted them to do. And this helps explain the first two moments I have recounted. In this regard, Morgenbesser was correct when he told me not to eat before completing my assignments and when he said, just outside his carrel, that doubt and genuine perplexity are the first philosophic steps. Morgenbesser could have told me a lot about Sorel or given me a long list of philosophy's characteristics, but, as Dewey would have observed, it would not have meant much. I needed to use philosophy to explore my own interests and to struggle toward understanding in my own way.

And Blau's response—that asking about the nature of philosophy should be put off until last—was in the same spirit. Although he did not give any clue about the nature of philosophy, he hinted at the misplaced confidence of freshmen who believed someone else could give them truth about the world. What Blau did offer about philosophy seemed, at the time, like a dodge. But to give him credit, Blau can be read as trying to tell me that the problem of the nature of philosophy is not simple, is not quite the same as the problem of getting from the Bronx to Manhattan. What looked for a long time like a question of finding the right professors, ones who would give me the answers I needed, now seems like a problem of having to shed high school attitudes of passive learning in a university setting which required active ones.

So Dewey's warning that ideas and bricks are significantly dissimilar—that, unlike bricks, ideas cannot be divided up and handed out—explains a major part of my dilemma. I came to college falsely believing that wisdom could be delivered piecemeal to me without my helping generate it, that wisdom was something separable from its development.

Deweyan Insight Number Two: The Need To Integrate The Classroom's Nested Dualisms

But something else was missing. Although it is true I had the mistaken notion that I could make someone else's ideas my own without struggling to use them, and this explains the first two university moments which haunt me, there is another piece to the puzzle. This is the third moment: Buchler's gesture toward his stomach. It took a long time, from 1959 until 1983, for me to begin understanding it, and, again, Dewey's thought was key to my clarification. For I now take Buchler's gesture to be a call to integrate myself and philosophy, to find continuity and interaction between my life and the new ideas I was encountering. Buchler's finger on his stomach was a pictorial graphic for Dewey's comment that, for a student, "having something to say" is very different from "having to say something" (*How* 246).

In interpreting Buchler's gesture this way, I do not want to imply that had he explained himself more fully, I would have understood well enough at the time to write a paper more closely related to my life. But I do believe Buchler's gesture hinted at an important part of the puzzle which no one else had even suggested: that student and curriculum need to be integrated (see Buchler, "Reconstruction" 127–35). Although Morgenbesser and Blau apparently knew that ideas could not be handed over like bricks—and wanted me to move me from passive knowing to active knowing—they failed to realize two things. First, the analytic thinking they were demonstrating needed to be balanced with synthetic, or constructive, thinking. And, second, my analytic and synthetic work, if it were to be original and worthwhile, had to have more of me in it, that is, be supported by better integration of student and curriculum. In other words, to improve the quality of my schoolwork, my teachers needed to help me find my own goals, or for-whats, so I could relate personal and academic concerns. Had I been encouraged to generate personally significant goals for reading philosophy, Dewey would say, I might have had a better chance to find appropriate to-whats and with-whichs to guide my entry into the subject matter. I would more likely have given schoolwork my wholehearted attention, interacting with the assigned material in deeper and more original ways.

My philosophy professors were not the only ones who failed to understand that without integration of student and curriculum, I could never approach my tasks wholeheartedly or produce quality work. As a junior, I sat through a year of Andrew Chiappe reciting Shakespeare, without understanding what I was supposed to be learning. I can still remember, "O tiger's heart wrapped in a woman's hide" and "lily in a gaol of snow." But that's all. As Dewey might have observed, although I memorized enough to pass, most of what I read, because discontinuous with my personal life, quickly became inaccessible (*Experience and Education* 47–48). And my longing for better integration was not limited to humanities courses. As a freshman I arm wrestled two semesters of calculus, asking, How is my life better, how am I wiser, for studying the parabola and its formulas? Is it obvious to everyone else except me how I might use this material and why it deserves my attention? Something told me it was foolish to even ask.

Looking back, it now seems my professors emphasized certain halves of the nested dualisms beneath the student-curriculum dichotomy: individual, interaction, criticism, and effort. But they failed to nurture the complementary halves: group, continuity, construction, and interest. Buchler failed to explain, for example, that if I had explored continuities between the little I knew about Spinoza and my own interests, I could have mounted a more sustained effort and interacted more deeply with Spinoza's work. With such continuities, I could have found more productive to-whats to attend to in the readings, thereby increasing my chances for growth or expanded interest. But Buchler and my other professors did not help me understand this. Nor did they encourage collegial conversations: not between me and my classmates as equals, not between me and them as junior and senior practitioners. And although these omissions may not have bothered other students, given my own hunger to shed a divided self for an integrated one, they remained strong contributors to my continuing hurt and puzzlement.

What I have said so far about ways to understand my university education has been the result of looking back through Deweyan lenses I myself have fashioned. Fortuitously, in "Construction and Criticism," Dewey himself comments about people who had college experiences similar to mine. He writes,

> I have heard intelligent persons say that their college education overdeveloped their critical faculties at the expense of their productive capacities.... [But the real problem is not the overcultivation of critical ability.] It is rather the

product of students being swamped with criticisms emanating from other minds. We forget that criticisms exist ready-made as much as anything else, and that absorption of ready-made criticisms is a very different thing from exercise of critical power. (134)

In effect, Dewey suggests, I was even worse off than I thought. My teachers were modeling critical thinking for me, but they were not helping me develop "the exercise of critical power." In other words, although my teachers wanted me to become an active learner, their demonstrating critical thinking was not by itself going to do the trick. Their approach was, "Watch me analyze. Now you analyze." But, according to Dewey, this was only "swamping" me with "ready-made" criticisms. I could only exercise critical powers when I was encouraged and motivated to generate my own analytic work.

However, I do not want to suggest my university courses were without significant value. After all, I was developing some level, however modest, of critical ability in that I was at least learning to question, doubt, and suspend belief. But Dewey helps explain why these analytic skills were not fulfilling. They were unsatisfying because, employed on material lacking apparent connection to my life, they failed to expand my own interests. In other words, they were not helping me grow. And, Dewey would continue, an important consequence of this lack of student-curriculum integration was that my schoolwork was at the mercy of forced rather than voluntary interests. With private life and school disconnected, all I had left as motives for school tasks were pleasing my teachers and obtaining passing grades. The hurt and puzzlement I felt, he would conclude, were my inner protests against an absence of intellectual integrity in my life. That is why, I figured out years later, I had "no heart" to go to my college graduation, why I refused to participate despite serious parental protest and disappointment.

In summary, to remedy my lack of intellectual integrity, to help me be more centered and wholehearted, Dewey would have wanted better integration of the nested dualisms he finds in the classroom. That is, until I could see the curriculum as a means to developing my own interests (for example, helping me articulate something I wanted to say or achieve a goal to which I was committed), I myself would not be fully present in my work. I would not really bring myself to it, and so my efforts could not find fulfillment. To exercise my constructive and critical powers, I had to make the curriculum my own. I had to use it to feed and expand genuine interests, and only when this occurred would I experience the moral integrity and meaningful integration I blindly sought.

CAUGHT IN THE PROFESSIONALIZATION OF PHILOSOPHY

I do not want to use Deweyan theory to underestimate my debts to Morgenbesser, Blau, Buchler, or my other Columbia professors. The fact that, more than 35 years after graduation, I still recall, mull, and profit from conversations I had with them is evidence of their positive influence. And, as Buchler—probably reflecting Peirce—once noted during the Santayana seminar, "A failed experiment is not really a failure if you learn from it" (see Buchler, *Peirce's* 74–78). Further, from my own teaching, I know it is not easy to integrate student and curriculum, to help students find genuine for-whats to guide their attention to course subject matter. In fact, it might be said that my entire 30-year teaching career has been an effort, sometimes ineffectual and confused, to help students make connections between themselves and course materials. I also know it can be difficult to develop cooperation among students and teachers, students and classmates. Given the university reward systems, the ways in which high grades and honors are distributed, it is no small task to conceive and stimulate interest in open dialogue and shared projects. But the difficulty of integrating student and curriculum, individual and group, as well as other classroom forces, only partly explains my professors' strong inclinations to keep them separate. A great deal of it also has to do with the reasons behind Dewey's philosophic eclipse, reasons why his method of doing philosophy fell out of favor.

Although I did not know it then, I was experiencing repercussions of a fight which Dewey, William James, and others were beginning to lose by the 1920s. My frustration was, in part, a product of the increasing professionalization of philosophy. Dewey could urge the integration of academic and personal life, not only because it made theoretic sense to him, but because he had lived it. He helped start the first New York teachers union, initiated efforts to develop a third political party in America, wrote for W.E.B. Du Bois's *Crisis* magazine and popular journals like the *New Republic* and the *Nation*, marched in the streets for women's rights, and chaired the famous Trotsky-in-exile trial in Mexico. However, by the time I got to Columbia, as I have said, Dewey's approach to philosophy had lost out (for Dewey's comments about this development, see *Problems* 3–20). There had been a fight for control of the American Philosophic Association in the early part of this century, with Arthur Lovejoy of Hopkins leading the argument for professionalization and people like William James of Harvard arguing against. Lovejoy's side won, and, increasingly, and especially through the 1950s and 1960s when I was at Columbia, philosophers saw themselves as specialists. They were moving away from larger cultural issues to more technical, epistemological ones, speaking more and more clearly, as John Herman Randall, Jr., once waggishly put it, about less and less.

So it is no wonder that I felt tacit prohibitions against questioning Morgenbesser or Blau or Buchler about philosophy's connections to my life. No wonder Buchler could only motion toward his stomach, hoping somehow I would give word and meaning to his gesture. These men had, after all, been working hard to step past questions like mine. Instead, they were engaged in professionalizing and upgrading their discipline, competing as individuals to develop a well-defined body of theoretical knowledge to be used in the service of increasingly technical tasks.

It has taken three decades for me to make some sense of the fragmentation and discontinuity I experienced during my university years. Given that Dewey's philosophy of education has been central to this process of clarification, you can see why I am in his debt. But insights about my own education did not come from reading Dewey in a vacuum. They came in the course of my own teaching—30 years of it—in which every problem I faced as a teacher reflected the problems I faced as a student. The same, slow process by which Dewey helped me look back with new clarity at my university education also enlightened my ongoing teaching. They are mutually embedded stories, each one mirroring the other.

Chapter Six

MY OWN TEACHING WITHOUT STUDENT-CURRICULUM INTEGRATION

Steve Fishman

HAVING TO SAY SOMETHING is a very different matter from having something to say.

— JOHN DEWEY,
How We Think, 1933: 246

Whereas in the previous chapter I explored—from my own student perspective—the consequences of neglecting Dewey's emphasis on student-curriculum integration, in the present one I look at the same problem from the standpoint of my own teaching. Borrowing Deweyan spectacles, I examine several pedagogical approaches I have used in attempting to resolve student-curriculum tensions during my 30-year career.

These are (1) teaching for critical thinking, (2) teaching for personal discovery, and (3) teaching for disciplinary initiation.

Teaching for Critical Thinking

When I left graduate school for my first full-time teaching job, in 1967, I did what in retrospect seems both paradoxical and predictable. I imitated my Civilization instructor. When I search for an explanation, I find no satisfactory one. Perhaps my freshman year—when I took Civilization—was not as frustrating as subsequent years. Or it may be that, despite pushing me toward fragmentation, Morgenbesser's approach was the lesser of alternative evils. Although he dominated the class (we were straight men to his high-powered Socrates) he did get students involved. So, in my first decade and a half of teaching, I did the opposite of what, as an undergraduate, I swore I would do. I stressed criticism rather than construction and presented philosophy without regard for student relevance.

My imitations of Morgenbesser were modestly successful; at least, students did not openly complain, and a few offered praise. But after my first years, questions surfaced which eerily mirrored ones I had asked in college and graduate school. As far as I could figure, the primary result of my teaching was planting seeds of doubt, getting students to see ideas in ways they had not previously considered. For example, in my Introduction class, when we studied traditional proofs for the existence of God, such as Anselm's and Aquinas's and Paley's, I would get students to agree that such proofs were not self-evident. And when we studied sections from Descartes's *Meditations*, I would show how difficult it was to decide the nature of the physical world. I would get students wondering if grass really was green, or if green was not just the color grass reflected. At worst, I was a trickster, showing the world was not as it appeared. At best, I was a weak-battery Socrates demonstrating that the worst form of ignorance is thinking you know when you do not.

As years of teaching added up, a number of my problems grew stronger. First, I was getting bored. Having taught the same way for almost 15 years, I was not discovering much. The only challenge was presenting things in ways which would catch students' attention, and my ennui was making that increasingly difficult. Second—and this was where questions from my own education kept surfacing—I did not clearly see the value of it. Yes, it was good to have students engage in self-questioning, but once I got them doubting, the best I could hope for was that they would leave class mildly puzzled. Perhaps it was better to be skeptical than naive, but that did not seem worthwhile in itself. Certainly, I thought, my classes should be doing more; my teaching should be adding up to more. And third, this Socratic skill I was demonstrating teetered on smugness, on what Dewey saw as learning for ostentatious display. Analyzing for analyzing's sake, at least without a lot more constructive work than I was promoting in class, could easily encourage students to become academic "sharps" (*Democracy* 9). So I was chalking up zeroes again, until I got assistance from an unexpected source, one which led me to see the value—as Dewey put it—of helping pupils find they have "something to say" (*How* 246). It was May of 1983, and like my reading of *Reconstruction in Philosophy*, I backed into it.

Help From a Writing Across the Curriculum Workshop

Earlier that month I noticed posters around campus announcing a first-time UNC Charlotte Writing Across the Curriculum (WAC) workshop, a 3-day retreat sponsored by our university's English department. A few announcements even appeared in my mailbox. But I'm a stick-in-the-mud, anxious about travel and change, so I ignored them until I got a handwritten note from Sam Watson, one of the workshop's organizers. He asked if there was any chance I could come, even going so far as to promise I would have a good time.

Of course, I dismissed his promise as innocent rhetoric. But what got me was the handwritten note. I figured Sam had to be pretty desperate if he was writing *me*. We had both been at UNC Charlotte for more than a decade and were pretty good friends. He knew well enough, therefore, that travel, adventure, and fun were not my things. I concluded no one from our campus was going and Sam was grasping at straws. When I left for the retreat that April weekend, I traveled thinking I would help save a drowning man. It turned out I was correct, only it was not Sam I saved; it was myself.

At the close of the first afternoon session, Dixie Goswami, who led the workshop, assigned a 10-minute freewrite about an article she asked everyone to study overnight. Around 10 that evening, as I made my way through the piece, I decided, perhaps wrongheadedly, that it was overly theoretical and pompous. This especially bothered me since we were at a retreat, something allegedly different from academics-as-usual, and so to my annoyance with scholarly obscurity was added my sense that I had been deceived.

What saved me was the freewrite. Goswami's instructions were to write for 10 minutes without interruption, without regard for grammar or transition or clarity. (The classic discussion of freewriting is Elbow, *Writing* ch 1.) Although I had never done such writing before, I found the time-limit attractive. Otherwise, I thought, I will have to spend all night working. Given that my writing was to be shared with colleagues, I would not want to look foolish next morning. But with only 10 minutes allowed, I figured no one could expect much. I was prepared to say, "Hey, if I'd only been allowed more time, I could obviously have composed a much better essay."

Toward midnight, as I read by a small desk lamp, I felt something new for me, the anticipation of writing. I could not wait. To heck with my high school English teachers, university professors, and journal editors. I'll let it rip. I did, and, next morning, my peers' reactions shocked me. Someone from religious studies, an associate professor with whom I once shared an office and article drafts, shook his head and said, "I've never heard your voice this strong before. The only way to account for it is you've just learned you have only 3 weeks to live." Well, it obviously was not that, but *I* couldn't figure it out either. The only thought that came to mind was Socrates's calling Ion "mad" because Ion claimed to be a medium for voices he could not explain.

Later that day, I recalled my undergraduate drifting. I remembered my disconnected and divided self. But I also remembered Buchler by the elevator, saw him point to his stomach and, almost 30 years later, began to sense what he meant. Having something to say really was different from having to say something.

It was by no means an instant understanding or teaching transformation. But the direction and sense of purpose personal writing generated for me was something I wanted to share with my students. I did not recognize it at the time, but, looking back, this was a large pedagogical step for me. My own teachers, as I have shown, had modeled skeptical questioning. But they had given me little to build with alongside all that belief-clearing doubt. In retrospect, freewriting appealed to me because, although I did not fully understand what was happening, I had been given a tool to start developing my own commitments or significant for-whats.

That summer, I was scheduled to teach Introduction to Philosophy, and the first thing I did was throw away my syllabus. I was on my way from my office to the classroom building when I realized I did not believe in the syllabus I was carrying. What was the use of having students memorize dozens of authors' arguments? Since they were discontinuous with most students' lives, pupils would forget them all by the following semester anyway (see *Experience and Education* 47–48). It was embarrassing, but I found a waste bin near the entry, ditched what I was carrying, and began class by saying I had been away and would give written course requirements next time.

TEACHING FOR PERSONAL DISCOVERY

In previous semesters, I had used an anthology edited by Edwards and Pap which was organized around classic philosophic themes: the nature of knowledge; freewill and determinism; ethical judgment; mind, self, and identity. Each section began with an historic selection, someone like Thomas Reid or David Hume, then went on to articles written in later periods, and concluded with pieces from the 1950s and 1960s, the language analysis period. But I did not want that anymore. What I now wanted was a chance for students to find their own direction, to realize they had something to contribute. Perhaps the reason students left my class with so little, I thought, was that by stressing the anthologized articles, students were intimidated and overwhelmed, unable to say anything of their own about the issues being considered. And recalling my own schooling, I had a sense this may have been one of the reasons I too had felt overwhelmed.

Once I decided the canonic voices were so loud students could not hear their own, I dropped the anthology and hunted for less intimidating philosophic readings. I decided on *Marriage and Morals*, by Bertrand Russell, *Essays on Sex Equality*, by John Stuart Mill and Harriett Taylor Mill, and Philip Slater's, *The Pursuit of Loneliness*. I also included Descartes's *Meditations*, a final gesture in the direction of the critical, analytic style. Besides changing the readings, I gave up both in-class exams and teacher-assigned, term paper topics. For these, I substituted journals and student-generated essays. I put a lot of time into these, responding each week to the journals and insisting on multiple drafts for the essays.

In addition to alterations in the readings and assignments, I was adjusting classroom activities. Whereas previously I had, in Morgenbesser fashion, demonstrated critical thinking, my classes now had a different purpose and tone. The idea was no longer to display my knowledge and root out student naivety. My new goal was to allow students to stretch their thinking, writing, and speaking. Rather than letting them sit passively as I filled blackboards with outlines of critical commentary, I wanted them active. I now saw lecture as something of a teaching failure, stealing valuable time from students' chances to develop their own purposes and skills.

The centerpiece of my new strategy was the freewrite. I began most classes with 10 minutes of it, about the topic I wanted to discuss that day. As a result, when I called on students, there would be a good chance they would have something to say. And writing along with them also fit my new strategy. Rather than stressing the finished, written product—what Dewey calls the map, as opposed to the actual trailblazing (see *How* 73)—I now believed it more helpful to stress the process, to share my own drafts, my own in-class work, so students could see that experienced writers were not geniuses. Mature writers also began with rough and poorly expressed ideas and then labored to polish them. In short, freewriting worked for me as a jump start on finding significant what-fors, deeply rooted attitudes and concerns. It was something of a miracle cure, a tonic I reached for when class discussion turned quiet, or students came to see me for essay topics, or when I myself needed ideas for an off-campus talk or presentation.

As for student reactions to my changed pedagogy, I cannot say. Although I was curious, I was not sure how to find out. When asked about the freewrites, a few students admitted they were helpful, but most seemed unimpressed. As for departmental, end-of-semester student evaluations, there seemed little change from my pre- to postworkshop scores. However, I did notice more active class discussions, especially on days when student texts, not outside ones, were the focus. On occasion, I would go so far as to keep silent, forcing students to lead their own class discussion, patiently waiting until someone came forward to get things going and get others involved. And hallway conversations indicated students enjoyed this emphasis, a number saying my class was unusual in this respect.

As late as spring semester, 1989, 6 years after the workshop, I was still pushing student-centered writing. I was continuing to tell Intro students I would consider the semester successful if everyone fell in love with just one sentence, preferably one of their own. However, during the fall of that year, things changed, and I began discovering that, as Dewey warned, student self-expression is not the be-all and end-all of education (*Experience and Education* 21–22). It was Sam Watson again.

Help From a College Composition and Communication Conference

The spring "4Cs" (Conference on College Composition and Communication) that year was in Seattle, and Sam pleaded with me to attend. Again, he sounded desperate. He had agreed to join groups headed by Toby

Fulwiler and Barbara Walvoord for a panel on "Student Writing in Content Areas." Although he had lined up faculty from other area schools, he could not get anyone from UNC Charlotte. No one attending from his school would look bad, he explained. He reminded me how much I had profited from the first writing retreat, and, besides, he added, I would be "performing a service" for disciplinary teachers who would be coming to our panel and were anxious to hear my story. I rolled my eyes and mumbled yes.

Our session in Seattle was hardly what Sam had promised. In fact, his 16 presenters were double the number in the audience. But Lucille McCarthy was one of the panelists, and I got to ask her about naturalistic research. Perhaps she felt sorry for me, or perhaps I had learned a few rhetorical tricks from Sam, but by the end of the conference, I had convinced her to help me study my Intro course. We began data collection that fall, and, from the start, I knew it would be complicated.

In our first interview, Lucille asked me the last question I wanted to hear. She asked what philosophy was. In doing this, she raised the issue of implicit versus explicit instruction which—at least in an inarticulate way—had haunted me since college. I was tempted to repeat Joseph Blau's comment, to say that this should be the last, not the first question. But I came clean. "I don't know," I said, "it's really complicated." "You mean you're teaching philosophy, and you don't know what it is?" I nodded. "How in the world can you expect your students to write philosophically if you can't even say what it is? Don't you have objectives for them?" I could see this was not what she expected. "I want them to fall in love with a sentence," I answered. She put down her pencil. "Look, you're not teaching biology, and you're not teaching literature. You're teaching philosophy. There must be a difference." What she said was reasonable, so I tried harder. "Well I can put my finger on one definition. In *Reconstruction in Philosophy*, Dewey says philosophy is exploration of cultural conflict, debate over moral values. But I don't think my students would understand that." "How do you know? Have you tried?" I had not, that was true, but, like my own professors, I really did not think it would do any good. Yet what she was saying made good sense.

After Lucille's initial questioning, I tried being more explicit with my students about what I wanted in their essays. Instead of asking them to write "about some problem which refuses to go away," I now suggested they focus on a conflict of values in their own lives. This seemed a good way of personalizing their essays while bringing them into line with Dewey's view of philosophy. I also substituted *Reconstruction in Philosophy* for Descartes's

Meditations, the epistemological concerns of the *Meditations* jarring rather than coinciding with the other books. But I left the Dewey for last, unwilling to be too explicit about the nature of philosophy until late in the course. I was unwilling, that is, to completely surrender my own professors' approach. I was dimly aware, perhaps, that to offer a block letter definition of philosophy too soon was to risk making students passive knowers, that teachers, as Dewey himself put it, must know "how to give information when curiosity has created an appetite that seeks to be fed, and how to abstain from giving information when, because of lack of a questioning attitude, it would be a burden and would dull the sharp edge of the inquiring spirit" (*How* 40). However, I did not understand that avoidance of premature explicit instruction—and the no-think rote products explicit instruction sometimes generates—is no automatic guarantee of successful implicit instruction. It would take me a long time to appreciate Dewey's claim that teaching indirectly requires much more planning and structure than a direct, lecture approach.

Alongside these efforts to be more forthcoming about my discipline, however, I maintained my commitment to student-centered writing, pushing the freewrites, urging students to compose essays that interested them (see Fishman and McCarthy, "Expressivism"; McCarthy and Fishman, "Boundary"). My teaching went on this way until, almost 4 years into my collaborative research with Lucille, in fall, 1993, a troubling dilemma emerged. Gearing up for our second study of my Intro class, I arranged to have my course videotaped in a specially equipped classroom with overhead cameras and microphones. What happened was that both the strongest and weakest aspects of my teaching-for-personal-discovery pedagogy came forward. Halfway through the semester, I thought it was my best class, the culmination of 10 years' emphasis on personal writing, but, by the end, I thought it was my worst and vowed never to teach the same way again. Before describing this teaching debacle, I first explain why I initially saw it as my instructional zenith.

Successes with Teaching for Personal Discovery: Student Change and Trusting Classrooms

Notwithstanding the disastrous way things ultimately turned out, Lucille McCarthy and I spent most of that fall, 1993, semester trying to explain why class was going so well. What stood out for both of us, on the positive side, was the cohesiveness of the class, its apparent communal solidarity despite the diversity of the students. It seemed a type of democratic, John-Dewey-settlement-house dream come true. Some of my pupils were from small North Carolina towns like Pilot Mountain, Iron Station, and Stanfield, whereas others came from urban centers like Los Angeles, New York, Dallas. One older student, Kent, was a firefighter; Aaron Wilhite, the starting power forward on the basketball team, an African American, was a former member of the Bloods, an LA street gang; Shannon was a no-nonsense senior business major who stressed women's rights; Myra seemed to take the role of group den mother, encouraging everyone; and then there was Bryan with his huge muscles, promising to become Mr. World while defending the Bible at every turn. In an effort to explain their self-proclaimed joy in coming to class and participating in discussion, Lucille and I decided students had formed an organic community, one in which everyone was valued for the unique role he or she played (Fishman and McCarthy, "Community").

A number of positive highlights involved Tate Osborne from Stanfield, a right-handed relief pitcher on the varsity baseball team. As a prelude to discussing Bertrand Russell's account of romantic love in *Marriage and Morals*, we talked about contemporary dating habits. Tate scoffed at my suggestion that males generally pay their date's expenses because they want to gain power. He said it was just a sign of respect, of how much a man values a woman. He described how he had been arrested by police outside the Palomino Club, a local country and western bar, when he came to the defense of a young woman being punched by her bruiser boyfriend in the parking lot. Although he did not know the woman, he thought it his duty to defend her. When the fight spread and police came, Tate confessed, he was thrown to the ground by a policewoman and jailed overnight.

On the other hand, Tate admitted that if he were married and found his wife interested in another man, he would throw her belongings in the garbage and be done with her. Aaron Wilhite, who was generally quiet, raised his hand to say he thought Tate crazy for getting involved at the Palomino. "In LA," he said, "you get killed if you don't mind your own business." Aaron also disagreed about a man's throwing his wife out if she cheated on him. "I'd blame myself," he explained. "I'd figure I wasn't taking care of things and should go talk to her." That was on a Tuesday. At the start of our next class, on Thursday, I was impressed when Tate waved his hand to relate that he had been thinking about Aaron's comments. "I've decided Aaron's probably right. If you find out your wife's been messing around, you really need to talk to her. It's probably partly your own fault." I came from class that day proud of Tate's openness to Aaron, attributing Tate's willingness to change to a high level of classroom trust.

What impressed me even more was a cooperative class discussion which occurred a few weeks later. As preliminary to exploring Harriet Taylor's essay on sexual equality, I handed out a series of questions about women's position in society. And to push my seriousness about student responsibility for class discussion, I announced at the start of the session that I intended to be quiet and simply take notes. After a minute of fidgety silence, Kent, the firefighter, got things started by answering the first question. He disagreed with Taylor that physical strength had become irrelevant in today's world. He said he feared a woman partner would not have the ability to drag him, if necessary, from a burning building, and he concluded women should not be considered equal to men. He then called on Shannon to answer question number two. She took a feminist position, stating that women could show their true abilities if given more of a chance, and she said she disagreed with the Citadel's resistance to admitting women cadets. As she finished, the class became quiet. When I glanced up, I saw Tate Osborne whispering to his teammate, Blue Pitman, sitting next to him. They were just a few feet from me, so I could hear Tate saying, "You take the next one, Blue, come on, you do it." But Blue would not volunteer. I kept my head averted and pretended to be busy with notes, hoping, along with Tate, that Blue or someone would come forward. After another half minute of silence, I glanced over and saw Tate switch from rubbing his goatee to fingering the gold cross at his neck. Finally he looked up and said quietly, "Well, I guess if no one else will, I'll do number three."

I felt wonderful. I wanted to cry. I was convinced the class had common purpose, a communal philosophic exploration in which everyone could share and to which everyone could contribute. Afterward, Lucille and I agreed my stress on personal writing and becoming a fellow student had fashioned strong communal responsibility that accounted for Tate's actions. This was mid-November, and over the following weekend, I smiled to myself, thinking my 10-year effort to put students at center stage was bearing sweet fruit.

Failures with Teaching for Personal Discovery

Inability to Integrate Student Writing and Philosophic Issues
Of course, there were some problems in the opening half of the Tate Osborne semester, but they were familiar and did not upset me. The most obvious of these I had encountered in previous terms, although it was one for which I still struggled to find solutions: It was the difficulty of integrat-

ing the student essays with the philosophic subject matter or assigned readings we were discussing. When it came to their papers, students seemed unable to make use of other class work. There was no continuity or interaction. For the two essays, I would ask students to begin with a personal conflict, some dilemma which exposed their loyalty to incompatible moral values. I tried to help by giving examples from previous semesters. I referred to a female student's paper which explored family loyalty versus her duty to report a drug-dealing parent, and I related a male student's paper which discussed divided commitments between his parents' plans for his future versus his own. I also responded to each student draft with a letter explaining how I would develop it and make it more philosophical if it were mine. Yet, by and large, I had little success helping students move from narrative accounts of their personal dilemma to philosophic essays which placed their problems in broader social and moral contexts. The Tate Osborne class, with each session videotaped and Lucille McCarthy doing extensive interviewing, gave me a chance to see this problem up close.

Colin Pharr usually took the seat next to Kent, the firefighter. He was a likeable, tall, midfielder on the soccer team, recruited from Dallas, Texas. In early conversations with Lucille, he described how much he enjoyed my Intro class, how he was having his first chance to speak his mind, how interested he was in the divergent views of his classmates. His initial essay was about his family. His father, a former star quarterback at Southern Methodist University, was still his hero, but his folks had recently divorced, and he felt that was unfair, that parents should not divorce when children are still young. My responses to Colin's draft ultimately proved inadequate, because his final essay remained a narrative without much effort at providing the larger moral or philosophic context I wanted. I gave him a C+, and, in later conversations with McCarthy, he expressed his strong disappointment. He told her the paper was the best he had ever written, had even initiated wound-healing conversations with his father. He said he thought he had done exactly what I had wanted, put himself into the essay and presented a dilemma central to his life.

Getting students to integrate their essays and larger philosophic issues had been a major difficulty for me ever since I began emphasizing student-centered writing. Once I did this, many students, like Colin, invoked a radical relativism when essay grades were below their expectations. Since I was interested in their opinions, they reasoned, and since everyone is entitled to his or her own view, how can Fishman give me anything but an A when I express myself honestly? It was not easy for me to answer. Although students seemed to want me to outline a satisfactory philosophic method in a list of declarative sentences, just as I had wanted many years before, I was now, in reluctant imitation of my own professors, unwilling to do that. I feared that if I did, it would result in nothing more than formulaic applications. Still, I was troubled by the problem of how to balance direct and indirect, explicit and implicit instruction for the purpose of integrating student and curriculum—undoubtedly because it mirrored my own college and graduate school questions. That is, I was now caught, without sufficient understanding, somewhere between the discipline-centered pedagogy I had wanted to leave and the more balanced place I wanted to go.

Interestingly, term papers which students completed in my early years of teaching usually looked philosophical and were easy to assign. I simply asked everyone, for example, to compare essays we had read by John Stuart Mill and William James on freedom of the will and, presto, everyone was using philosophic concepts and writing in a way which bore family resemblance to at least one well-known philosophic genre. But this sort of project no longer seemed satisfactory to me, its results too routine and shallowly rooted. To paraphrase Dewey, these sorts of essays lacked something of the students themselves, "something of [their] own spontaneity, something of [their] own originality" ("How the Mind" 220). Missing was the blend of the student's life and academic subject matter, feeling and thinking, which I wanted but which my limited understanding of indirect instruction kept me from achieving.

As I have already mentioned, however, problems with student essays had been a lingering difficulty since my WAC workshop, one I had by now almost learned to live with. What really forced radical changes in my approach had to do with a problem I had not noticed prior to fall, 1993, and, interestingly, it was Tate Osborne who made it clear.

Insufficient Motivation for Assigned Readings

Since the moment in 1983 when I started downplaying canonic texts (postponing their introduction until the fifth week of class and eliminating midterms and finals), I knew getting students to complete reading assignments—extending their interests, to borrow Deweyan language, to new areas of subject matter—might be difficult. As an incentive, I instituted a series of short-answer quizzes, usually 10 questions, which I scheduled throughout the semester. I stressed, however, that I did not want anyone studying for these quizzes, that it would be enough to simply read the assignments carefully. I also indicated that students should not worry if they failed one or two, since what was most important was showing they had made a serious, good-faith effort to understand the readings. Although many of my students were not doing well on the quizzes, I was not much concerned until one day, as I was handing them out, Kent, my firefighter, asked Tate, who had come in late, if he had done the assignment. Tate laughed and, addressing the entire class, said, "No, I've given up doing the readings, since I do just as well on the quizzes by guessing." This surprised me, and, perhaps because I knew, and still know, Tate to be honest, I was both grateful for his candor and, at the same time, disturbed. Afterward, when I mentioned it to Lucille, she told me that what she had heard from other students reinforced Tate's remarks. Very few students were attempting the readings or taking them seriously. What hurt me was that I had misread the enthusiasm of my students. I thought my respect for their points of view, supplemented by their desire to participate in class discussion, would motivate them to make a strong effort with assigned readings. But I was wrong.

Not to paint a totally bleak picture, there was evidence I had helped some of my students gain academic confidence that semester. Many of them, including Tate, Blue, and Kent, were hardly scholarly types. Myra even told McCarthy that my class was the first in which any teacher had taken her seriously. She said she was beginning to believe she was "not as dumb as she thought." Further, I suspected many students who had good attendance in my class were frequent no-shows in others.

Despite these modest signs of positive student residue, I was deeply worried about the view of philosophy with which they would leave my class. As it stood, most of them, with such little attention to the texts, would be hard pressed to distinguish late-night dorm discussions from informed philosophic inquiry. This left me feeling I had failed them. Although I wanted students to be alert to personal discovery, I also wanted them to know that entrance into the arena of philosophic thinking involved special effort. I wanted them to know that expressing one's own opinion was not in itself to think philosophically. More was required: at the minimum, a beginning sense of the arguments and conceptual frameworks of those who had previously addressed their cultures' moral and social problems.

My failure to get students to do the readings was not just surface deep. After sharing my dilemma with the class—and coming to a joint agreement that we switch from short quizzes about the readings to take-home study questions—very few, despite my pleas, did the assignments in more than summary fashion. The class was so structured that the readings—the sources of new subject matter—just were not seen as important. Blue Pitman pointed out in his journal that, since class conversation was more vigorous when I gave up attempts to discuss assigned texts, the obvious solution was to eliminate these readings altogether. At that moment, I decided to change, suddenly aware, at some level, that in focusing on student self-expression, I had neglected what Dewey saw as our need to challenge students ("Interest" 275). Next semester, spring, 1994, I reintroduced the Edwards and Pap anthology, the best collection of rigorous philosophic thinking that I knew.

TEACHING FOR DISCIPLINARY INITIATION

Besides adding articles from Edwards and Pap to the books I had used the previous term, I decided not to delay the philosophic texts but assign them the first week. And since I was concerned students might be expecting a repeat of immediately preceding semesters, I determined to make clear my style had changed. To this end, I assigned two Platonic dialogues, the *Apology* and *Crito*, for the first week and scheduled an in-class essay exam for the second. This way I could establish high standards early enough so students could drop without penalty if they found them unreasonable. Further, to help insure the readings would be taken seriously, I assigned take-home study questions for each assignment. These took a traditional academic form: "Present three arguments Socrates gives Crito for refusing to escape from prison," or "After outlining Paul Ree's arguments against freedom of the will, present two ways you might resist or criticize his thinking." Answers to these questions were to be turned in at the start of class prior to our discussion of the reading. I did this reluctantly, fearing it was busywork and an insult. After all, there would be little excitement for students searching the readings for answers they suspected I already knew. But what was I to do?

At this point, it may seem I was going back fully to Morgenbesser imitations, but I was not. For better or worse, I could not set aside what I still saw as attractive features of teaching for personal discovery. We still sat in a circle. My first class of the semester continued to be devoted to learning about each student's home community and its primary values. I still asked a different student to start each class with written impressions of the previous period. And I still privileged student-centered writing and multiple drafts. Although I did reduce from two to one the number of student essays, I continued to value freewriting and used it extensively along with other writing-to-learn techniques.

Given that many of my Intro students were often friends or teammates of students I had taught previously, I expected a coup d'état, if not open rebellion, in spring, 1994. But, to my surprise, students did not flinch. At least a quarter of the class seemed to enjoy the more traditional work. Matt McWilliams was one such student. A transfer from a community college in Kansas and starting pitcher on the baseball team, Matt wrote three- and four-page responses to the study questions and looked with disdain upon classmates who suggested the workload was excessive. When this issue arose in class, Matt said that study questions and readings were what college was all about. Bruce Lovell, a 23-year-old African American Gulf War veteran from Gastonia, North Carolina, was excited by Hume's article on self-identity. He volunteered to do further library research and report back to the class. Donna Allen, a senior nursing student, who rarely spoke and whose facial expression read "keep away" when I merely looked in her direction, tape recorded each session and wrote even longer responses than Matt McWilliams. I thought her approach unimaginative, but she eventually began thinking for herself and, to my joy and hers, had become less of a passive learner by the time she wrote her essay and final exam. And there was Tammy Gardner, a 30-year-old San Francisco flight attendant and English major. She was as serious as Donna Allen but with a smile. She never quite put things together as well as Donna, but she tried hard throughout the semester. When she graduated a year later, she wrote me a note saying she would always keep her copies of Dewey's *Reconstruction in Philosophy* and the Edwards and Pap anthology for inspiration.

In sum, things seemed to go quite well that semester—at least students seemed to be taking the subject matter of the course more seriously—and I attributed it to making course requirements clear and setting high standards from the start. Of course, there were students who I thought did poorly, about four or five who, sorry to say, received Ds or Fs. But it was obvious to me and, I think, to them that they were not doing the work or turning in their assignments, and deserved the grades I ultimately assigned. And what about the nagging problem of getting students to write essays which integrated personal and disciplinary concerns? Were student essays this semester any more philosophic than ones from previous semesters? Sadly, I have to say no. And that bothered me. But, again, I had no new solutions and could only work harder with strategies I had already tried.

My new emphasis on the philosophic canon, showing students that initiation into the philosophic community requires familiarity with classic texts and conversations, seemed successful for two semesters, spring and fall of 1994. But a year after the Matt McWilliams class, my teaching sled felt like it was scraping dry ground again.

Failures With Teaching for Disciplinary Initiation: Lifeless Writing and Dull Class Discussion

In the second week of the spring, 1995, semester, two groups of Intro students came to my office. The first consisted of five freshmen and sophomores who were on the women's softball team. In response to their initial sets of study questions, I had given a number of them low passes. They said they had never gotten poor grades before and needed advice. I suggested more detailed answers, more effort to relate issues from the readings to their own lives. Later that same week, four freshman baseball players came with similar questions, and I offered similar answers. Word must have spread, because, soon after, I began getting lengthier responses from the majority of my Intro students. I was impressed at first, but after a few weeks I sensed students were simply filling pages, not using philosophic subject matter for significant purposes—as Dewey would have hoped (*How* 278–79)—but copying extensively from the assigned texts without acknowledging it, employing language, like oversized clothing, which did not fit. And students who cited events from their own lives also seemed to be filling pages, making little effort to integrate their personal examples and the disciplinary texts.

Several other developments revealed an absence of sufficient student-curriculum integration as well. About a month into the course, a couple of students each period would turn in their answers to study questions at the end of the hour, rather than at the beginning as required. After noticing this, I watched more carefully, and, although I could not be sure, I suspected a few students were copying friends' work during class discussion. Since I wanted everyone to read the material before we discussed it, if this was not cheating, it was certainly outside the spirit of the assignments. But aside from harsh stares, I kept quiet, not wanting to falsely accuse anyone. As the semester wore on, I was also troubled by reductions in student-to-student exchanges. When I called on people in class, I had trouble provoking them into heightened interest. And on the rare times I did, the energy failed to spread. I felt as if the responding student and I were isolated, everyone else's attention lost.

This lack of classroom energy in spring, 1995—my failures to help students use philosophic texts to achieve personally significant goals—actually contrasted sharply with the first weeks that semester when two of the three older women in class directly challenged some of the young baseball players across from them in the class circle. These exchanges were lively and biting, but I did not build on them for fear they might get out of hand.

For example, during the third class, B.J., 45 years old and angry about two ex-husbands, called Socrates a "jerk." She said he had abandoned his family for the sake of public reputation. Having myself been through marital difficulties, I was somewhat sympathetic with B.J.'s interpretation, but Joe Lopez and Steve Michael, both from Florida on baseball scholarships and all of 18 years old, were not. Barely polite, they made it clear they thought B.J. was "out of it," had totally missed the nobility of Socrates's dying for principle. This disagreement was just one of many between B.J. and some of the younger students in the first weeks. As these disagreements continued, they seemed to mask a growing personal animosity, so I played them down. Unfortunately, I failed to stimulate other student-to-student interactions, and as we moved into the second half of the semester, I felt the course grow moribund. If I had had more courage, I would have declared it dead at Easter break and sent everyone home. But I didn't. Instead, as my strategies to interest students kept failing, I simply tried harder, voice growing louder, hand gestures wilder, resorting eventually to personal testimonials about the value of philosophy and the readings I had chosen. It was time to examine my pedagogy once again.

DEWEYAN INSIGHTS ABOUT MY PEDAGOGICAL PROBLEMS

I've outlined three pedagogical shifts, each initiated by a turning-point experience. The first was Dixie Goswami's WAC workshop in April, 1983. This led me to teaching for personal discovery. The second was my finding, 10 years later, in the Tate Osborne class of fall, 1993, that philosophy texts had become strangers in my Intro course. This led to my version of teaching for disciplinary initiation. And my third turning point, just two semesters later, in the B.J. class of spring, 1995, was when I sensed that teaching for disciplinary initiation had reversed things, and it was students who had now become classroom strangers. Quite a dilemma. In the following sections, I detail how Dewey might respond to my pedagogical problems.

Failure To Integrate The Forces Underlying the Student-Curriculum Dichotomy

To open my Deweyan analysis, I speculate he would characterize my three teaching shifts as failed efforts to integrate the nested polarities I describe in Chapter 2: continuity and interaction, construction and criticism, interest and effort. After graduate school, I started with a criticism-centered pedagogy, focusing on close textual analysis, insensitive to the need to help students find reasons for engaging with my course subject matter. At the WAC workshop with Dixie Goswami in 1983, I experienced freewriting. And impressed by its power to generate something to say, I shifted toward a more student-centered pedagogy, developing the personalized essay into a type of philosophy "project." Without my understanding it very well at the time, this advanced me, Dewey might say, beyond my own teachers. Whereas my professors had for the most part stressed criticism's role in knowledge building, they failed to help me understand the partnership of criticism and construction, how criticism needs the integrating, connecting potential of construction and how construction needs the strengthening of criticism.

But after 10 years of my emphasizing student-centered writing and a trusting classroom environment, Dewey might continue, I finally sensed, thanks to Tate Osborne, that teaching for self-discovery has its own problems, can keep students from the course subject matter they need in order to enrich what they want to say. At this point, by the end of the Tate class, I intuitively knew I should be doing better at integrating my students and my discipline, at using student essays to more effectively promote what Dewey saw as the project method's primary goal—student "inquiry into fresh fields of subject matter" (*Way* 31; see also *How* 218). But I really did not know how, and, desperate to do something, I turned, as I have shown, to reemphasizing philosophic texts, to my third pedagogical shift, which I call teaching for disciplinary initiation. In particular, I introduced sets of study questions to make students read, and, by and large, this worked: Most students were motivated to complete the assigned materials. But the study questions were so constituted, Dewey might note, that student interest was forced rather than voluntary. As a result, many pupils completed their answers in routine, inattentive ways. This was evidenced by the lifeless quality of the writing I received in the B.J. class and by the fact that various students resorted to copying classmates' work.

To summarize, I speculate that, for Dewey, my early Morgenbesser teaching used criticism to dissolve student belief but gave few tools for constructing new ones. After the 1983 WAC workshop, I encouraged students to find what they wanted to say through personal writing and class-room sharing, but I left them without the proper motivation to use and develop my disciplinary subject matter. My third pedagogy was another unsuccessful attempt to integrate student and curriculum, because, like my first approach, its emphasis on the curriculum was forced and insufficiently related to students' nonschool concerns.

The Cause of My Problem: An Undertheorized Workshop

My hunch is that Dewey would say the workshop which propelled my pedagogical inquiry was certainly an educational experience. It prompted me to pause, think, and begin reconstructing my teaching. It left what he would call a positive residue, making me sensitive to classroom possibilities previously overlooked, increasing my own and my students' chances for meaningful classroom experiences. In subsequent semesters, I would never again teach without incorporating large doses of freewriting, attempts to generate collegial discussion, and emphasis on the personally relevant philosophic essay. However, from a Deweyan outlook, the workshop also had serious flaws. These became evident when, in the following decade, I continued to have only modest success integrating the personal and the disciplinary, the student and curriculum. Why?

I believe Dewey would say the major problem with my first WAC workshop was that it was undertheorized, that it left me with a limited vision of freewriting that hindered my effectiveness when I incorporated it in my own courses. Despite my excitement about such writing and the pedagogical journey it launched, I had little understanding of what had happened. I had gained a new realization—that people can write to discover, not just to report—but I had too narrow a view of it. Dewey might argue that the joy of self-discovery I felt was more complicated than I appreciated. I had experienced writing from the heart, and that was important. Put in Deweyan terms, I had experienced moments when writing and the material it was organizing had become one, when my method and subject matter had become so seamless my writing ceased to be self-conscious (*Democracy*, ch. 13; for a similar view of attentive activity, see Polanyi 18). So far so good, but Dewey would argue there is more to wholeheartedness than that. There is also brain and body and history. What made my "new" voice powerful was not just that it was personal, but that it was also being filtered through a long, critical, philosophic training, through disciplinary methods and materials with which I was deeply familiar. Whereas at the time of the retreat I saw my workshop experience as simply new freedom, Dewey would say it was really a complicated transaction among multiple, newly connected forces.

Further, for Dewey, the nourishing tonic I felt when freewriting in class with my students was not just everyone enjoying his or her own creativity. Its power was also the connection and integration of individual and group, the sort of mentoring and collegiality, the social cooperation I myself had longed for as a student. Unlike in-class exam or test work, freewriting values individual difference, not just as personal expression, but as contribution to group discussion and enriched, more diverse community life. Although, again, it was not until years later that I had the conceptual framework to understand the positive feelings I experienced with in-class freewriting, that such writing was connecting individual and group was evidenced by the organic, cooperative quality which Lucille McCarthy and I noted and prized in the Tate Osborne class.

Overall, from a Deweyan perspective, the sponsors of my first WAC workshop were correct to emphasize writing experience, to plead you cannot teach composition well if you yourself are not actively composing. Yet, presenting writing-to-learn techniques as they did, using the potentially misleading language of "new freedom" and "inner voice," risked handing out classroom practices as if they were bricks. After all, personal writing and freewriting can be used in many contexts and for many purposes, each presenting its own set of problems. Given this variety of potential problems, theory becomes essential to successful adaptation of new classroom practices, for, as Dewey reminds us, there is nothing more practical than theory ("Sources" 8). "[Teachers need] to know," he tells us, "not merely as a matter of brute fact that [techniques] do work, but to know how and why they work. Thus, [they] will be independent judge[s] and critic[s] of their proper use and adaptation" ("Relation" 325). Applied to my own situation, I take Dewey to mean that, without more educational theory at my disposal, my classroom observations about freewriting lacked breadth and organization. I was in a trial-and-error—as opposed to experimental—situation, my questions lacking the direction, system, and imagination which theory provides (*Democracy* 144–45, 264; "Sources" 11).

And this is what was missing at my retreat. To have understood the effectiveness of personal writing and freewriting, I needed more philosophizing about education. I needed a richer set of concepts—including ideas about the importance of voluntary interest, expanded attention, and sustained effort—to probe educative experience in general and my first WAC workshop experience in particular. I needed to understand that using student-centered writing to help pupils discover they had something to say was only the starting point of their engagement with my course material. I also needed to help them see philosophy as an important to-what, a means they needed to expand their interests and reach goals (for-whats) to which they were genuinely committed.

A Deweyan Solution: Integrating Student
and Curriculum *In*directly

As for specific solutions to my failures to integrate student and curriculum, Dewey, as I have previously indicated, does not offer concrete suggestions. He leaves such experimentation to practitioners. But given the spirit of his pedagogical principles, I believe he would say I was, however clumsily, struggling in the right direction. Ever since I experienced freewriting, I had at some level sensed the importance of the personally relevant philosophic essay as a project. And I had sensed the need of a supportive environment if that project were to succeed, if the interests of my students and my discipline were to be integrated. I also sensed that this integration involved helping students find good reasons to do the readings, showing them that the road to developing their own interests ran through the heartland of my philosophic texts. But lack of educational theory hindered my classroom vision. As shifts in my teaching show, I was alternatively failing either my students or my discipline.

Things stayed this way until, after the failures of the B.J. class, I began planning my Intro course for the following semester, for fall, 1995. Preparing for that class, and further reflecting on Dewey, helped me envision new solutions to my dilemma. These preparations made it seem as if my previous attempts at connecting students and philosophy had been done with a shoehorn. They suggested that better integration of student and curriculum would only come with better interaction of more specific educational resources. That is, I now believe I failed to reconcile student and curriculum because I only went at it directly. In presenting the essay as a type of philosophic project, I had urged students to read philosophy texts and write personal papers, hoping that each activity would influence the other. But no amount of telling students to put these resources together did much good. In this regard, my own experience points to the wisdom of Dewey's refusal to tout the project or problem method as anything more than an invitation to teachers to do serious classroom experimenting. What my own trials, and reflections on those trials, taught me is that, however useful projects like student essays may be as tools for integrating student and curriculum, they would not work in my own classroom without a lot more effective, day-to-day text and student interaction than I was facilitating.

Put another way, the centerpiece of my student-curriculum integration strategy was the term project essay. The results were disappointing, however, because I had provided pupils with too few genuine reasons for tilling the soil of my disciplinary texts, and, as a consequence, they were unable to use these texts to enrich their essay projects. I had failed to heed one of Dewey's often repeated principles: "The educator [must] *determine the environment of the child*, and thus by indirection to direct" (*Child* 209, italics in the original).

That is, since philosophy was not an existing "direct interest" of my students, my best strategy, according to Dewey, was to help them see philosophy as an "indirect interest," a tool for expanding their already existing direct ones (see *Interest and Effort* 16–45). If I succeeded, then students' attention would turn in earnest to my course subject matter. But I failed in this regard because I failed to sufficiently understand the idea of working indirectly, of setting the conditions within which students would need philosophy and the two could better connect. I was leaving important classroom activities, less obvious to me than student and curriculum, but equally significant, in watertight compartments. Without integrating these overlooked processes, I was beginning to realize, I would never make progress with the larger integration I sought. In what follows, I discuss four pairs of these "less obvious" activities which also needed to be reconciled if my essay projects were to improve. These activities are teaching and studenting, questioning and answering, homework and classwork, students and their classmates.

Integrating Teaching and Studenting, Questioning and Answering

With regard to class activities, Dewey says teachers should become students, and students should become teachers, and the less we know about which function we are performing the better (*Democracy* 159–60). And he could cite me as a technicolor example of that principle. As I have shown, only when I began teaching did I begin understanding my own education. The troubles of one became troubles of the other, and I could not understand either without attending to their mutual shaping. Yet in my own classes, I was doing little to help students become teachers—to me or to one another. After my first workshop, I had succeeded, through freewriting, in becoming something of a student in my own classes, but my students, by and large, remained students. And without a more serious reversal of roles, according to Dewey, it would be difficult for them to become effective learners.

In order for my students to become teachers, Dewey would say, they needed experience with both answering *and* questioning. After Tate Osborne's class, I went back to providing lots of questions, but that meant my students were restricted to answering, and, even I have to admit, it must have been counterproductive for students to keep responding to questions throughout the semester when almost none of these were their own.

Integrating Homework and Classroom Work, Students and Classmates

As important as it is, following Deweyan guidelines, to promote interaction between teaching and studenting, questioning and answering, it is equally important to facilitate exchange among students. I was hoping for classmate-to-classmate responses during discussions I led, but it was not happening. And the homework, the study questions, were additional classroom resources which remained isolated. After the B.J. semester, I knew I needed to experiment so homework could better interact with class debate; and the same with students and their classmates. They could not care about or learn from one another, because I had left them isolates. I had done too little to facilitate shared and cooperative work.

Dewey would conclude, as I have already suggested, that focusing on integration of student and curriculum was in itself too broad, an ideal I could not reach with the course I had structured. What was wanting was a finer-grained look at my classroom activities and resources.

LEARNING FROM DEWEY: PREPARATIONS FOR AN IMPROVED INTRO COURSE

Ideas for better integrating the specific educational resources I have just discussed did not come to me clean but were a result, once again, of mulling my own learning and teaching histories, reflecting on Dewey's educational principles, and reading accounts of specific pedagogical experiments.

Helping Students Question

In June of 1995, I received an article Art Young had just completed for an anthology on writing. I was struck by an assignment Young called student letter exchanges. In these, students developed questions about novels covered in his literature class. The assignments involved the exchange of two letters. In the first, students explained their understanding of a work and posed a question about something they still found troubling. In the second, students responded to a classmate's letter, answering the question presented by that classmate.

I was also struck by Young's reminder to avoid assigning writing which we as teachers are not excited to read. This reinforced my doubts about my own study questions, and I decided to plan a version of Young's letter exchange for my Intro course. What especially appealed to me was students' generating their own questions for one another and receiving comments on their work from a classmate as well as from me.

Helping Students Work in Groups

Over the years, I had tried writing groups for student essays, but these had not been effective. Students claimed either that their classmates were not helpful because they simply said, "Your draft is great," or because their classmates had no better idea how to write a philosophic essay than they had. In July of that summer, I was reading articles by Carolyn Shrewsbury and Nancy Schniedewind which stressed, echoing Dewey, the power of group work, its capacity for helping students switch roles and become reflective about group interactions. So in addition to Young's letter exchanges, I prepared to experiment with assignments combining features of Shrewsbury's and Schniedewind's suggestions. I planned to form small student groups which would jointly develop text-based questions, exchange these with other small groups, and then generate joint answers.

Helping Students Identify With Texts:
Changes in Assigned Readings

Ever since my first WAC workshop, when I sensed the intimidating potential of philosophic texts, I had been on the lookout for accessible and relevant ones. In the B.J. class of spring, 1995, I used a combination of Russell's *Marriage and Morals*, Dewey's *Reconstruction*, two Platonic dialogues, and a dozen selections from the Edwards and Pap anthology. Toward the close of the following July, however, I had the itch once again to alter the readings. So, as I had done many times in the past, I scoured my colleagues' stacks of Intro anthologies. In one of these, I discovered a volume which interested me, a book which had just been published by Wadsworth (and edited by Max Hallman) titled, *Expanding Philosophical Horizons, A Nontraditional Philosophy Reader*. When I checked the table of contents, I was impressed by the length of the selections and the number of women and minority authors. Although fearful some of the articles would not be representative of philosophy's academic tradition, yet mindful of Dewey's claim that student interest and identification with things coincide (*Democracy* 352), I thought it worth a try, a chance, if nothing else, to help female and minority students better relate to the assigned texts. So in place of a chapter from Dewey and six articles from Edwards and Pap, I decided to modify my curriculum with authors I had read but never previously assigned, including Elizabeth Spelman, Mary Daly, bell hooks, and Simone de Beauvoir.

Helping to Integrate Student Essays and Philosophic Issues: Audiotaped Responses to Drafts

In the packet in which I received Art Young's article, I also found one by Chris Anson for the same anthology. Anson discussed alternative ways of responding to student drafts, including a positive account of his experiment with audiotapes. As I have already noted, for a long time I had been writing letters to students suggesting ways to make their essays more philosophic, to broaden the contexts of their personal conflicts. When I read Anson's idea about audiotapes, it appealed to me because I thought that in this way I could be a better colleague-mentor to my students, more effectively thinking along with them and exploring—trailblazing rather than mapping, as Dewey would say—ways they might develop their essays. Although I worried about the time such tapings would require and the logistics of collecting and returning them, I decided to try it.

Integrating Homework and Classwork: Typing Daily Assignments

Although I did not know it at the time, it would turn out that one of the more significant innovations I was considering—one which would have great impact on classroom interaction—was also one of the simplest. Tired of attempting to prevent students from copying one another's homework instead of paying attention to class discussion, I thought of simply demanding that homework be typed; I could then reduce my policing duties. With that worry set aside, I could let students exchange their homework in class, in pairs or groups, thereby better promoting better the cooperative interaction of students and classmates for which Dewey calls ("Need for a Philosophy" 13).

In retrospect, I see that these specific plans for adjustment led to better integration of student and curriculum in my Intro class the following fall. Details of the twists and turns of that fall, 1995, semester—my attempts to carry out Deweyan classroom experiments—are the subject of Lucille McCarthy's ensuing chapters.

DEWEYAN CLASSROOM EXPERIMENTS

———————— ✤ ————————

Part Two

[RESEARCH IN EDUCATION] REQUIRES JUDGMENT and art to select from the total circumstances of a case just what elements are the causal conditions of learning. . . . It requires candor and sincerity to keep track of failures as well as successes. . . . It requires trained and acute observation to note the indications of progress in learning. . . —a much more highly skilled kind of observation than is needed to note the results of mechanically applied tests.

— JOHN DEWEY,
"Progressive Education and the Science of Education" 1928: 126

Chapter Seven

QUALITATIVE RESEARCH IN A DEWEYAN CLASSROOM

❖

Lucille McCarthy

Before discussing our findings about Steve Fishman's Deweyan experiments in his fall, 1995, Introduction to Philosophy course, I will describe our research approach. In systematically examining Deweyan pedagogy in action, we offer an account of teaching and learning which goes beyond previous studies of Deweyan classrooms which offer only retrospective teacher reports or broad surveys of curricula (see, for example, Mayhew and Edwards; Rugg and Shumaker). Although we obviously cannot make up for what some bemoan as the "regret[able lack of]...systematic and objective inquiry" into Dewey's own school and its effects on students (Rugg 555–56), we do mount such an inquiry in Fishman's classroom.

In doing so, we employ the type of social scientific methodology Dewey himself believes most appropriate for studying progressive classrooms. Specifically, we use a qualitative or naturalistic approach which allows us to focus on actual transactions among students and teacher in a local classroom setting. This is in keeping with Dewey's warning that the quantitative approach—the research alternative which became the order of the day in schools of education following World War I—is better suited to traditional classrooms. This is true, according to Dewey, because traditional classrooms are geared more to the transmission of particular skills and information than to the development of student attitudes and habits, such as initiative, openness to learning, and cooperative inquiry. Dewey sees traditional schooling as based on a flawed understanding of human faculties, namely, that imagination, thinking, feeling, and doing can be trained separately. In his view, this encourages the teaching of skills without concern for students' "collateral learning," that is, the impact of these skills on pupils' dispositions and desires (*Experience and Education* 48). Because quantitative research isolates specific variables, its appropriateness is limited to classes which decontextualize learning and neglect questions about the formation of enduring student habits. In effect, Dewey believes, quantitative research takes responsibility away from teachers, casting them as empty conduits rather than as informed and sensitive practitioners of what he calls "the most difficult and important of the human arts" ("Progressive" 126).

As opposed to the quantitative approach, Dewey calls for teacher research which is context-dependent yet organized and sharpened by philosophic theory and knowledge of the social sciences. Ironically, however, it has not been until the last quarter century that educationists, borrowing from anthropology and sociolinguistics, have developed the sort of qualitative research alternative Dewey thought appropriate in progressive classrooms. Fishman and I employ this qualitative approach in the present study, drawing upon many of the same methods we have used across our history of collaboration, techniques which have had special power for us. I will describe the strengths of the naturalistic approach as we have experienced them, highlighting differences between qualitative and quantitative orientations.

THE STRENGTHS OF QUALITATIVE RESEARCH
FOR CLASSROOM INQUIRY

A Broad Research Gaze

In scientific or quantitative inquiry, believable ("objective") findings result when researchers distance themselves from their subjects and work to control variables. They are, in essence, narrowing their gaze to particular features of similar subjects across settings. But this sort of research, according to Dewey, has limited value in classrooms, where the "number of variables that enter in is enormous" ("Sources" 33). Dewey argues,

> That which can be measured is the specific... that which can be isolated.... [But] how far is education a matter of forming specific skills and acquiring special bodies of information which are capable of isolated treatment?... [T]he *educational* issue is what *other* things in the way of desires, tastes, aversions, abilities and disabilities is [the student] learning along with the specific acquisitions.... The intelligence of the teacher is dependent upon [his or her ability] to take into account the variables that are not obviously involved in the immediate special task. Judgment in such matter is of qualitative situations and must itself be qualitative. ("Sources" 33, emphases in the original)

Furthermore, Dewey continues, the sort of quantitative determinations resulting from isolating and testing specific variables presuppose repetitions and exact uniformities. However, educators deal with situations which never repeat themselves.

By contrast, naturalistic researchers like ourselves do not attempt to isolate variables, joining Dewey in believing that to do so may lead to concentration on "unimportant by-products" of classroom activities rather than on these activities' "*quality*... and ... consequence" ("Progressive" 118, emphasis in the original). Instead, as naturalistic inquirers, we range widely within a single locale, refining our hypotheses within the context of a broader, more general view. In order to establish credible findings, we explore numerous data sources, acknowledging that all sources and collection methods (as well as we investigators ourselves) are limited and incomplete. However, when we combine various types of data, "triangulating" among them—using them to cross-check, augment, and refine one another

—the limitations of one, we believe, are compensated for by the strengths of others. In this procedure, naturalists liken themselves to fishermen layering flawed nets such that the intact parts of some cover holes in others. This triangulation process results in conclusions which rest on a strong database and, therefore, may be considered "trustworthy" (Lincoln and Guba 306).

Throughout our study, Fishman and I triangulated among the data sources and collection methods I outline below. We also triangulated among theories as well as between ourselves as investigators. In addition, we followed several other procedures to insure credible results. These included (1) prolonged engagement in the setting—enough time to build trust, identify important shapers of context, and test for misinformation; (2) persistent observation—enough experience in the setting to determine salient features for further inquiry; (3) and member checks—tests of our interpretations with informants themselves. In sum, our findings are credible because of the multiple angles, the diverse voices, we bring to bear, not, as in scientific paradigm inquiry, because of limitations we impose on our gaze (for discussions of triangulation, credibility, and trustworthiness in qualitative inquiry, see Denzin; Doheny-Farina and Odell; Lincoln and Guba; Mathison; Spindler).

Because naturalistic inquirers do not control variables, however, we cannot generalize our findings to other locales, as scientific researchers can. Instead, we present a detailed account of participants and setting so readers may determine for themselves the transferability of our findings to their own settings. In the present study, Fishman and I spotlight only a single college philosophy instructor at work in a particular classroom—"another country heard from," as Clifford Geertz says, "nothing more or less." Yet, "small facts speak to large issues" (*Interpretation* 23). From our account of Fishman's teaching and his students' learning, readers may gain a number of insights. First, we offer information about one teacher's efforts to use Deweyan principles and pedagogy to integrate student and curriculum. We also show the operations and effects of Fishman's approach upon his students, describing what Dewey calls the residue, or habits, that pupils take with them from his course (*How* 153, 268).

In-Progress Emergence of Research Foci and Theory

Naturalistic inquirers, very much in the Deweyan spirit, do not treat theory as fixed rules with which to build a kit of procedures applicable in all classrooms. Instead, we immerse ourselves in the classroom situation, allowing that situation to set the table of problems and the foci of our attention. But our observations are not simply random; they are informed by an understanding of those systems of inquiry most relevant to teaching practice, namely, social sciences like psychology, sociology, and anthropology as well as philosophies of education. In this way, naturalistic researchers understand philosophy and social science not as road maps for educators but, rather, as instruments whereby educators become more inventive and imaginative in their exploration and resolution of practical problems. This mixing of theory and practice is consistent with Dewey's repeated caution that science and philosophy in the abstract run the danger of becoming arid and irrelevant, and that practice uninformed by theory runs the risk of being too limited by tradition and routine.

Thus, as naturalistic inquirers, we enter the research scene with numerous questions and theories, but once there, we try to remain open to all that is going on in the particular setting under study. In this regard, we are quite different from inquirers working within the scientific paradigm. Whereas scientific researchers design hypotheses in advance and then test them using predetermined tools, we, as naturalistic researchers, are ourselves the primary instruments of inquiry. Although we too enter the scene with "working hypotheses" which direct initial observation, it is our own intuitions and "qualitative" judgments, our own immersion in the local situation, rather than predetermined tools and tests, which focus inquiry (see Dewey "Sources" 27–28, 33). As we take in information from as many perspectives as possible, we continually test and modify our working hypotheses and, thereby, the project's direction. It is, then, the inquirers themselves who play a powerful and creative role in naturalistic research, shaping the project's emerging foci and design (see Dewey "Progressive"; Doheny-Farina and Odell; Heath; Lincoln and Guba; Spindler).

In the present case, although this book is about John Dewey's educational philosophy, it did not start out that way. Steve Fishman and I began our observations of his classroom in fall, 1995, with several foci of interest. It is true, as Fishman has said, that we were aware of his teaching problems during the previous semester and his newly devised pedagogical techniques to address them, and it is also true that we knew the work of John Dewey. But these were just a few of our concerns as the semester began, and we did not feature them originally. Instead, we initiated our inquiry as we always do, casting a wide net of observation, collecting as many types of data from as many sources as possible. And then we waited to see how these data would sharpen and recast the general questions with which we began. We also would discover, as our inquiry progressed, which of several possible theoretical frameworks would best clarify Fishman's practical problems.

As our project progressed, then, Fishman and I were like Geiger counters, using ourselves to register what was significant. We noted striking moments during data collection, alert to the importance of our saying "That was a class!" or "What a paper!" or "Listen to this interview!" These moments helped us develop a clearer idea of where we were going and suggested ways to refine our hypotheses and refocus our design. I interviewed students who offered their perspectives, and, depending on what I learned, Steve at times redesigned student-reflection log questions or daily assignments to further explore certain classroom events. And as we looked back at already reviewed data, they also took on new meaning.

Our researcher intuitions flashed, for example, as we left the final class of the fall, 1995, semester. Walking back across campus toward Steve's office, we looked at one another and asked, "What happened today? Why was that so special? You felt it too?" Although it was mysterious to us, we sensed we had witnessed the fulfillment of semester-long developments. We were aware, for example, that Fishman had often referred to the energy in this class, greater this semester than usual, he claimed. In his log entries he had mentioned "motion" and "live electrons" and "nuclei of interest," and he had marveled that he felt relieved this semester of the usually exhausting business of carrying the discussion by himself. Class structure, rather than the force of his personality, seemed to generate interaction. Because this final session, one fundamentally influenced by Fishman's Deweyan experiments, struck us as related to this energy theme, we agreed to explore it further. I report our findings about it in the following chapter.

Just as certain key moments became crystallizing threads which focused data collection and analysis, these moments also helped clarify theory. As we examined them with various theoretical lenses, we determined which theory provided most illumination, which best helped us explain or synthesize our data. In this process, we were once again instruments of inquiry, and we worked to balance theory with data, never theorizing too long without returning to classroom facts. Fishman, who is keenly aware of the dangers of theoretical panaceas for complex social problems, put it like this: "In this work, we're not just singing theoretical arias to ourselves. I can't solve my teaching problems with a theoretical swoop, a final, pie-in-the-sky answer, because just when I do, I have to go to class. I have to test what I'm thinking all the time." In Fishman's strong desire to unite theory and practice, he echoes Dewey, who inveighs against "arm-chair science," that is, educational research which does not begin and end with actual classroom problems ("Sources" 21–23).

At the start of this project, Fishman and I considered applying feminist pedagogical theory to his teaching dilemmas. In mid-November, however, we reread Dewey, and several of his key concepts resonated powerfully with the classroom data we were collecting. Although feminist and Deweyan theories share a number of features, Dewey's principles seemed to offer richer interpretive possibilities. In particular, I remember our satisfaction as we related Dewey to a theme in our data: Fishman's in-class "Ahhhh"s, an expression of discovery which made most of his students laugh. However, one member of the class, Sean Wilson, a 25-year-old Marine Corps officer in training, did not find Steve's Ahhhh's funny. Sean took them very seriously, telling me that he wanted to "reach that Ahhhh zone we all make fun of." Although not exactly sure what that zone was, he knew it was some "rush" of insight Fishman was enjoying. As we pondered Sean's comments, we found his desire to experience Fishman's rush interesting, but we could not do much with it. However, when we connected it to Dewey's notions of wholeheartedness and intellectual integrity, as I explain in Chapter 9, Sean's longing took on larger meaning. This sort of help from Deweyan educational philosophy led us to adopt it as fundamental for our study.

Promotion of Teacher Change

As I have said, the goal of educational research for Dewey is not pedagogical recipes or educational "laws" but more sensitive teacher observation, invention, planning, and judgment ("Sources" 14). Because teachers who are involved in naturalistic classroom inquiry are responsible for observing and judging the teaching and learning going on in their courses, it is an approach which fosters change. The potential for teacher transformation is pronounced because the teacher is both researcher and researched, subject and object. Rather than worry, as scientific paradigm inquirers would, that such intimacy limits researcher objectivity, naturalistic inquirers assume that knower and known are intimately bound. In fact, we view neutrality, the separation of observer and observed, as undesirable because it encourages the observer to overlook biases and assumptions he or she brings to the setting (Kirsch and Ritchie; Lincoln and Guba; see also Gergen; Harding "Feminism").

This uniting of researcher and teacher would be especially attractive to Dewey because it invites the teacher, in this case Fishman, to be a full partner in the inquiry, studying himself in a hands-on, potentially transformative, and personally risky business. As Fishman and I examine his classroom, he plays a double role. He is, first, the object of our inquiry, the theorist-practitioner living out with his students his pedagogical experiments. But he also must step away from his teacherly role and join me as observer of classroom events; at these moments, he is analyst, interpreter, and, once again, theorist. Yet, even in this more distanced stance, Steve still cannot be detached, because we are exploring his practical teaching problems. Our findings are immediately useful to him. As he puts it, "This is compelling work. It's about what I do in class tomorrow. And the students we're talking about are ones I have to deal with. This is not research at a remove; it's about my life."

This potential for immediate classroom reform is what makes naturalistic teacher research especially vital. The findings are "presold," needed by the teacher-researcher who contracted for them in advance, the teacher who must, then, decide what to do with them. As Fishman explains in Chapter 6, the conclusions of our previous studies have sometimes been gratifying to him, at other times painful. But in either case, his deep involvement in the inquiry—pursuing his own questions, generating his own data, and formulating his own interpretations—has repeatedly led him to revise his practices (for discussions of the transformatory goals of naturalistic teacher research, see Cochran-Smith and Lytle; Daiker and Morenberg; Fleischer; Goswami and Stillman; Hubbard and Power; Lincoln; Ray).

The transformatory power of naturalistic classroom research for teachers, then, results from its encouraging them to be practitioner, researcher, and theoretician all in one. As for me, the outside researcher, I too have changed as I have brought together theory and practice. Despite my training in qualitative methods, in my early observations of Fishman's class, I tried to hang on to the "arm-chair" approach Dewey distrusted, that is, the white-coated, neutral social scientist's stance I had recently adopted in my dissertation (completed at the University of Pennsylvania in 1985). In that project, I examined student learning in several college disciplinary classrooms, but I remained aloof from the instructors, never inviting them to join me in coconstructing their stories (McCarthy). The politics of this bothered me, especially when I was critical of the teacher, and it was dawning on me that teacher change is more likely to occur in response to findings constructed *with* teachers than to findings constructed *about* them. In the equal partnership Fishman and I have developed, we combine our expertise, each of us responsible for both theory and practice (our separate bylines notwithstanding.) Our collaboration has been for me, then, a testimony to the power of theory and practice to enrich one another. Borrowing Dewey's terms, I have come to appreciate the power of theory to act as "a lamp to the feet," and the ability of practice to provide a "light to the eyes" ("Sources" 7; for further discussion of teacher-researcher collaborations and researcher reflexivity, see Florio-Ruane and deTar; Harding *Whose* 138–63, "Introduction" 9; Latour and Woolgar 273–86; McCarthy and Fishman "Text"; McCarthy and Walvoord; Mohr and MacLean; Tedlock).

Heightened Student Interest and Self-Reflection

Not only does naturalistic classroom research lead to teacher and investigator change, our projects, we have also noticed, provoke keener student interest in the class, greater attention that manifests itself in a variety of ways. In the current study, for example, one informant, a junior medical technology major, said she devèloped the habit of watching herself do classwork so she would be in a better position to report to me during her interviews. This made her more aware of her struggles to hear other students and be an effective respondent to their written work. Another student claimed she did the written assignments more carefully because she knew her pieces would be read by the outside researcher as well as her classmates and Fishman. Other students said that Fishman's caring enough about them to videotape each class and xerox all their written work led them to try harder than they might otherwise have.

In addition to their claiming increased self-awareness and attention to classwork, several students also indicated that they felt part of a larger project, valued as sources of information about their class experiences. A senior journalism major wrote, "These reflection logs make me feel I have a working relation with the teacher." And she was right; she did have important research status. In projects such as ours, students become expert informants, and this cooperative relationship subtly reshapes student-teacher interaction. For example, students who are doing poorly, instead of being seen as failures or nuisances, may hold particular interest for the teacher-researcher. This occurred in the present study, and Fishman's and my questioning these students led some to view their difficulties in a new light.

Representation of Diverse Voices and Perspectives

When, as naturalistic researchers, we write reports, we face quite different challenges from those of scientific paradigm inquirers. As opposed to reports of scientific research, which are, most often, rendered in prose which has been characterized as "author-evacuated," naturalistic accounts are "author-saturated" (Geertz *Works* 9). That is, reports of naturalistic inquiry are narratives by particular observers making limited claims about local activities (see Fraser and Nicholson 26). And, given the goal of naturalistic inquiry to reconstruct the multiple realities of participants within a setting, the research report must represent not only the inquirer's perspective but also the diverse voices in that locale, their interplay and mutual influence. In other words, readers should hear participants' diverse ways of conceiving, imagining, and telling their stories (see Hartsock 158–64; Kirsch and Ritchie 16–24).

In the last few years, naturalistic investigators have increasingly experimented with textual forms, seeking styles more reflective of the goals of naturalistic research. We have created forms, that is, which represent the dialogic, mutually shaping interactions among investigators and informants. Texts of this sort have been called "heteroglossic" by Clifford (119), and they have offered Fishman and me territory on which to negotiate our collaborative roles and research authority. In his and my early struggles to equalize authority, we tried to find a single researcher voice in which to report our findings. But any blending of his teacherly voice and my outside-researcher voice left one or the other of us feeling cheated. We resolved our impasse by agreeing that each of us would write our own sections, exploring our questions in our unique ways, and that we would then connect these with coauthored sections. In this fashion, we could finally be satisfied that our different perspectives and ways of speaking were adequately represented (for further discussions of textual representation in naturalistic research, see Berkenkotter, "Rhetoric"; Clifford; Clifford and Marcus; Geertz, *Works*; Herndl; McCarthy and Fishman, "Text"; and Zeller).

Since Fishman's and my first heteroglossic article appeared in 1991 ("Boundary"), we have constantly renegotiated textual representations and research authority. In the present volume, for example, we shape our coauthorship in a variety of ways. In Part I, Fishman speaks as a philosopher-autobiographer, authorizing his account through academic citation and confessional narrative. In Part II, we form a partnership, my voice dominant, Steve's consulting, as I tell our research stories, buttressing my authority with citations and classroom evidence. In yet other arrangements of our voices, our coauthored Introduction presents a series of individually authored statements, whereas in our coauthored Conclusion, we adopt a single, shared point of view. But despite our various bylines, each of us has been involved in all aspects of this project. I have read Dewey extensively, and Steve knows the classroom data very well, playing a crucial role in shaping our research findings. But no matter Fishman's and my exact management of textual space, in all our reports we try to represent our differing viewpoints and our diverse ways of telling our stories. We strive, that is, to represent textually our unique contributions to our communal enterprise.

RESEARCH QUESTIONS, SETTING, AND PARTICIPANTS

Our overarching questions in this project concern Steve Fishman's Deweyan goal of enriched experience through student-curriculum integration. Did he succeed in helping his students connect philosophic subject matter to their personal lives? If so, what did this expansion of interest and integration look like, and what were its consequences for students? And what can we learn from Fishman's experiences about Deweyan principles themselves, the "nested dualisms" underlying the student-curriculum dichotomy? Our secondary aim is to explicate these principles so they may become for our teacher readers useful instruments in their own classroom observation, planning, and evaluation.

The Students

Fishman's introductory philosophy class in the fall of 1995 was comprised of 25 undergraduates from a variety of majors, all of whom enrolled to satisfy graduation requirements. The course was designated writing intensive and satisfied a humanities distribution as well as writing requirement for non-humanities majors. The 25 students ranged in age from 19 to 25. Fourteen were female and 11 were male. Six were African American (three men and three women), and all except one were native speakers of English. About 80% of the class came from North Carolina. With very few exceptions, these students did not know one another before the semester began, and none knew Fishman.

I selected the students I concentrated on (my "focus students") with an eye to diversity of race, class, gender, and geographic origin. (I originally approached 16 of the 24 students in the class, and of those 16, 12 agreed to participate.) I aimed also for a range of quiet and talkative students, ultimately choosing people who I thought would be willing and able to participate in extensive interviewing and think-aloud taping. Across the semester, nearly all became increasingly adept at self-reflection, and all took care to uphold their commitments to me. Of these 12 focus students, 5 receive special attention in subsequent chapters. The advantage of limiting my report in this way is that it enables me to present more detailed accounts than had I attempted to provide the stories of all 12. The 5 I chose represent a range of success and failure in Fishman's class as well as a variety of majors and the diversity noted earlier.

All students in Fishman's class, focus and nonfocus, were aware of our research from the first day of the semester when videotaping began. Fishman told them, "Don't mind the camera. I try to study my classes to make them better. I'm not sure where it goes, and it's a lot of work, but I believe in this research. It keeps my teaching alive." He also explained that their reflection logs would be an "informal way of finding out what you're experiencing." On September 5, the fourth class meeting, I made my initial visit, and Steve presented me as Dr. McCarthy, a researcher from the University of Maryland. He explained, "She watches these videotapes along with me, and she will be speaking with some of you." Throughout the semester, I felt that most students liked and trusted Fishman and wanted to cooperate with him. Because they understood that I was his research partner, I benefited from the good will he earned for us both.

The Teacher and the Institution

As Fishman has indicated, he has taught for 30 years—all of them at the University of North Carolina Charlotte. During these three decades, he has watched the institution grow from 2,500 students on a 7-building campus to its current enrollment of 12,000 students living and taking classes in some 50 buildings. The university is comprised of schools of architecture, business, education, engineering, and nursing as well as of arts and sciences, and it offers doctorates in a small number of fields.

Steve Fishman is a full professor of philosophy who, like other members of his department, teaches three courses per semester, generally including one Intro course, one Logic, and one advanced course on a topic of his choice. Because there are so few philosophy majors at UNCC, and no philosophy graduate students, the greatest proportion of Fishman's students will only ever take one philosophy course. This was true of virtually all of the students in the Intro class we studied.

Fishman's eight colleagues in the philosophy department have had, with one exception, tenures nearly as long as his, and it is a department which generally reflects university values. That is, although efforts to improve teaching in the philosophy department are appreciated—for example, Fishman's continuing service of offering writing-intensive courses—it is research and publication that are rewarded. Nonetheless, the department chair has, since the early 1980s, supported faculty development programs such as the Writing Across the Curriculum initiative sponsored by the English department. As Fishman has explained, this program was crucial to his career, and several other philosophy professors have participated over the years as well.

In fall, 1995, Fishman's Intro course met in Smith Engineering Building, across campus from his office, in a small classroom stuffed with movable chairs and individual, detached desks. Because the room was so full of furniture, Fishman's usual classroom circle became a closely packed, two-tiered horseshoe with him in the opening. The negative aspect of this arrangement was that some students looked at the backs of others' heads. The positive was that students were physically close to one another, a benefit especially during frequent paired and small group conversations.

Fishman's classroom demeanor and appearance were, according to students, somewhat unusual. As a tall, thin, greying man in his late 50s, a full professor and longtime faculty member, he carried a great deal of authority. Yet Steve's behavior defied their expectations of such a professor. His class was "totally different," they said, because, unlike most of their teachers, he never lectured or even stepped up to the blackboard. It was, in fact, the only course they had ever taken in which students talked as much as the professor and where the teacher sat among them and listened. Students also commented on Fishman's casual dress—his T-shirts, sweatshirts, and shorts—and some even referred to him as Steve, the name he signed on his notes to them. And Fishman's sense of humor, they told me, "relaxed" them. They laughed at his self-denigrating stories, accounts of his ineptitude as a boy growing up in the Bronx, the grandson of Eastern European Jewish immigrants, and his struggles as a student, the first in his family, like many of them, to attend college.

The Outside Researcher

Although Fishman and I share many personal and professional traits, I present a more formal appearance to students. Like Steve, I am tall, thin, white, and in my 50s (although WASP and second-generation college), and I too have an Ivy League background. Yet, by contrast with Fishman, I hold tight to my professorial authority, wearing a suit and heels and carrying a stack of notebooks. And Steve helped me construct this professor persona when he introduced me to students as an experienced researcher. During my class observations, although I sat among students in the horseshoe, I did not join the discussion but instead watched and took notes. As the semester progressed, I often joked with students, and I occasionally revealed parts of my own autobiography. Yet, generally, I maintained my formal stance, the outside researcher seriously trying to understand students' experiences.

When I entered Fishman's fall, 1995, Introduction to Philosophy classroom, as is by now abundantly clear, I was hardly a neutral observer. Not only had I studied Steve's teaching since 1989, I knew about his woes in the B.J. class the previous semester as well as about the new techniques he hoped would ameliorate the situation. In fact, he and I had discussed these pedagogies at some length. Therefore, I began this project not only well acquainted with the teacher but actually having helped shape the classroom I would observe.

DATA COLLECTION PROCEDURES

Data Generated by the Teacher

Teacher Reflection Log
As soon after its completion as possible, Fishman described each class meeting in a two-page reflection. He recalled vivid moments and offered tentative interpretations.

Teacher Interviews
On five occasions, at regular intervals across the semester, I audiotaped interviews with Fishman. In these 60-minute sessions, I asked him to reflect on his own and his students' experiences. These interviews were open ended (see Spradley, *Interview*), often beginning with requests for clarification about classroom transactions I had just witnessed. During these interviews we also

discussed—and at times readjusted—Fishman's future assignments and classroom activities.

Teacher's Audiotaped Responses to Student Drafts

Fishman recorded an 8- to 12-minute response to every student's essay draft in early November. A month later, when he collected their completed essays, he asked them to return these tapes, and before reading their papers, he replayed them. When he had completed responding to each student's paper, he again spoke into each tape, this time recording for our research his impressions of that student's achievement.

Teacher-Student Conferences

Late in the semester, Fishman audiotaped a conversation in his office with each of three students who came for help with their papers.

Data Generated by Students

Student Class Reflection Logs (CRLs)

Students responded to 22 questions across the 14-week semester. Fishman handed a question to students at the end of most class periods, which they were to complete at home, writing as much as they wanted. He collected students' logs three times during the semester, responding briefly in the margins, often thanking them for particularly detailed or candid reflections. These logs received credit but no grade.

Fishman and I constructed reflection log questions together, shaping them with particular research interests in mind. For example, we asked students about (a) their responses to particular classroom exchanges, (b) their reading and writing experiences during particular assignments, (c) their sense of their own progress in the class and their current understanding of what constituted philosophic thinking, (d) their relations with Fishman and their classmates, (e) their own and their families' schooling histories, (f) their understanding of the relation of philosophic discourse to other, more familiar discourses, and (g) their comparative analysis of Fishman's pedagogy and that employed in their other classes. Students' answers to these questions often provided a starting point for my interviews with them. (See Appendix A for a complete list of reflection log questions.)

Student Interviews

During the semester, I interviewed 16 of the 25 students enrolled in the class, 12 of them extensively, that is, four or five times at regular intervals across the semester. (These 12 students I refer to as "focus" or "focal" students, the others as "nonfocus.") My 30- to 40-minute audiotaped interviews with students took place in Fishman's office or in a nearby seminar room and combined features of discourse-based and open-ended approaches (Odell, Goswami, and Herrington; Spradley, *Interview*). That is, although I began with particular questions in mind, I generally followed students' lead into other issues when I thought it would be productive. Throughout the semester, I was open with students about my specific interests, making clear that they were experts who could help me gain insight into their experiences in this class. In these interviews, I also obtained information about students' lives outside the classroom, including their family, work, and educational histories.

Student Follow-up Interviews
In addition to interviews during the semester, I conducted an additional follow-up interview with each of my 12 informants 3 to 5 months after the course ended. These 30- to 90-minute interviews were conducted on the telephone as I took notes. They provided information about the residue that students took from Fishman's class as well as gave me a chance to conduct "member checks," in which I tested my reconstructions of their experiences with the informants themselves (Lincoln and Guba 314–16).

Student Think-Aloud Tapes
I asked 8 of my 12 student informants to speak their thoughts out loud— and tape-record them—as they did their reading and writing assignments outside class. These 8 students interested me particularly, and I believed they would be willing and able to undertake such a task. Six agreed, and five of these, at semester's end, gave me audiotapes of between 2 and 6 hours, in which they, at home or in their dorm rooms, detailed their reading and writing processes. These think-aloud tapes provided useful information about these students. That is, I could hear them actually engaged in processes that they had summarized for me in interviews and which resulted in written products I could examine. In addition to their composing aloud, students also recorded their reflections about class discussions. (See Appendix B for my letter to students instructing them on their think-aloud taping. For more on this instrument, see Walvoord and McCarthy 28–31.)

Student Texts

Fishman and I made copies of all student writing across the semester, an average of some 45 pages per student. These documents included all 22 homework assignments as well as all in-class writing. The forms of student writing varied widely, including letters to classmates; in-class freewrites; in-class, triple-entry notetaking exercises; essay exams; reflection log entries; answers to Fishman's homework study questions; students' questions about texts for their small groups; two drafts of their 5- to 10-page essay; and class notes, written by one student each session and duplicated for everyone to read aloud at the start of the next.

Data Generated by the Outside Researcher

Class Observations

I observed ten 75-minute class sessions during the semester, participating in small groups, and taking field notes throughout (see Spradley, *Observation*). In addition, all classes were videotaped by one of Fishman's former Intro students whom we employed. This visual record of class interactions was especially valuable for what it revealed about nonverbal as well as verbal communication among participants. In addition to what students said and their tone of voice, we were able to observe meanings carried in body language, eye contact, facial expression, choice of seating, and dress.

Observation of Teacher Evaluation Sessions

I observed Fishman in three evaluation sessions as he responded to students' work—their midterms, final exams, and essays. During and after these grading sessions, we discussed his responses in terms of our emerging research foci. We audiotaped these conversations for later transcription.

DATA ANALYSIS PROCEDURES: CONSTRUCTING THEMES AND PATTERNS

Proponents of naturalistic research assume, as I have said, that the researcher is the primary instrument of inquiry. In Fishman's and my case, our analytic instrument was a complex chemistry of our two ways of going at the world—perspectives shaped by our unique dispositions and training, our different relations to the classroom, and our diverse ways of telling our stories. Our data analysis procedures throughout the project were guided by the work of Gilmore and Glatthorn; Lincoln and Guba; Miles and Huberman; Odell et al.; and Spradley (*Interview; Observation*). They can be divided into three stages.

Transcribing Audio- and Videotapes

From hundreds of hours of tapes, I transcribed those I believed would prove most useful. I did as many of these as possible myself because the slow-motion listening during transcription is generative for me. It puts participant language under a microscope, and I hear tones, tempos, nuances of overlap and interruption, fine points of affect, which help me construct my interpretations. However, because transcription is so time-consuming, and, for this project, my body of tape-recorded data so large, I had to employ assistants. In all, about three quarters of the tapes were transcribed and analyzed.

Refining Analytic Categories

Working with Fishman, I read and reread the data—triangulating among transcripts of interviews, field notes, student and teacher documents, and videotapes and constructing tentative themes and patterns. In collaboration with him, I continually modified these categories, my alterations shaped in part by my ongoing "member checks" with him, that is, my continual query, "Did I get you right? Did I get the teacher right?" During this process I paid special attention to "negative cases" in the data, cases which conflicted with or fell outside my emerging interpretations (see Lincoln and Guba 309-16).

Although it may appear that Fishman and I were focused solely on classroom data during this period, we were actually engaged in a complex theory-practice dialogue. While Steve was commenting on my interpretations of data, I was, at the same time, responding to drafts of his theoretic chapters. Our development of our empiric and theoretical arguments, then, took place in tandem and was dynamic and mutually conditioning.

Composing Data Reduction Drafts

Finally, drawing on the themes and patterns we had tentatively agreed on, I composed drafts of my chapters, "data reduction" efforts in which I narrated various partipants' versions of what happened in Fishman's class (Miles and Huberman 21). These initial drafts were extremely long, full of voices and possibilities, but, compared to my raw data, they provided Fishman and me a greatly reduced field on which to continue refining our analysis. Clarification of our findings continued as I created further drafts, in each one sharpening my arguments and story lines.

I turn now in Chapters 8 through 11 to the analyses Fishman and I produced, the findings we constructed. I choose to start at the end, examining, in Chapter 8, the final class meeting of the semester.

REAL, GENUINE ATTENTION MEANS MENTAL MOVEMENT, not only on the part of the individual but also on the part of the class. It means that ideas come into the class, various persons follow out those ideas, and new points are brought out; and yet the teacher harmonizes it all, combining this play of variety, this expression of different elements, so that it leads consistently and consecutively in a definite direction.

— JOHN DEWEY,
"Attention" 1902: 283

outlined at the end of Chapter 6. This was the letter exchange, a pedagogy which worked indirectly in a number of ways. First of all, Fishman's objective was to get students to come up with their own foci of interest in the assigned text, what Dewey would call their own "to-whats" (see Chapter 2, this volume). In other words, instead of Fishman's telling students "to what" he wanted them to attend in their readings, he set the conditions so they would have to do it themselves. And he did this indirectly. That is, he asked students to write a letter to a classmate posing a question about difficulties they were experiencing with the text.

What is the advantage of working indirectly like this, of not simply telling students to come up with their own ways of reading the material but, instead, asking them to write a letter to a classmate? Following Deweyan thinking, the letter assignment gave students an additional reason for reading the assignment. Besides their usual motivation or "for-what"—their desire to get a passing grade—students had a new and more social one: to uphold their end of a shared project. To do this, they needed to work through some philosophic subject matter, accessing it in their own ways.

In addition to these for-whats—getting the grade and pleasing a partner —Fishman had two more goals or for-whats in mind. He envisioned that, as students generated their own text-based questions for their letter partners, their own to-whats, they might find the reading relevant to ongoing issues in their lives and be able to use this new subject matter for their own purposes. Philosophy might, that is, become a vehicle for achieving some personal goals, ones in which students had direct and genuine interest. Finally, Fishman hoped that a few of his pupils might even develop an interest in the assigned texts themselves, perhaps mastering some of philosophy's methods well enough to be able to apply them to practical situations in the future. These latter two goals represent the sort of expanded interest in subject matter which is, for Dewey, the ultimate sign of student-curriculum integration.

These, then, are the mechanics and goals of the indirect pedagogy you are about to watch. As I play my tape, I will illustrate them, and in this process, spotlight Fishman's struggle to harmonize disparate student ideas. Because Fishman, in enacting his indirect pedagogy, made student homework the center of class discussion, he had less control of what Dewey calls the class's "mental movement" than if he had simply lectured ("Attention" 282). Instead, with pupils' letter exchanges as the basis for classroom conversation, ideas put on the table did not necessarily have built-in coherence or development. Therefore, we will watch Fishman work to weave continuities among these reports, making split-second decisions about which student contributions to develop and which to drop. We will also observe his decision making about when to remain in the background because students were hearing and responding fruitfully to one another and when to step forward with explicit instruction.

In my account of the last session, I report not only Fishman's decisions about harmonizing class discussion but also his second-guessing in this regard. His self-doubts remind us that Dewey is right about the teacherly burdens of indirect instruction. As Dewey puts it, teachers employing this method must bring to class a wide understanding of their subject matter as well as a keen sensitivity to student learning, to signs of potential mastery of the curriculum (*Experience and Education* 57–59; *How* 274–77). However, alongside the challenges of indirect teaching we also see opportunities for teacher discovery and growth. When Fishman successfully sifted disparate student contributions to find the uniting thread, his sense of fulfillment was evident. This served for some students as an instructive example of risk and discovery, of what Dewey calls intellectual integrity (*Democracy* 176; *How* 32).

LAST CLASS DISCUSSION:
STUDENTS QUESTIONING AND ANSWERING,
TEACHING AND LEARNING

Fishman began the final class session with a freewrite intended to make use of students' homework to inform class discussion. He asked them to write for 10 minutes on the letters they had brought to class with them, letters in which they had responded to their partners' questions about chapter 1 of Dewey's *Reconstruction in Philosophy* (See Appendix C for the assignment; see also Young.) More specifically, Fishman asked, "What did you learn about Dewey's chapter 1 from answering your partner's question?"

I begin my tape about 50 minutes into the 75-minute period. The class has already heard from one exchange pair, and Fishman has just called on Demika Braxton, a junior medical technology major from Winston-Salem, North Carolina, and one of my focus students.

"Demika, who was your partner?"

"John."

John Lucas, a senior English major from Charlotte, North Carolina, and another of my focus students, was sitting behind Demika and to her right. As partners, John and Demika were, in many ways, the proverbial odd couple. John was a young man who sought the spotlight as much as Demika tried to avoid it. He spoke glibly; she painstakingly; he was tall, thin, and white; she short, heavyset, and African American. Yet both students were respected by their classmates, and both were, at this moment, stage center.

On the videotape, we see Fishman acknowledge John with a nod and then look back to Demika.

"Okay, okay, Demika. Did you learn anything by trying to respond to John's question?"

"Sure."

The class laughed, Demika's short answer implying a long story. She then explained that, although she had read the wrong assignment when she formulated her letter to John—Dewey's 45-page introduction to *Reconstruction* instead of chapter 1—she had later gone back and read chapter 1 to prepare for John's question to her.

"But then," Demika sighed, "after I read chapter 1, John didn't even ask me about it. Instead, he asked for my personal opinion." She looked down at his typed letter to her on the desk in front of her, reading the first of its five paragraphs to the class:

> Knowing that you are a fellow Christian, do you find that Dewey's theory of philosophy undermines our Christian beliefs? Because we are Christians, does that not make us traditionalists to an extent? Do you personally feel that we should question *everything* in an attempt to gain a better understanding of the world? In my own Christian walk I have been taught never to question God. Have you found this to be a bit of a struggle in this class?

Fishman nodded thoughtfully as Demika read. He was pleased that John had hit upon an issue at the center of philosophy, namely, the value of questioning, but he was dismayed that John's question led away from, rather than into, the assigned reading. Still, hoping to salvage something, Fishman responded appreciatively and tried to relate John's question to chapter 1.

"Okay, yes, Demika. Well, John asks for your personal opinion, but his question is relevant to what Dewey is talking about in chapter 1. So, what happened when you answered John?"

The videotape shows Demika glance down once again, this time at her own typed letter, as she prepared to explain her response to John's question. Speaking deliberately, she began:

> Well, the way I thought about it is that if God doesn't want us to figure out certain things, then we don't figure them out. There's a reason why we can't figure out certain things—like the afterlife and ghosts or whatever. But the things we do know have benefited our world. So to answer John's question, I

think we are traditionalists to a certain extent. I think we cannot question God's commandments. However, as far as questioning how the world functions, I think we can do that.

"Okay, Demika," Fishman responded, accepting her answer in his usual supportive manner. "So it is a delicate balance you're working for."

"That's right," she replied.

Although still unhappy with the drift away from the assigned text, Fishman thought Demika's answer was provocative. In effect, she was saying both yes and no to John's question. She assumed God's intentions were clear enough so we would know which questions to ask and which not. That is, we had better not challenge the Ten Commandments or Christian moral principles, but it is okay to investigate nature or "how the world functions." And for those who go too far, according to Demika, God stops them by giving no answers to questions they have no business asking. Fishman also knew that because she was a medical technology major, this compromise was an important one for Demika, not just one she dreamed up for John. In previous class discussions dealing with evolution and creationism, she had used some of the assigned readings to develop a similar compromise in order to reconcile her church and laboratory lives.

As Demika concluded her answer to John's question, Ashley Posten, a freckle-faced redhead from Ohio, sitting two seats away, raised her hand. Ashley, a sophomore health and fitness major and a five-foot-six-inch starter on the women's basketball team, contributed regularly to class discussion. Like Demika and John, Ashley was a focus student, and, like them, a Christian. Yet her furrowed brow indicated that Demika's answer left her troubled.

Fishman turned to his left "Ashley wants to speak. Do you want to question Demika?"

"Yes."

Ashley faced Demika and challenged her statement that God knows best and only lets us understand and do what is good. "Demika," Ashley began, "you know how you said God doesn't let us figure out some things. I've been thinking about that recently. Like with science coming up with creating babies by just using a sperm and egg, messing with chromosomes to get someone perfect. I think that's bad, but God let us figure it out."

"That's a good question, Ashley," Fishman commented. "Demika, you're a medical technology major; you know all about that stuff. Is that right? They're some day hoping to make babies outside the uterus?"

As Fishman later explained, he was pleased at Ashley's response because it indicated she had heard Demika and was interested in questioning her. It was the kind of student-to-student exchange Fishman hoped for. He remarked, "You know that students are paying attention when they want to jump in, when they want to forward discussion by challenging or adding or clarifying." And, Fishman was pleased with the question itself, another one at the heart of philosophy and theology. On the table now was not only John's query, Is it good to question? Also up for consideration was Ashley's question: What sort of God allows evil to happen?

However, despite the fact that Fishman was gratified by Ashley's attentive response to Demika, at another level he remained worried. The to-what which John had given Demika—her own view of philosophic questioning— and the line of classroom thinking it was provoking were still skirting chapter 1 of Dewey's *Reconstruction*. So although Fishman was allowing the conversation to go on (after all, it was spirited and well within the philosophic tradition), he still remained uneasy. It had the negative glow of some discussions in previous semesters, ones in which the line between class inquiry and dorm bull session became blurred. Because the discussion was not moving into the center of the reading assignment, Fishman felt his indirect teaching had, so far, failed.

Ashley's question about the place of genetic engineering in Demika's scheme had put Demika on the line once again.

Once more seeking words, Demika began slowly, "Well . . . I think man can take things to a certain extent, like us figuring out how to do genetics. That helps us cure birth defects. But man in his quest for superiority sometimes goes too far. But that's our fault, not God's."

Ashley: "But why isn't God stopping us from knowing? Why is He allowing us to do that?"

Demika: (pause) "Well, I'm not God, so/"

Ashley: (amiably, not wanting to corner Demika) "I know."

Fishman: (smiling at Ashley) "Ashley, have you mistaken Demika for God?!" (The class erupts in laughter.)

Demika: (reentering the conversation quietly) "Well, I'm not sure what to say."

At this point, despite Fishman's disappointment that the discussion was still skirting the text, he decided to join Ashley in pushing Demika a bit. He knew from past experience that Demika's retreat did not mean she was closed to further exploration, and he wanted to see what would happen if he made more explicit the idea behind Ashley's follow-up question, namely, that if God is all good and all powerful, how do we explain the presence of evil in the world? He thought Demika had given a classic answer to Ashley: the evil in the world is of human rather than divine origin. In effect, he thought she was saying it is our free will that gets us in trouble, not God. In return, Ashley also echoed a classic strategy. She countered, if God is good and knows everything, then you cannot blame moral evil on humans' free will. So although the topic was not quite what Fishman hoped for, the high level of interest, as well as its philosophic import, made him decide it was worth pursuing, at least for a while longer.

So Fishman pressed Demika, reiterating Ashley's challenge. He began with what was for him a typical attempt to let Demika know he was not attacking but trying to work with her.

"Oh, Demika, while I have you here, let me ask you this. How do we know what God wants us to know or not know? It looks like we are going to figure out ways for children to be produced without women being involved. I think Ashley was a little upset about that. She wants to know, if God is in charge, why is He letting us figure out things we shouldn't be figuring out. Am I right, Ashley?"

"Yes, that bothers me," Ashley admitted. "If we can figure this out, why not other things that lead to no good?"

Despite Demika's history of willingness to "dig deeper," as she put it, she had, at least for the moment, gone as far as she was willing to go. She shrugged and smiled. Fishman accepted her refusal, realizing that reconciling God's omnipotence and the presence of evil was not so easy.

Fishman thanked Demika and turned to John, who was waiting to report his half of the letter exchange. Fishman was hoping that, although Demika had read the wrong chapter, her question to John might be a way of leading the class back to the assigned reading.

At this point, Fishman asked John the same question he had posed to Demika: "John, we have already heard from Demika about your question. Now, what did she ask you? Did you learn something by trying to answer her?"

In what follows, John, like Demika, described his experience in a complex medley of teaching and learning, questioning and answering.

"Yeah, I learned something. Her question comes from Dewey's introduction. It was," (he read):

Why does Dewey bash science? Being a medical technology major, I took offense at some of his assumptions about science. I see him as saying that to be a philosopher, you cannot possibly trust science. He portrays science as being destructive.

Although John admitted he had not read the introduction to *Reconstruction*, he said he knew enough to answer Demika. From his own typed letter to her, John read, "Is Dewey really bashing science, or is he showing it is parallel to philosophy?" From what he understood, John explained, Dewey sees philosophy and science as more aligned than opposed.

Fishman nodded as John read, but he decided not to press John further. Although John was generally correct in what he had said, Fishman felt that it would be difficult through questioning either John or Demika to get back to *Reconstruction*, chapter 1. He was also somewhat disturbed that John had circumvented Demika's to-what invitation to look, even in cursory fashion, at Dewey's introduction. Yet despite Fishman's fear that neither Demika nor John had pursued the issue sufficiently to profit from direct teaching, he decided to fill out John's answer to Demika himself. At this point, he just hoped to tie the knot quickly on their letter exchange and move on to another. Fishman began:

> Well, Demika, I haven't read the introduction in a while. Dewey wrote it in the 1940s just after we dropped the atomic bomb, and so I think he's not so much against science as he is against how science is sometimes used. I think he is saying science isn't used in a vacuum but in the context of various values and goals. And he fears that until we develop more intelligent ways for reassessing our values and goals, science may continue to be used destructively.

Demika listened, and John's (as well as most other students') eyes were on Fishman as well. Although things in this exchange had not gone quite as Fishman hoped, the students involved, as well as those just listening, seemed satisfied, as if they had successfully explored to-whats in which they had a real stake.

With about 12 minutes left in the period, Sean Wilson, seated to Demika's left, waved his hand, and Fishman acknowledged him. "Sean, you wanted to say something?"

In what followed, Sean—a senior health and fitness major from Charlotte, North Carolina, a short, crew-cut, 25-year-old Marine officer-in-training and a focus student—finally brought the class back to Dewey's chapter 1. He questioned Fishman directly about the text:

> In my letter, I asked my partner about Dewey's contrast between traditional and practical knowledge. If we do what Dewey says, and take away the emotion that is involved with tradition, does that not make Dewey's new philosophy an abstract science? . . . Does Dewey want to keep traces of past philosophy and

intertwine them with his new science of philosophy? I couldn't figure exactly what he was getting at.

"That's a great question, Sean," Fishman responded. "How does Dewey see philosophy, the new philosophy? Is it going to be abstract and cold, or is it going to be emotional? What is the proper function of philosophy? How does it work?"

Fishman commented later that he was excited that Sean had finally returned class discussion to the assignment. Furthermore, although Sean's inference about Dewey's view of philosophy—that it would be abstract and as unemotional as science—was a little off target, Fishman thought his question revealed a serious reading of chapter 1 and a good attempt to make something of it on his own. Unfortunately, however, with so little time remaining, Fishman felt he had no choice but once again to resort to a direct answer.

Well, Sean, I think you're right. Dewey does want philosophy to be more like science, but not in the sense it should do lab work or rely on elaborate equipment. I believe he's referring to science in the broad sense of a way of thinking, a way of analyzing problems, framing hypothetical solutions, and revising these in light of future experience. And, although Dewey wouldn't want us to be carried away by our own emotions, I think he would say that this sort of thinking, like all thinking, has important emotional dimensions.

Fishman then asked Sean to read to the class from *Reconstruction*, inviting him, essentially, to be teacher to the class: "Sean, you're going to read this as we close the semester. Page 26."

Fishman's direct teaching pointed Sean to the culminating pages of Dewey's chapter 1, to the to-what (object of focus) Fishman believed Sean was ready for. Fishman sensed that Sean was using the assigned text for his own purposes, that genuine for-whats (goals) were driving him to understand what Dewey was saying about the relation among science, philosophy, and tradition. Fishman also sensed a momentum in Sean's questions because they resembled ones he had raised in earlier class periods. He thought Sean's curiosity and the work he had already done made it likely that a direct answer would now serve him well. In other words, this was one of those circumstances where direct teaching would be neither a waste of time nor a burden but would actually fuel a student's curiosity. In addition, Fishman believed his response to Sean about the nature of philosophy might be productive for other class members as well.

With only 5 minutes remaining in the semester, Sean opened Dewey's *Reconstruction* and read to the class:

> When it is acknowledged that under disguise of dealing with ultimate reality, philosophy has been occupied with the precious values embedded in social traditions, that it has sprung from a clash of social ends and from a conflict of inherited institutions with incompatible contemporary tendencies, it will be seen that the task of future philosophy is to clarify men's ideas as to the social and moral strifes of their own day.

Sean looked up from the page and leaned forward. He squinted at Fishman and, in the next moment, he revealed his for-what, the purpose which was sustaining his attention and directing his reading of Dewey. "So what you're saying is that when our parents sit us down and lecture us and try to give us their philosophic view of life, they are possibly wrong because they are not in the same generation we are?"

Fishman responded, "Exactly! Dewey has a view of life as evolving, and therefore every generation must be philosophers. We live in an uncertain and changing world, so we constantly have to adjust.... But Dewey doesn't say throw away the past; we want to conserve what we can use of it. However, we also want to be sensitive to present experience and try to move openly toward the future. Does that make any sense, Sean?"

"Yes, sir. It sure does."

In fact, Sean told me later that afternoon, this exchange with Fishman "just enlightened everything for me." Understanding Dewey's view of philosophy, he reported, "just opened my mind. It was the point I've been looking for, the approach I'm going to pursue in resolving the biggest conflict in my life, the one I'm writing my paper about. Dewey says solutions are ever changing, and that's how I see things. But I've had trouble saying that to my father and grandmother.... It was like Dewey touched a part of me none of these other authors have."

Following Sean's and Fishman's in-class exchange, there were only 2 minutes left, and Fishman concluded the semester by doing something unusual. Although he always wrote in class with his students, he had never read his freewrite aloud. At this moment, however, he decided to do that in an effort to bring together the theme about God and questioning with Dewey's efforts to reform philosophy. Fishman was not sure he would succeed, but, given what he had written in his freewrite, he thought he might be able to leave students with new ways of looking at religion as well as new ways of looking at Dewey.

Fishman also wanted to share the excitement he felt while freewriting that morning, "to show students," as he put it later, "how I myself play pupil. I wanted them to know I had learned something from being in class with them, from using the same techniques they did." Borrowing a term from Dewey's Carus lectures, Fishman concluded, "It was a kind of 'intellectual disrobing.' I wasn't just another adult imposing the truth on them. I was someone trying to expand my own interests—like they were trying to do."

Fishman read to the circle of students around him what he had written:

> Dewey tells us he wants to change the direction of philosophy. He wants to reform it and emphasize the strand he most likes. Dewey is, then, in the forefront of what might be called a Protestant revolution in philosophy, an attempt to discard what he considers excess baggage and get to the kernal of philosophy.

Fishman looked up. Students were watching him closely, their body language indicating attention despite the fact that class had run a minute overtime. Sean Wilson and John Lucas each told me later that at that moment Fishman looked straight at him. Steve concluded class by telling students,

> This is the first time I have ever thought of Dewey as a reformer like those in religious traditions—like the Protestants who wanted to reform the Catholic church or like Jesus who wanted to reform Judaism. Yet none of these reformers wanted to reject the past entirely. They all wanted to look at traditional practices and beliefs and keep what was pure while reshaping what no longer worked. They all wanted to move forward.

Fishman paused. After a moment's silence, he said, "See you Tuesday at noon for the final. Please give one copy of your letter to me, one to your partner."

Before leaving the room, students picked their way through the densely packed desks, hailed their partners, and handed their letters to one another. Several pairs chatted for a moment. I heard one student apologize for his too-quick job; another wished her partner good luck deciphering her thinking and prose. Another pair indicated their satisfaction that both of their questions had been touched on in class. Students then passed by Fishman on their way out, dropping a copy of their work on his desk.

In the class we have just watched, Fishman labored to give coherence to the disparate ideas generated by the letter exchange. The ultimate aim of the exercise was to give students reasons to drive through the heartland of the class reading, in other words, to integrate student and curriculum. Unfortunately, as we saw, Fishman, to a large extent, failed. Although questions from John Lucas and Demika Braxton were certainly prompted by their reading of Dewey, for various reasons they did not provide to-whats which led the class to productive analysis of the assigned text. In this situation, Fishman did his best to balance his desire to get into the subject matter with his desire to encourage a coherent and expanding discussion of the issues which students did raise. Although at moments he felt the ghosts of previous semesters when philosophy and dorm bull session merged, at least the John-Demika-Ashley conversation was grounded in efforts, however modest, to engage the assigned reading.

As for Sean Wilson's question, it was what Fishman had hoped for all along. Coming so late in the class, however, it presented a dilemma. Ideally, Fishman would have had time to question Sean and his letter partner, allowing them to say more about why they focused on certain aspects of the reading. But because time was so limited, Fishman made the decision to answer directly, hoping that such an answer would be productive for Sean as well as for his classmates. Unlike his direct answer to Demika's question, Fishman had some confidence his response to Sean might be effective. This was because Sean had led a spirited fight earlier in the semester to get Fishman to outline precisely what philosophy was. Although Steve side-stepped Sean's questions on those occasions because Sean had simply raised his hand and demanded a definition, Sean did not lose interest. Instead, he persisted all semester trying to figure out the nature of philosophy and philosophic thinking. As a result, on the last day, when Sean, reporting on his letter, asked about the nature of philosophy once more, it was in a very different way. In this context, Fishman believed Sean could profit from a direct answer.

Regarding Fishman's freewrite, this was an instance where indirect pedagogy offered a teacher an opportunity to think on his feet as he tried to pull together the odd pieces on the discussion table and push them into a unified direction. Looking back, Fishman at first said he was "embarrassed" he had "grabbed the microphone like that," but, after further reflection, he decided he was glad he did. Ultimately, he saw it as a lucky stroke that he was able to use his own freewrite about the Protestant Reformation, Jesus, and Dewey to connect the discussion, leaving class on what he hoped would be a provocative note.

FINDINGS ABOUT FISHMAN'S INDIRECT PEDAGOGY

As I explained in the previous chapter, Steve Fishman and I originally decided to study the last class session to try to explain the energy we felt that day, a level of excitement surprising to us since it was the end of the semester and students were discussing a text on which they knew they would not be tested. As we left that class on December 7, Steve remarked that the student pairings in the letter exchange may have been in part responsible. These were inherently dramatic, he said, because when he called on a student, he "got two for the price of one." For example, when Fishman called on Demika, it was she, in effect, who beckoned John forward. Steve recalled, "It was like I was watching one of those maps where lights switch on in various parts of the country to record telephone use or energy consumption." Because Fishman did not remember who Demika's partner was, he waited with interest as the light blinked on at John's seat.

In addition to calling on one another, students also had to report and evaluate their partner's question. In this regard, Fishman upset familiar class-room scripts by asking one student to assess another while the latter was present and capable of disagreeing. This created interest for Demika and her partner, John, as well as for their classmates and teacher, because both Demika and John were at risk. Demika had to show she understood John's question and had developed an adequate answer, but she was also in a position to expose him, reporting, as Fishman had asked, on the quality of reflection his question provoked.

Class attention on the last day was also due to the fact that John's and Sean's questions took up ongoing class themes. John's concern about philosophy and its relation to religion was interesting to the class because it was a group heavily populated with fundamentalist Christians. Of these, John and Demika were among the most committed, and their beliefs had been repeatedly challenged by class discussions not only on evolution, but on such topics as the nature of God and immortality, marriage and the status of women. Similarly, Sean's question about the nature and method of philosophy was of interest because, as I will show, it too fed into a long-term class focus.

Before further exploring the sources of class energy on the final day, I note that the session actually began very differently. In fact, the period opened with typical end-of-semester discourse which Fishman said he found depressing. "Can we get out early?" asked Jaime Klinger, a sophomore communications major and one of the most serious pupils in the class. Ashley

Posten wanted to know about grades, and Todd Bell, a senior education major, asked if he could sell back his books. And beneath these questions was a hum of student complaint about stress and overwork, and, I had to admit, from where I sat, several did look exhausted. The energetic discussion which developed, then, was all the more striking.

Fishman's Indirect Pedagogy Promoted Voluntary Student Interest and Self-Discipline

As Fishman and I analyzed the sources of energy in the last class, several Deweyan concepts were helpful. The first of these is "voluntary interest" and attention. We found evidence that, during the last class, student interest in assigned texts and class issues was, at least in some measure, voluntary. That is, instead of "forced" interest—students paying attention simply to pass the course—for some, at least, completing the assignment had become a voluntary or "direct" interest, a goal, or for-what, worth pursuing for its own sake.

I turn for evidence of voluntary interest to the three-person conversation which began with John Lucas' question to Demika Braxton. Although John never forgot about grades, the letter exchange allowed him to develop additional positive for-whats. First, as we saw, he asked Demika a question in which he was directly interested: Is it all right for Christians to question? In effect, John was asking, Is it fair what Fishman has been asking us to do all semester? He remarked in an interview the next day, "I really wanted to know what Demika had to say. All this questioning we do in philosophy pulls at me, and sometimes I wonder if you can be both a Christian and a competent philosopher. I think you can, but I wanted to see if Demika had the same response."

In addition to a question which genuinely interested him, a second for-what motivating John was the live audience that Fishman's class provided. In his follow-up interview 3 months after the course finished, John said his most vivid memory of philosophy class was his classmates reading and appreciating his work. "It was always exciting," he recalled, "when my ideas got taken up by the class." John was a young man who cared about impressing his classmates (and Fishman), and during the last class session, they obviously took him very seriously. In short, John and his interests were featured in Intro to Philosophy in ways he found gratifying.

Demika Braxton also showed signs of voluntary interest. Despite her initial disappointment that John did not question her about the assigned text, she offered a provocative response to his query regarding her view of philosophic questioning. She told me not long afterward that she ultimately "enjoyed" answering John's question: "I knew he was a Christian, and he asked my opinion as a Christian. It felt good to finally talk to someone who wanted to know what I thought about this subject. John made me think about the things we know and don't know and why."

In addition to Demika's voluntary interest in the issue John raised, Ashley appeared genuinely attentive as well. This attitude was evident not only in what they said but in her body language. The videotape shows Ashley leaning sideways toward Demika, her brow furrowed as she listened, and then turning in her chair to face Demika as she questioned her. And from his seat behind Demika, John watched all this intently, his interest and ego on the line.

By contrast, Demika's own question about Dewey's view of science was less successful than John's both in terms of attention level and amount of development. Demika did pose a problem which interested her, one in which she brought together her concerns as a medical technology major with Dewey's text. However, because her question about the relation of science and philosophy had never been a class theme and because it was based on Dewey's introduction, which no one else had read, Fishman was unable to help Demika and her classmates do much to expand it.

As the John-Demika-Ashley conversation shows, then, voluntary student interest resulted from two aspects of Fishman's indirect pedagogy: First, the letter exchange provided students a chance to shape their own to-whats or questions, and, second, it gave them the opportunity to develop these in cooperation with classmates. This social component of the letter assignment—students' teaching-learning responsibility to a classmate—was something most took very seriously. In fact, when I questioned Ashley about the high level of student involvement in the last class, she was surprised I could not see the reasons myself. It was obvious to her that everyone came to class and participated because they did not want let their letter partner down. That had happened to her once, and she felt silly, she said, her response a waste because her correspondent did not care enough to come get her answer. This was particularly disheartening, Ashley recounted, because she had worked harder for her classmate than she would have for the teacher. If she were writing solely for Fishman, she explained, she could have just said, "I don't get it, and let him fill in the blanks. But for someone on my level, I had to explain *why* I was confused."

The classroom energy Fishman and I observed, then, is explained in part by voluntary student interest and attention. What we were witnessing, as I have said, was what Dewey would describe as student "self-discipline" rather than teacher-imposed, external control. Although at the beginning of class

Fishman actually doubted that he would be able to motivate students at all, they ultimately paid attention, because his indirect pedagogy worked. That is, control during the final session resided not in the teacher but in the activity itself. Students' collaborative work generated voluntary interest and self-direction.

In this way Fishman's indirect pedagogy fulfilled at least some criteria for what Dewey would call moral education. When discipline in classrooms is inherent in common projects, according to Dewey, that is, when the teacher does not have to "keep order" because it is in the hands of students who are pursuing voluntary interests together, then schooling may be considered ethical. Such classrooms encourage students "to give out, to do, and [thus] to serve" (*Experience and Education* 55; "Ethical" 119, 130). This was something Fishman and I glimpsed, at least in modest measure, on the final day of the semester.

Fishman's Indirect Pedagogy Promoted Some Student-Curriculum Integration

Although voluntary interest and student self-control are essential components of effective education for Dewey, they are only part of the story. As Dewey points out, and as Fishman himself had painfully learned, interest and attention are only good to the extent they lead students into new areas of subject matter and promote mastery of the curriculum. In this regard, Dewey's concept of "expanded interest" is helpful (*Interest* 39–40). When students' voluntary interests lead them though new subject matter, he argues, their interests expand. Learners in this situation, ideally, use the curriculum to solve their own problems and, in the process, become interested in the subject matter itself. Because, for Dewey, one's interests and one's self are identical, expanded interests mean personal growth. This growth is the primary aim of Dewey's student-curriculum integration and the center of Fishman's concerns as well.

Unfortunately, Fishman's letter assignment failed John Lucas in this way, as I have said. Although John was interested in his question, and although he paid close attention to his classmates' development of it, this exercise did not take him or the class very far into the assigned reading. Similarly, Demika's question, in part because she read the wrong assignment, did little to expand her own or her classmates' interests. That is, neither John's nor Demika's question promoted integration of student and new subject matter.

The student who illustrates expanded interest is Sean Wilson. Sean's for-whats drove him to the core of the assigned text, and in the process of exploring new subject matter, he developed his interests and enriched himself. The reason for this, I believe, is that a number of for-whats were alive and working for him in the last class. His purposes for reading included (1) his desire for a high grade on the letter homework, (2) his belief that he could use the assigned reading to clarify longstanding family problems, and (3) his hope that the reading would help him answer his ongoing question about the nature of philosophy. Further, I have some evidence that Sean was developing yet another goal or interest, namely, (4) understanding Dewey's work itself.

When I asked Sean about the reasons for his obvious excitement on the last day, he mentioned the second of these purposes. "I think Dewey can help me deal with 25 years of family pain. . . . Even though I don't understand all Dewey's points, once his main idea was clarified for me at the end of class, it snapped. . . . After reading Dewey and listening to Dr. Fishman, I know what I have to do."

What Sean "had to do" was apply Dewey's philosophy to his family conflicts; specifically, to his mother's alcoholism and his family members' clashing recipes for how to deal with it. This was the problem on which Sean was focusing in his term project essay, a draft of which he had written a month earlier and which was due in final form the following day. He believed he could get help for this conflict from Dewey's view that traditional wisdom must be tested against current and future experience. It would give him a leg to stand on, Sean believed, when dealing with his father and grandmother, both of whom claimed he should embrace his mother regardless of his negative feelings toward her. Sean explained,

> I think I may get some kind of solace from what I've discovered from Dewey. My grandmother's truths about honoring my mother are from another era; so are my father's. I have tried to make them work for me, but they won't. . . . Dewey says truths change; you must take into account present experience . . . I've always had that mindset, but I've never really voiced it because I doubted I could communicate it correctly. Dewey will help.

Sean's academic project, his reading of the assignment in *Reconstruction*, was driven in part, then, by the for-what I have just mentioned: his hope for help with a serious family problem. But it was also motivated by the third for-what or purpose I listed above, his interest in learning about the nature of philosophy. In this regard, Sean was not unique in the class, but, of the four students I have so far described, he was the most articulate and wholehearted in his efforts to understand philosophy. Sean's interest in learning about Fishman's discipline led him to read the Dewey assignment in a particular way. It also led him to attend closely to Fishman's behavior, because, in doing so, Sean hoped to figure out how philosophers think.

In fact, it might be said that Sean had spent the entire term preparing for Dewey's definition of philosophy and Fishman's direct response to him on the last day. In Sean's interviews across the semester, he had often described for me Fishman's Ahhhh's of discovery, his fist-waving and hand-slapping. In early November, Sean confided, "I want to feel that.... Philosophers are analytical, and Dr. Fishman takes apart so many things and cracks them open, and there he is, almost euphoric. Man, he's enjoying himself, getting a rush, and I'm like, Put me in that zone." Although Sean worried that a semester might not be long enough "to discover true philo- sophic thinking," and that maybe he did not have the self-discipline to read and reread the texts, he felt that if he "clawed just a little harder, maybe [he] too would see the light."

Thus, when Sean, in his letter exchange, asked if Dewey's view of philosophy was, like science, unemotional and abstract, he was not only completing the assignment. He was also trying to determine appropriate behavior toward his mother as well as gain further insight into the "What is philosophy?" question which had disturbed him all semester. These interests all came together for Sean in the last class, and he experienced something akin to Fishman's Ahhhh. In addition, he appeared to transfer his interest in and identification with Fishman to Dewey himself.

When Sean and I spoke after the last class, he began by describing his interaction with Fishman, his remarks typifying the close attention he had paid to Steve all semester. "You saw how Dr. Fishman and I were feeding off each other. I felt like we had found common ground. First I made a state- ment, and then Dr. Fishman said, Yes, you're right, and here's a little bit more to add to that. Then I said, Hey, wait a minute, he's right, and then I contributed my two cents to that." Sean only lamented that time had run out and that he and Fishman had to cut short their exchange.

Although Sean began the interview focused on Fishman, his attention shifted to Dewey's work, a move suggesting a fourth for-what, or purpose for reading: Sean's developing interest in the assigned text itself. He appeared to identify with Dewey and, thus, to see himself in new light. Toward the close of our 30-minute interview, Sean exclaimed,

Now I understand why I was so excited in class! Dewey thinks a lot like I do! I have always known I had to create knowledge myself. I have always known I am a different person today than I was last week. Remember, I told you that when we first talked.

Sean concluded by rehearsing some Deweyan phrases, apparently trying them out to be sure he had made them his own.

"To set aside traditions and pay attention to present experience, to come up with solutions for the social and moral strife of our own day." Boy, that struck home!

In conclusion, Sean's multiple goals, or for-whats, organized his reading of chapter 1, the letter assignment allowing him to direct his attention to those to-whats in the text he believed would help him achieve his ends. This resulted, for Sean, in expanded interests and, therefore, Dewey would argue, in an expanded self.

Yet I want to be cautious in my claims. Although Fishman was pleased that Sean had accessed subject matter in personally productive ways—and although my post-semester interviews indicate Sean believed he took a positive residue from the course in the form of increased patience for careful thinking—this does not mean Sean understood Dewey perfectly or that he would continue reading Dewey after the semester concluded. Nor do I have evidence Sean developed an abiding interest in philosophy or would ever take another philosophy course. Nevertheless, he felt satisfied that something special had happened in those final minutes of the semester. He had had the experience of being excited by academic work. He felt the "coming full circle," as he later put it, the "surge" of fulfillment when he connected his interests with the assigned reading.

Of the four students I spotlighted in the final class, only Sean Wilson, as I have said, integrated student and curriculum in ways Fishman hoped. That is, Sean is the only one who used the assigned reading to deal with personal problems and, at the same time, expand his interests to include subject matter itself. Although Fishman's success rate regarding expanded interests was poor for the other three, his indirect pedagogy did succeed in generating voluntary interest and attention in these students. The letter assignment, as I have shown, allowed them to develop for-whats, or reasons for reading, that were internally motivating rather than teacher imposed. And even though their goals did not lead to exploration of the assigned text, they did at least promote discussion of broad philosophic issues.

Chapter Nine

CLASSROOM CONTINUITIES AND INTERACTIONS

———————— ✤ ————————

Lucille McCarthy with Steve Fishman

I n the previous chapter, we saw how Steve Fishman's attempt to enact Dewey's indirect pedagogy yielded significant student self-discipline, voluntary interest, and some small measure of student-curriculum integration. In the present chapter, I examine students' experiences which lay behind that last class of the semester. That is, I look at the continuities students built to the philosophy curriculum and their interactions with it as they exchanged letters about their reading. Following Fishman's theoretical analysis in Chapter 2, I define continuities as the connections students make between present and past and between present and future, and I define interactions as their give-and-take with their present environment. In particular, I study the ways student continuities and interactions determine not only the content of the letters but also the roles pupils play in them and the moral traits of character they exhibit as they complete the assignment.

In the sections which follow, I analyze a number of letter texts, including those of the four students I introduced in the previous chapter. In carrying out my analysis, I rely heavily on Dewey's view of the importance of the mechanisms of interest and effort for understanding continuity and interaction. Drawing upon Fishman's discussion of these mechanisms in Chapter 2, I use what Dewey calls student with-which(s) (bridges) to identify the continuities with which they link Introduction to Philosophy to their past, and I use what Dewey calls their for-whats (goals) to locate the continuities students construct between philosophy and their future. Finally, I use the foci of student interest, or what Dewey labels their to-whats, to clarify the nature of their interactions with Fishman's classroom.

As I attempt to connect students' continuities and interactions with their classroom roles and the moral traits of character they display, I am able to examine a dimension of student experience which is highly important to Dewey. As he advises, education is a social process, and, therefore, effective teachers must attend to the roles students play, especially providing opportunities for them to alternate studenting and teaching. Teachers must also give students the chance to build character, to cooperate and show self-discipline and initiative (*Democracy* 159; *Experience and Education* 58–59). The letter assignment offered these opportunities.

STUDENT ROLES AND THE LETTER EXCHANGE ASSIGNMENT

Steve Fishman's expectation for the letter assignment was that students would see a classmate rather than the teacher as their primary audience, and they would thus adopt two cooperative roles. First, he hoped they would play pupil to each other; and this was unorthodox in that most school writing asks students to display as much knowledge as possible and hide any shortcomings (Applebee; Britton et al.). In the letter situation, however, students wrote to peers, to people "as confused as I am," as one student put it, people for whom they did not have to "fakely pretend to understand everything." Ideally, then, Fishman hoped they would adopt the role of student exploring his or her uncertainties about a new text in cooperation with a classmate in a similar position (a role we call cooperative classmate inquirer). He trusted that with such an audience, students would be candid and unintimidated, more willing to ask questions they might otherwise fear were too elementary. And he offered them the letter, a familiar, nonacademic genre to which all had equal access.

In their follow-up or response letter, Fishman expected students to adopt a second role, one we call colleague mentor. That is, he wanted students to carefully read their letter partner's question, interpret it sympathetically and go back to the text to find, if not an answer, at least suggestions about parts of the text from which an answer could be developed. Or he hoped that, when appropriate, they might point to other aspects of the reading they thought relevant. In short, Fishman wanted students to put their heads together, seeing themselves as paired trailblazers into difficult academic terrain, able to penetrate further into this territory working together than they could alone.

This chapter explores the roles that five students actually did create for themselves and their partners in their letters. The first, John Lucas, the senior English major whose final letter of the semester was introduced in Chapter 8, constructs for himself and his partner, Demika Braxton, a writer-audience relationship Fishman did not anticipate: one we call conversation pal. In this role, as we saw, John, when writing to Demika about the first chapter of *Reconstruction in Philosophy*, asks her to skirt new subject matter. He is, apparently, a victim of what Dewey would have seen as the worst excesses of so-called progressive education, his attitude reflecting previous instruction which valued the student at the expense of the curriculum. John says to Demika, in effect, that there is not much to see in the land of the assigned text, so we can remain safely anchored, chatting about ourselves, a good distance from shore.

By contrast, Sean Wilson, whom we also met in Chapter 8, adopts the stance Fishman hoped for, that of cooperative classmate inquirer. He speaks as someone who has spent some time in the land of the assigned reading, taken field notes, and constructed preliminary findings which he wants to share and develop with a classmate coresearcher. In the process, Sean achieves student-curriculum integration and practices the moral trait of wholeheartedness.

After contrasting John and Sean, who are almost opposites in terms of what Dewey would consider successful student-curriculum integration, I introduce a student we have not encountered before. Emily Parrish, a senior political science major from Winston-Salem, goes into the reading as does Sean, with a pronounced focus, takes field notes, and returns with preliminary findings to share with her partner. But unlike Sean, Emily organizes her reading and writing with persuasive intent. She adopts the cooperative classmate inquirer role in order to play agent of social change. As we will see, she says to her partner, in effect: "I have been to this new curricular territory, and I think you need to see some things there, things which, once observed, will have a direct impact on your life." In this assignment, Emily, like Sean, builds continuities to the class and interacts within it in ways which help her integrate student and curriculum. Further, she exercises what Dewey would recognize as an important social power, confronting inequality and working toward what he calls "a bettered community life" (*Public* 201).

I conclude by returning to two students who received attention in the previous chapter, junior Demika Braxton and sophomore Ashley Posten. In particular, I examine letters they exchanged about Bertrand Russell's *Marriage and Morals*. Although, like Sean and Emily, they adopt the cooperative classmate inquirer role, Demika and Ashley do so in a different way. Whereas Sean and Emily root their questions for their partners in interpretations of the assigned readings, Demika and Ashley do not get that far. Although they struggle to treat each other as coresearchers, they sound more like frightened tourists in the territory of Bertrand Russell, each apologetic that she needs help with even the first signposts in this foreign text. Nevertheless, Fishman's indirect pedagogy allows them, for reasons I will describe, to work together in remarkably rich ways, exhibiting tolerance, openmindedness, and cooperation—attributes Dewey sees as the best qualities of "social intelligence" (*Experience and Education* 72).

JOHN LUCAS'S CONTINUITIES AND INTERACTIONS AS SHAPING HIS CONVERSATION PAL ROLE

As we saw in Chapter 8, the role John Lucas adopts in his exchange with Demika Braxton about the first chapter of Dewey's *Reconstruction in Philosophy* allows both him and Demika to skirt the text. And, as we also saw, this keeps both of them from experiencing much student-curriculum integration in this assignment.

John Lucas's Question Letter to Demika Braxton

John's December 5 letter begins with a claim that he understands the reading because it was relatively easy, and he offers Demika a quick summary of his understanding of Dewey's view of philosophy, namely, that philosophy questions tradition. But rather than explaining how he arrived at this interpretation, he leaves it and goes on to question Demika about her personal experience. His question is, in fact, one he could have asked early in the semester and without reading Dewey at all: Is it all right for Christians to question? John begins his one-and-a-half-page letter:

> Well, what do you think about Dewey? Does he have a good definition of philosophy? I think so.... Dewey seems to say we traditionalists should question.... And he gives the example of Socrates.... Dewey believes that traditional views deal with the individual, whereas if people can learn to think in a more positivistic way, solutions to the problems of the greater society will result. I agree with him on this aspect of philosophy....
>
> This is my question to you: Knowing you are a fellow Christian, do you find that Dewey's theory of philosophy undermines our Christian beliefs? Because we are Christian, does that not make us traditionalists to an extent? Do you personally feel that we should question *everything* in an attempt to gain a better understanding of the world? In my own Christian walk I have been taught never to question God. Have you found this to be a bit of a struggle in this class?

John's letter shows he has attempted to read the text. He uses the word *positivistic*, a term Dewey employs frequently in *Reconstruction*, chapter 1, and he refers to philosophy as criticism or questioning. However, John focuses exclusively on Dewey's account of Socrates's challenge to the foundations of Greek tradition. And he leaves it at that, showing little sensitivity to the complexities in chapter 1, that is, to Dewey's idea that philosophy is not just questioning but, at its best, also a special sort of experimental and open-minded answering. John's interpretation, in short, reflects a superficial reading.

Although John's letter is an improvement over earlier ones in which he paid almost no attention to the assigned reading, he continues to be primarily the conversation pal to Demika. After speaking briefly and self-assuredly about Dewey, breezily answering his own questions, John moves on to what Fishman calls dorm buddy talk.

John Lucas's Continuities and Interactions with Intro to Philosophy

Why did John adopt the conversation pal role? To answer this question, I employ the conceptual tools outlined in Deweyan theory. I examine John's classroom experiences, that is, his interactions as shaped by continuities he develops among Introduction to Philosophy, his previous schoolwork, and his future goals.

John's First Continuity with Previous Classes

In his interviews with me, John revealed that he entered Fishman's class with a particularly powerful with-which, that is, a powerful continuity he built between Intro to Philosophy and his English classes which privileged personal experience. This led him to focus, not on the curriculum, but on those aspects of Intro in which Fishman attempted to elicit students' personal responses. John therefore argued that reading the texts was secondary, that what was most important was personal opinion, and that all interpretations, no matter their sensitivity to the text, were equally good.

In a September interview, for example, John explained that he was in his final semester of college, an English major who did not like to read, preferring creative writing. He particularly enjoyed philosophy class, he said, because it was, like his English courses, "a point-of-view class" in which he could learn from himself and other students. John further described the class in a reflection log entry which made Fishman cringe: "It's like English in that your own particular interpretation is as good as anybody else's. There are no wrong answers as long as you can pull out examples from your own experience."

John did the philosophy reading, he told me, at 10 o'clock the night before class, a time when he was tired from playing basketball or delivering pizzas, and his answers to study questions were often a single line long. The assigned texts, he insisted, "belong to the person who reads them, not the author. What everyone takes from the reading is different, so you can't really be graded on that." He maintained until the last few weeks of the semester that philosophic writing was just "personal opinion," and that his pithy "one-liner" responses were successful because they made his readers puzzle.

John's Second Continuity with Previous Classes

John's continuities with his past, then, included connections between philosophy and classes which emphasized personal response. In addition, he built a second continuity to previous schooling which, following a Deweyan line of thinking, also shaped his experiences in philosophy. This was the frequent inconsistency he noted between his teachers' evaluations of his work and his own. Although John was very concerned about grades, he described to me his unusual habit of neither checking them nor speaking directly to the teacher about them. In fact, it was 5 weeks into the semester, an hour before the midterm, when John first went to his folder, kept in a cabinet in the philosophy office, where Fishman returned all student work. There he discovered he had done poorly on many of his early homework assignments, some of them the one-line responses he continued to defend as "my own brand" of philosophy. As John and I spoke about his unwillingness to monitor his grades or be open to the teacher's evaluation, he explained that because his own estimate of his work was often significantly higher than his instructors'—a pattern he suspected would repeat itself in philosophy— it was depressing to learn their views. This continuity, then, shaped John's experiences in Intro. In particular, it kept him from interacting with or attending to Fishman's feedback.

This continuity, I believe, also contributed to his adoption of the conversation pal role in his letters. Just as John was reluctant to learn Fishman's evaluation of his work, he seemed not to want to share his real thinking— especially not his questions and doubts—with other students for fear of the "grade" they might give him. Thus a consequence of this particular continuity was that it closed John to interaction with classmates in the cooperative classmate inquirer role.

John's Continuity with Future Goals

From my interviews with John, it seemed that when he looked to the future, the only use of the course he could see was its impact on his grade point average. John's desire for an A—and his wish to be known among classmates as a good student—also seemed to underlie the breezy style of his conversation pal role, a style which admitted no uncertainties or confusions. It was an approach which led John to respond to Fishman on the first day of class, saying he expected nothing to surprise him during the semester, that he already knew or could anticipate the positions of most classmates and assigned authors. I suspect that John believed that if he sounded knowledgeable, if he declared that he found the texts quite transparent, he might impress both classmates and teacher and receive the A he sought.

Stuck with the for-what of wanting a high grade, and saddled with with-which(s) that led him to attend to personal experience and avoid evaluation of his work, John lost valuable opportunities to interact with the texts and achieve the kind of expanded interest and growth which, for Dewey, mark student-curriculum integration. And this affected not only John but each of his partners. As I have already shown in Chapter 8, Demika Braxton went back to read the proper assignment for the last week of class, preparing herself to play colleague mentor to John. When John's conversation pal role denied her the opportunity to participate in that way, to be responsible and, in Dewey's words, "to give out," she openly expressed her disappointment ("Ethical" 119).

And Demika was not the only one of John's letter partners who sensed something was wrong, who felt that John had denied him or her a learning opportunity. His other partners protested even more strongly. To illustrate, Todd Bell, a senior education major, was John's partner for the October letter exchange focusing on Russell's *Marriage and Morals*. Unlike Demika, whom I described in the previous chapter as being, in many ways, quite different from John, Todd was much like him. Although quieter than John, Todd was also a tall, thin, white male who grew up in North Carolina. In fact, Todd and John were friends. And, although Todd played out the conversation pal role in his letter response to John, when Fishman called on Todd in class, he, like Demika, complained. When asked by Fishman what he learned from answering John's questions, Todd embarrassed John. "I didn't learn anything," he replied. "John's questions were not about Russell at all— although they did make me think about what I want in a wife."

Todd was right. In his question letter, John barely refers to the assigned text before offering his own experience with a former girlfriend and eliciting Todd's views about criteria for a good wife. Despite John's show of collegial interest in both Demika and Todd, he refused to be a good colleague to either. He was unwilling to open the door so they might coexplore subject matter, engaging in the sort of teaching-learning role exchanges Dewey sees as educationally vital.

For Fishman and me, two things stand out in our reflections on John Lucas, both brought to light by our Deweyan analysis. First, John's case makes clear the wisdom of Dewey's resistance to atomism in all its forms. John is a powerful reminder that students do not come to our classes as empty vessels or passive recipients of what we offer. To the contrary, as John shows, they immediately set out to relate our courses to previous school experiences and to fit them into the demands of their insistent futures.

In particular, we are struck by the liabilities John is saddled with because of the continuities he creates between Fishman's class and previous ones. Although there were, no doubt, other causal factors at work—senioritis, John's work schedule, his lack of patience with the rigors of philosophic discourse—his continuities seem to serve as iron barriers, preventing him from adopting the sort of roles in Fishman's class which might have helped him attend to the subject matter and interact with it fruitfully. Nevertheless, given these barriers, John, had, by the end of the semester, actually accomplished quite a lot. As I will describe in the next chapter, he finally alters his original view that philosophy is pithy one-liners and that personal opinion is more important than textual analysis, succeeding in his term project essay in ways which surprised both Fishman and me.

Second, Fishman and I are also struck by the reactions of John's letter partners, particularly their protests at John's failure to cooperate with them in the letter exchange. We take this as evidence for Dewey's claim that learning is a social and cooperative affair. When opportunities for cooperation were offered and then frustrated, John's partners were disappointed.

SEAN WILSON'S CONTINUITIES AND INTERACTIONS AS SHAPING HIS "COOPERATIVE CLASSMATE INQUIRER" ROLE

Sean Wilson, in contrast to John, used his letter about Dewey's *Reconstruction*, chapter 1, to expand his interests and achieve personally significant goals, and this required openness to assigned texts. Although Sean also wanted a high grade in Fishman's course, he managed during the semester, as already noted, to generate three additional goals, or for-whats. These were his desire to resolve a longstanding family conflict, to learn about the nature of philosophic method, and, by the time of the last class, to get a clear hold on Dewey's ideas. These continuities which Sean built between future goals and Fishman's class were, then, very different from John's and, as Deweyan theory would predict, so were his interactions with the class and the role he adopted. More specifically, Sean's letter displays the earmarks of the cooperative classmate inquirer that Fishman wanted. What does his letter look like?

Sean Wilson's Question Letter to David Miller

Sean begins his page-long letter in a no-nonsense way, outlining his understanding of Dewey and offering several quotes as if to show his partner, David Miller, how he arrived at his interpretation, as if inviting David to follow and evaluate his work. He then asks a question about Dewey's reconstructed view of philosophy, the one we heard him paraphrase in class discussion on the final day of the term. In sum, Sean sets up his and his partner's cooperative inquiry in ways which allow him to play the alternate roles Dewey advocates, first teaching David and then opening himself to learn from him. In his question letter, Sean constructs himself as an inquirer whose work is underway but whose progress now depends upon getting help from a colleague mentor. Sean writes,

> I was able to surmise that Dewey recognizes that philosophy, in the old way of thinking, dealt with the traditional hopes and fears of a community. He states that men are "governed by memory rather than by thought, and that memory is not a remembering of actual facts, but is association, suggestion, dramatic fancy" (6).... However, Dewey seems to think the best way for Philosophy to reach a new plateau is for individuals "to search out the reason for things and not accept them from custom and political authority" (17).
>
> David, I understand what Dewey means by past philosophic thinking, how it has been tied in with the human psyche and emotional congeniality. What I do not understand is what Dewey means by the "New Philosophy." Is he saying that philosophers should abandon all feelings when attempting to solve philosophic problems? Wouldn't that make Philosophy more like science? Would that not eliminate room for ambiguity and multiple answers to a problem?...
>
> David, if your understanding of Dewey allows, please help me understand exactly what a Philosopher in the "new" philosophic mind-think should be involved with.

Although Sean, like John Lucas in his letter to Demika, contrasts philosophy and tradition, his understanding of Dewey's position is sensitive to the fact that Dewey says more than just that philosophy criticizes and challenges. That is, Sean does not stop with Dewey's account of Socrates as a questioner. He goes on, realizing Dewey is up to something more elaborate, namely, identifying his reconstructed view of philosophy with science. And Sean's criticism of the Deweyan position is a kind of reductio ad absurdum argument directed against Dewey. At the end of his letter, he asks, If philosophy is really the same as science, is that not going to have odd repercussions? Science is precise and technical, whereas philosophy is ambiguous and uncertain. Thus, in effect, Sean says to his partner, either Dewey's view of philosophy does not make much sense, or I have misunderstood it.

What we see here is Sean's struggle to master new material, trying to use what is familiar, his with-which(s), to make sense of the unfamiliar, the to-what on which he is focusing. We see Sean trying to bridge to Dewey's view of a scientific, experimental philosophy by calling up his own ideas about science. Yet when Sean goes to complete construction of this bridge, he senses something is not working. When he tries to combine his views of science and philosophy, he finds they are not quite compatible, and so he asks David for help.

Sean Wilson's Continuities and Interactions with Intro to Philosophy

I have already mentioned four continuities Sean built between Fishman's class and the future. I now turn to the continuities he developed between Fishman's class and his past, connections which shaped his interactions in Intro and the role he adopted.

Sean's Continuity with Previous Classes
During my conversations with Sean, he mentioned that Intro to Philosophy reminded him of an Eastern Religions class he had taken the year before, an experience, he said, which opened him to questions regarding his Southern Baptist background. More important, it showed him the value of looking at situations from multiple perspectives. He explained that he had found that course "expanding" and thus in philosophy class he paid special attention to the differing viewpoints of his classmates and the assigned authors.

Sean's Continuity with Previous Experience
Sean had, when he entered Fishman's course, just come from summer Marine Corps officer training camp, and he described it to me across the semester in ways that connected it to philosophy class. For example, he mentioned that group work in Intro was similar to group work in the marines. He also remarked that things that are worthwhile often require effort and concentration, so he was willing to struggle if that was what it took to get a hold on philosophy. "In the marines we pay attention to detail," he said. "Although we are a small branch of the armed services, we take pride in what we do. It's like a tight-knit family of men and women. There's an esprit de corps. I'd say we're almost a perfectionist family." In both his officer-training work and in philosophy, Sean told me, he was "very methodical."

When I compare these two students, the case of Sean Wilson is, as I have said, very different from that of John Lucas. Whereas continuities shaping John's experiences in Intro to Philosophy seemed to erect barriers between him and the roles Fishman hoped for, those which Sean could develop provided a fertile context for achieving them. John read assigned texts super-ficially, with "divided interest" (Dewey, *Democracy* 177), whereas Sean, a self-described "perfectionist," was willing to give them his full attention, struggling with them in ways Dewey would celebrate as wholehearted.

Despite these differences, Sean Wilson's case, like John's, adds weight to Dewey's view that experiences are continuous rather than atomistic. Both cases put the lie to classroom appearances. That is, the first day of the term is never the first day. It may seem to us that students sitting quietly in their rows are waiting patiently to receive our instruction, but, as both Sean and John show, their past experiences are, from the first bell, shaping what they will attend to and what they will ignore, how they will use the class, and the ways in which they will participate.

The stories of the first two students I have discussed present important cautions about teachers' ability to affect the roles pupils adopt in our classes. Given the strength of John's past experiences and the pressure of Sean's future ones, Fishman can hardly take full blame or credit for their performances in philosophy. By contrast, the next three students seem to adopt roles for which Fishman's indirect pedagogy is more responsible. Let me now turn to the first of these three, Emily Parrish.

EMILY PARRISH'S CONTINUITIES AND INTERACTIONS AS SHAPING HER COOPERATIVE CLASSMATE INQUIRER ROLE

Emily, like Sean, integrates student and curriculum. But, unlike Sean, who focuses on a longstanding family conflict, Emily's primary goal or for-what in Intro does not emerge until almost midterm. And although her concern was deeply rooted in her life, it appears to come to her suddenly. This happened during class on September 26 when Emily reacted to a problem which concerned her: demeaning stereotypes of women.

In that late-September class session, Fishman proceeded as usual, orches-trating discussion by eliciting students' ideas about the assigned reading, a feminist text by Carol Christ titled, "Why Women Need the Goddess." Toward the middle of the period, Warren Murray, a junior education major and African American focus student from Red Springs, North Carolina, articulated his position in a straightforward way. Warren, who had been president of his freshman class and was used to public speaking, concluded his remarks in a self-assured tone, seemingly unaware of their potential to offend. He declared, "Well, from what I have seen, beautiful young women are usually dumb."

Although Emily until that moment had never volunteered in class, the videotape shows her sit bolt upright and ask Warren, whom she did not know personally, "Why do you say that? How do you know? What in society makes you think that way?" It was at that moment, Emily told me in an interview a few days later, that she first felt part of the group. In fact, she and two other women walked outside after class and carried on the conversation. "We couldn't believe Warren said that," Emily told me. Despite support from these women, however, Emily still felt frustrated, because Warren, she believed, had remained closed to her. "He wasn't getting what I was trying to say," she told me, "And when I asked him why he thought that, he just said, 'Because I do.'"

Emily Parrish's Continuities and Interactions with Intro to Philosophy

Emily's Continuities with Previous Experience

From a Deweyan perspective, Emily's anger at Warren's comment, compounded by her frustration that he would not explore his position, marked the awakening in her of an important class continuity and focus of interaction. From that point on, her growing awareness of the culture's misogynist tendencies—and their impact on her life—shaped her reading and writing in Fishman's course. As I will show in greater detail in the following chapter, an important continuity in Emily's past had prepared her to hear Warren and interact with him in special ways. At age 15, Emily had experienced what she believed to be a mistreatment of women in her church. In this incident, which she explores in her term project essay, Emily observed the all-male leadership of her church make a judgment and then silence women in the congregation who disagreed. Emily was shocked, she writes, and her response to this "institution which brushed women aside" was to abandon churchgoing altogether. Her experience with misogyny 7 years earlier provided the continuity which conditioned Emily's reaction to Warren's remark.

Emily's Continuity with a Future Goal

Emily's continuity with the church incident in her past also shaped her future goal in Fishman's class: to focus on and be an activist about women's issues.

The first opportunity for Emily to work toward her activist goal occurred a month after the Carol Christ assignment. She found herself paired with Warren in a letter exchange about *Reconstruction*, chapter 2, and she realized she had been handed another chance to influence him. As a result, she read Dewey's work with unusual energy and direction. She told me, "I focused toward Warren because I wanted to get something which would make him think about his views." And she found what she needed in Dewey's discussion of modernism. "As I was reading," Emily explained, "I was thinking, how can I write this, and then I found these quotes, and I thought, this is great! This is exactly what I want to tell him. Dewey was describing how Francis Bacon wanted people to question things and not just take ideas as truth." Although Emily assured me she felt no hostility toward Warren personally—in fact, they now spoke in friendly ways when they met on campus—she "hope[d] these quotes would make him think."

Emily Parrish's Question Letter to Warren Murray

> I guess I have more observations than actual questions, but hopefully you can comment on these and give me more insight....
>
> I read Dewey's description of Bacon's "true method," and what I found most interesting was something similar to what we discussed in class concerning modernism and open-mindedness. On page 33, Dewey refers to "inert conservatism...which accustoms the mind to think of truth as already known, [habituating] men to fall back on intellectual attainments of the past and accept them without critical scrutiny." He then goes on to say that the "logic...of truths already possessed by the mind blunts the spirit of investigation and confines the mind."
>
> Warren, isn't the idea to question your beliefs and not be closed-minded to what others are saying, even if you don't agree? Isn't this the point Dewey is trying to make? What do you think?

In her two-page letter to Warren, Emily plays cooperative classmate inquirer, asking Warren to consider passages regarding Dewey's conception of the modern mind, specifically, Dewey's valuing of cultural critique and his understanding of ideas as socially agreed upon and fallible. Although Emily constructs Warren as a colleague mentor, her goal is not to learn from him but to change him. In an interesting mirroring of Fishman's indirect approach, Emily never tells Warren she thinks he is wrong, nor does she explicitly indicate her disapproval of what she sees to be his closed-mindedness. Instead, she invites him, through her letter, to relate his life to the text, to see its relevance to his views and thereby enlarge his perspective on women. Emily is, in this way, demonstrating social responsibility, a moral trait Dewey would applaud. That is, Emily is working toward social change, while, at the same time, showing respect for Warren's individuality and need for self-determination.

Although Emily's letter ultimately fails to get Warren to use the text in the way she hopes, the assignment is, nevertheless, successful for her in two Deweyan respects. First, she is able to use the reading for personally significant ends. As Dewey teaches us, the main stratagem of indirect pedagogy is to get students to employ the curriculum for their own purposes. The hope of indirect pedagogy is that, on occasion, as students use subject matter for their own purposes, their concerns expand to include the curriculum itself. We have seen it happen for Sean with his new interest in Dewey. Does it happen for Emily? Yes. She, like Sean, extends her concerns to include Dewey, but, in addition, her interests expand to encompass feminist writers she has encountered in the class as well.

Second, Emily also grows in that she practices social responsibility. As her letter suggests, Emily's expanded interests are not limited to subject matter but also include important social problems about which she is becoming increasingly aware. Insofar as she better understands relations within the culture, the practices and institutions around her, she is more "socially intelligent" ("Ethical" 130). And, as a result, she is in a position to work toward community betterment (see *Public* 200–01). In Emily's final reflection log entry, we hear her practice social responsibility, a moral trait of character which, as we have said, Dewey advocates. She writes:

> The feminist authors we have read, along with our class discussions, have shown me I will have to work harder to prove myself, especially if I decide to run for political office some day. Even in this class many "traditional" views about women prevail: Women can't do the same work as men. They belong in the kitchen. And beautiful women are assumed to have no brains. I am already made to feel a stereotypical "dumb blonde" by some guys my age who explain things to me as if I am a 5-year-old. Naturally there are differences between men and women, but we all deserve equal opportunities. I want to be able to achieve anything I decide to do, even if it means I have to fight to insure myself that right.

Although we obviously cannot predict which steps, if any, Emily will actually take to render society more just, we believe that her increased political awareness is a positive moral repercussion of Fishman's indirect pedagogy.

DEMIKA BRAXTON'S AND ASHLEY POSTEN'S CONTINUITIES AND INTERACTIONS AS SHAPING THEIR COOPERATIVE INQUIRER ROLES

Whereas Sean and Emily, in their letters, employed genuine for-whats— continuities they built to Fishman's class—to integrate student and curriculum, not all students were in this position. How did the assignment work for pupils who did not bring to it meaningful personal objectives?

To try to answer this question, I offer the cases of Demika Braxton and Ashley Posten who, in their October exchange about Bertrand Russell's *Marriage and Morals*, did not see it as a means to achieving personally valued ends. Yet these students engaged seriously and productively with the text because the letter assignment provided them a social motive or for-what: a desire to cooperate, to uphold their part of the bargain. They both adopted the cooperative roles Fishman hoped for. In this situation, I found that although these students did not achieve significant student-curriculum integration, they did achieve another important Deweyan goal. That is, their correspondence shows many of the features of what Dewey calls intelligent, tolerant, and democratic collaboration.

Demika Braxton's Question Letter to Ashley Posten

Unlike Sean's and Emily's focus on aspects of the text which will help them achieve their goals, Demika simply chooses a passage which confuses her. She begins by admitting she is "lost" and then lays out clues so Ashley can help her find her way:

> The section which puzzled me came from "The Dominion of the Father." For the most part I understood it, but when Russell began discussing the "element of jealousy" in fathers and husbands, I got lost. I think Russell is saying that a man who has a wife and a mistress would be more jealous where his wife is concerned. . . . This point makes sense. What husband wouldn't be upset about another man trying to move in on his wife?
>
> But unfortunately I cannot understand how children fit into this category. What is the relation between the husband, wife, mistress, and illegitimate children? Russell says, "If, on the other hand, the child is not legitimate, the putative father is tricked into lavishing care upon a child with whom he has no biological connection." I understand what Russell is trying to say, that some women do "trick" men into caring for their children. But how does this relate

to the husband being jealous? What do illegitimate children have to do with this scenario?

In her question letter, Demika requests help in understanding Russell's historical account of patriarchy and the status of women and children as property. She relates his account to her own notions about jealousy and paternity, struggling to construct with-which(s) between familiar and unfamiliar territory, but, unlike Sean and Emily, Demika has not gone far enough into the text to have preliminary interpretations of her own. Yet Fishman's indirect pedagogy is effective. It gives Demika a social for-what—a desire to cooperate with Ashley—which, despite her confusion about Russell, and despite her lack of genuine interest in the text, motivates her to take her partner seriously. That is, she reads and writes carefully, describing the landscape in which she has lost her way, so Ashley will be able to mentor her.

Demika Braxton's Continuities and Interactions with Intro to Philosophy

Continuing to operationalize Dewey's notion of experience as it relates to the classroom, I examine the continuities Demika built among Fishman's class, her previous experiences, and her future goals. Specifically, which continuities led her to interact with her letter partner in serious and responsible ways? In our interviews, Demika did not mention similarities between Fishman's class and previous ones, as did John and Sean. Rather, she marveled at the differences.

Demika's Continuity with Previous Classes
In her other college courses, Demika told me in a November interview, "it's always easy to hide." In biology, for example, she takes notes during lectures, her mind "sometimes not in the same room," and if the professor calls on people, she said, she just keeps her head down. In Intro to Philosophy, by contrast, "Dr. Fishman *makes* us participate because of the questions he asks. He won't let us off the hook or let us just summarize the reading. We have to bring ourselves into it. . . . And in class, we have to listen to each other."

Demika's excitement about her class participation is interesting in light of the fact that she actually began the semester in philosophy trying to "hide." A new transfer to UNCC, she sat in the back corner of the class, the videotape recording her averted eyes and her body language, which seemed to warn both teacher and students: Keep away. However, as Fishman drew her into class discussion, Demika was repeatedly surprised and pleased by how much she knew. Not only was she not "wrong," as she had feared, or accidentally "offensive to others," but Fishman and her classmates praised her comments, remembering and referring to them in subsequent class discussions. Intro to Philosophy was different, then, she felt, in that she was valued for her own ideas.

This continuity which Demika built between Intro and her other classes, a continuity based on contrast, helps explain her openness to Fishman's assignments and the interactions they required. It is as if her sense that this class was unusual allowed her to modify some of her well-established class-room habits and be open to more cooperative ones. In this way, she is unlike John and Sean, who found similarities which led them, with very different results, to believe that habits honed in other classes were appropriate in Intro to Philosophy.

Demika's Continuity with a Future Goal

By October, then, Demika had had numerous cooperative experiences with Fishman and her classmates, and her goal was to pay back. Commenting on her exchange with Ashley in a follow-up interview 6 months later, she recalled, "It meant a lot to me. I didn't want to write just any old thing to Ashley. I really wanted to answer her question, but it was hard. I couldn't just use my personal experience, and I couldn't just go to the book for the answer. Instead, I had to climb out on a limb and use my own reasonings about what Russell intended. I'm not sure I was right, but I hope I helped her. I had generally gotten good answers from other students, and I didn't want to give Ashley a half-done job."

An example of the sort of "good answers" which set the stage for Demika's cooperation with Ashley was one she recounted to me in early September. During the fifth class meeting, she was paired with Sean Wilson for a 10-minute, in-class conversation about their study question homework on a feminist article by Elizabeth Spelman. Not only was Demika new to UNCC, but, because of schedule mix-up, she had missed the first 3 days of Fishman's class. In this "depressing" situation, her conversation with Sean reassured her, Demika told me. His treatment of her answer "made me begin to believe I could do the work." In discussion that day, when Fishman asked Sean to explain Demika's perspective to the class, Sean prefaced his remarks by saying he had learned a lot from Demika because she spoke from the perspective of a woman. The class laughed—apparently at his assumption she might do otherwise—and then Sean summarized her point. Fishman took up where Sean had left off, saying, "Let me see if I understand you, Demika. You seem to be saying. . . . " He refined Sean's version of Demika's position while she nodded vigorously. She told me later, "It was like Dr. Fishman read my mind. Sean understood me, but Dr. Fishman really helped me out." Demika's appreciation of this sort of cooperation shaped her goal: her determination to be a good letter partner to Ashley.

Ashley Posten's Question Letter to Demika Braxton

I switch now to Ashley's question letter, which, in many ways, mirrors Demika's own question letter to Ashley. Like Demika, Ashley does not connect the assigned text to personal goals. Instead, she attends primarily to her responsibility to be a good collaborator, reading the text carefully and laying out a problem that she is having with it. Although Ashley's question is more sophisticated than Demika's, she also tries to articulate it—"to describe my confusion clearly," as she put it—so Demika can mentor her. To do this, Ashley told me, required that she work hard, spelling her problem out more carefully than she would have needed to do for the teacher. Ashley writes to Demika:

> As soon as I started chapter 5, questions started hitting me. In fact, I was lost when I read his first sentence: "Marriage is rooted in family rather than family in marriage." Although I began to understand a bit better as I read on, I still have some confusion. . . .
>
>   Russell explains that some people see the purpose of marriage, [as] not to reproduce, but to avoid fornication. St. Paul is referred to often. I understand how this might be saying that family is not important in marriage, but I have yet to understand what is meant by "Marriage is rooted in family rather than family in marriage.". . . Later Russell writes, "The art of love was forgotten and marriage was brutalized." This sentence also allowed me to understand my question a little more because if the family was the most important part of the marriage, there would not be any wrongdoing in it. I feel that I am really stroking to answer my own question, but I'm afraid it's is the best I can do. I hope you can assist me.

In this letter, Ashley focuses on a key quotation, a puzzling idea central to understanding Russell's point. Unlike Sean and Emily, she neither presents her own interpretation nor uses the text to achieve genuine for-whats of her own. Instead, like Demika, she focuses on clarifying her confusion in order to help her partner become her mentor. What were the continuities in Ashley's classroom experience which led her to adopt this cooperative role?

Ashley Posten's Continuity with Previous Classes

Like Demika, Ashley was influenced by previous experiences within Fishman's class. However, by contrast with the pleasant cooperative experiences Demika describes, the context for Ashley's role was supplied by an unpleasant event: the time, earlier in the semester, when a philosophy partner let her down. She had worked hard on a response letter for him, but when he did not show up to get it, she said, she felt silly, her effort futile. She explained that although she realized Fishman would read her letter, she really had not written it for him but for the classmate who did not show up. This experience left a bad taste, Ashley said, and she did not want to betray someone else in this way. And indeed, on one occasion, when she feared she might be absent on a letter exchange day, she phoned Fishman to make special arrangements to keep up her end of the contract. For Ashley, then, the continuities she forged with this negative experience helped fashion the cooperative classmate inquirer she became.

I turn now to the response letters these two young women wrote to one another in order to demonstrate what happens when students without a powerful interest in the text itself are directed to to-whats their partners dictate. I found that both Demika and Ashley, motivated by the for-what of helping one another, worked very hard, expending more effort, they claimed, than they would have done for Fishman alone. And both developed interpretations which Fishman deemed remarkable, especially in the absence of such understanding in their initial question letters to one another. Although their work was not always accurate in terms of expositing Russell, their letters and their think-aloud data reveal deep interaction with the reading and persistent, if not fully successful, efforts to connect the material to their lives.

Demika Braxton's Response Letter to Ashley Posten

As Demika worked to fulfill the colleague mentor role to Ashley, she wrestled with the confusing statement from Russell. On the hour-long think-aloud tape she recorded while composing, she repeated it numerous times, as if repetition might force its meaning to emerge. Eventually, she sighed deeply: "Maybe the best way for me to explain my thinking is to write that statement as a question." But after working with it in question form for a few minutes, she gave up, saying, "No, the best way might be to break it in half." And this is what she did.

Demika begins her response to Ashley by confessing her inadequacies. However, she then does her best to mentor Ashley, not only breaking the quote in half, but also trying out several familiar ideas as possible with-which(s) to bridge to Russell's unfamiliar ideas. Demika writes,

> Well, Ashley, to tell the honest to goodness truth, after reading your letter, I was as lost as you were. I had to read parts of the chapter over and over just to begin to formulate an interpretation. I will, however, try to help you as much as I possibly can. The best way to explain what I got out of the statement is to break it apart and analyze each half.
>
> The first half of the statement says: "Marriage is rooted in family." I believe this could mean that for generations marriage was seen as important to the welfare of families. That is, it helped the family if a daughter married a rich man. Another meaning could be that the lives of parents come to a halt when their children are living at home, but once they are gone, the parents' relationship can continue....
>
> The second half of the statement says, "rather than family in marriage." This one is a little harder to analyze. I feel it means marriage should not come about just because the two people want to procreate....Family should begin with love between two people. Personally, I've never seen a happy family that didn't start that way.

Demika concludes her think-aloud, apparently exhausted: "Well, if that wasn't philosophic thinking, I don't know what was! I'm still not sure I answered Ashley's question. I used the book, but basically I had to formulate my own ideas."

Although Demika apologizes in her concluding paragraph "for using my own opinion," she is actually an excellent student to Ashley as well as a worthy colleague. She accomplishes what Fishman had hoped for. Motivated by the for-what of mentoring her classmate, she spends an hour mulling over the to-what that Ashley gives her, a puzzling sentence containing a key idea. A closer look shows that Demika misunderstands Russell's point as she analyzes the first half of the sentence. Because she interprets "family" to mean the couple's parents rather than their children, she misses Russell's argument that the couple's romantic love for one another is less important than their commitment to their offspring. The second half of the sentence she interprets accurately—marriage (love between the couple) is more important than children—but she fails to understand that, while she may agree with this popular romantic view, Russell opposes it. Yet despite her failure to fully grasp Russell's meaning, Demika, according to Fishman, "mounted a wonderful effort" to explore Russell's idea. Using her own best understanding of what marriage and family is, Demika grappled with Ashley's to-what, analyzing and interpreting it in a self-disciplined attempt to clarify her partner's confusion.

Ashley Posten's Response Letter to Demika Braxton

Ashley worked equally hard to mentor Demika, also "climbing out on a limb," to use Demika's phrase, to construct her interpretation of Russell. Ashley tells Demika at the beginning of her response: "I am answering you from my own view because I do not totally understand how Russell fits husband, wife, mistress, and illegitimate children together.... However, in some ways, I feel Russell's opinions are similar to mine." The interpretation Ashley constructs for Demika draws not only on her own ideas, but also on a recent class discussion. She writes,

> I think in a round about way Russell is saying there is a double standard of sexual morality, like we discussed in our freewrites in class the other day. Although Russell does not come out and say it, I feel he fits husband, wife, mistress, and illegitimate children together in this way. He is saying it is okay for a man to perform an act with his mistress which might result in children, but it is not okay for him to have to support an illegitimate child.... He also says, "a legitimate child is a continuation of a man's ego." So Russell is bringing men and their women and children together by suggesting a very big double-standard. This is not obvious, however, until his writing is broken down.

After offering her interpretation, Ashley also apologizes, saying she regrets she cannot clear up Demika's question once and for all. She concludes, "I hope I have been of some help to you, Demika. I am sorry I couldn't give more concrete proof of my answer, but hopefully you can accept my opinion as worthwhile."

The serious effort Ashley puts forward as she struggles to mentor

Demika is recorded in the think-aloud tape she made for me while composing her letter. For nearly an hour, we hear her work with the to-what Demika presents her. Comparing and contrasting Russell's contentions with her own ideas, she tries, just as Demika does, to find with-which(s) to bridge between the familiar and unfamiliar. Finally she recalls the class's discussion of the double standard, the system which applies stricter moral standards to women than to men. It is a with-which she knows Demika will recognize, and she seizes on it as a way of building continuity with Russell. And, according to Fishman, the interpretation she constructs, although it is not what Russell has in mind, is "ingenious," quite consistent with Russell's account of women and children within patriarchy. Although Ashley's account, then, like Demika's, is not completely accurate, and although she, too, fails to find significant relations between the text and her personal life, her interpretation is, Fishman believes, one with which Bertrand Russell would not disagree. The double standard and the male ego are indeed important factors in the sexual morality of patriarchy.

To summarize, Demika Braxton and Ashley Posten both produce letters marked by significant shortcomings. Neither Demika nor Ashley gets Bertrand Russell's full meaning, and neither integrates the text with her own life. Why, then, do Fishman and I praise Demika's and Ashley's experiences? Why do we celebrate them as educative? For three reasons, all of them methodological, that is, all concerning these students' habits and attitudes.

First, Ashley and Demika learn something about cooperating and sharing knowledge to achieve common goals. As we have seen, they carefully tune to one another's needs as they compose, genuinely interested in mentoring and sharing with one another. Although Fishman and I have considered the possibility that Demika's and Ashley's behaviors might be accounted for by their gender, we believe it is more complicated than that. This is because we also saw paired men demonstrate sensitive listening and cooperation in various situations. For example, John and Sean, two of the most dominant men in the class, helped one another in the computer lab, where they completed their assignments, Sean even asking John, on one occasion, to type his homework and hand it in for him when he had to go out of town. John was pleased to do it.

In addition to Demika's and Ashley's experience with collaboration, Fishman's and my second reason for celebrating their exchange is that we believe they learned something about integrity and self-discipline. That is, in their letters and think-alouds, we see evidence of the sort of self-directed attention which, Dewey tells us, results from voluntary interest and internal motivation (*Experience and Education* 51–60). Both students put forward remarkable effort, and they do that because they want to. By contrast, I observed both Demika and Ashley at other times during the semester when they were bored or rushed, when they were working, in Dewey's terms, with "divided interest." In their letter exchange about Russell, however, they appeared single-minded and intent on helping one another. These were not students simply completing an assignment with one eye on the clock and the other on a passing grade.

Finally, we praise Demika's and Ashley's correspondence because, despite the fact their final accounts of Russell are not quite on target and despite the fact they fail to use the curriculum to expand their own interests, they do have the experience of struggling and succeeding with new material. They show the sort of commitment and initiative which Dewey says helps students over the "dead places" in the curriculum (*Experience and Education* 38). That is, Demika and Ashley come face-to-face with a difficult text in which they have no particular interest, and, starting from nothing, they engage with it, explore it, and, finally, "climb out on a limb" to articulate an interpretation. Being able to articulate their positions, both told me, built self-confidence. Ashley, in a late-semester reflection log, writes:

> I had to read into Russell deeper and assume a lot about him that I was not sure of....But I felt good about that. I now realize the more you read something the more you see the thinking pattern of the author—or at least the more you believe you see it.... Trying to help Demika think about her problem was a lot different from high school where we answered ten questions for the teacher at the end of every assignment.

I will return to Ashley and Demika in Chapter 11, commenting further about what they got from this particular assignment as well as the "residue" they took from Fishman's course in general.

FINDINGS ABOUT CONTINUITIES AND INTERACTIONS

I return to the general questions with which I began this chapter. Applying Dewey's view of experience—his ideas of continuity and interaction—to Fishman's classroom, what do we learn about his students' student-curriculum integration, and what do we learn about their development of what Dewey considers important moral traits of character?

Cooperative Roles, in the Presence of Meaningful Continuities, Resulted in Student-Curriculum Integration

I find that when Fishman's students came to the assignment with significant continuities or personal objectives (important for-whats) and adopted the roles of cooperative classmate inquirer and colleague mentor, they were able to achieve student-curriculum integration. However, in terms of percentages of students actually fulfilling this Deweyan criterion of classroom success, Fishman's rating is poor. For the students whose letter exchanges I have presented in this chapter, my scorecard shows only two out of five, with only Sean Wilson and Emily Parrish able to use the assigned reading to achieve personally valued ends. Only these two have genuine for-whats which promote mastery of course material and expanded interest in subject matter.

Cooperative Roles Led to Moral Development

As Fishman and I have repeatedly noted, Dewey wants more for students than mastery of curriculum; he also wants moral development. What is our finding when we apply this Deweyan standard to Fishman's letter exchange? Before giving our answer, I point out that in using this criterion, we proceed with caution, employing the idea of moral development in Dewey's broad sense. As Fishman explains in chapters 1 and 3, intelligent inquiry, for Dewey, requires not only clear and informed thinking but also specific attitudes or moral traits (*How* 28–29). That is, while intelligent inquiry depends upon cognitive skills and disciplinary knowledge, it also requires open-mindedness, wholeheartedness, self-discipline, cooperation, and social responsibility. Dewey regards these moral traits of character as both important ends of education as well as means.

Using this Deweyan measure, I find that Fishman's scorecard is better. Of the five students we spotlight in this chapter, four develop in this way. In particular, Sean Wilson experiences wholeheartedness, and Emily Parrish learns something about social responsibility. Even more striking, in Fishman's and my view, are Demika Braxton's and Ashley Posten's practice with democratic collaboration. Although neither of these students fully masters the assigned reading or integrates it with personal concerns, both make a sincere effort to help one another, and their work is characterized by self-discipline and mutual regard.

Only John Lucas appears neither to expand his interest in philosophy nor develop the moral habits and attitudes Dewey values. Because John continues for most of the semester to read superficially while pretending to do otherwise, we deem the letter assignment a failure for him. Pretense or "divided interest" of this sort, Dewey would say, hardly builds character or leads a student into new areas of subject matter (*Democracy* 176–77). Instead, John constructs letters which allow him to avoid assigned texts and encourage his partners to do likewise. Although the reasons for John's stance are numerous and complex, as I have shown, and although he does eventually recognize the need to take subject matter more seriously, for much of the semester John represents Dewey's progressive education nightmare. That is, John is a student who attempts little beyond personal response, never challenging his own views with serious interaction with new material. He remains, therefore, an interesting case for us because he makes clear the challenge for teachers who, like Fishman, attempt to integrate student interest and disciplinary methods.

I find, then, with regard to the letter assignments I examine in this chapter, a mixed scorecard. Fishman's indirect pedagogy is only modestly successful in promoting student-curriculum integration, but his record is somewhat better concerning Dewey's ideal of intelligent, moral practice.

CONCLUSION: THE VALUE OF APPLYING DEWEY'S CONCEPT OF CONTINUITY AND INTERACTION

Leaving my specific findings about students' experiences with the letter exchange, I now ask a more general question about our research: What are the advantages of studying the classroom from the standpoint of Dewey's view of experience? Do we gain anything more than clarification of the theoretical constructions—theoretical terms like continuity and interaction—of an influential American philosopher? Our answer is yes. First of all, our Deweyan study reveals students as more than discrete atoms and their classroom experiences as more than isolated events. After employing Dewey's theory of experience to organize the stories of five Intro students, what strikes us is the contrast of a Deweyan perspective to cognitive and sociolinguistic frameworks. Whereas cognitivists tend to zero in on decontextualized problem-solving strategies and sociolinguists tend to examine students' language competence in particular discourse communities, a Deweyan researcher focuses on students' integrative work: the continuities pupils forge across time, diverse activities, and multiple roles. (For a discussion of various research perspectives, see Berkenkotter, "Paradigm") As we have shown, students like Sean and Emily, who find connections between their work in

Philosophy class and their nonschool goals, are highly motivated to master new subject matter and, as a result, succeed in enriching their experience and expanding their interests.

Dewey does not deny that students without such continuities can perform well enough in classes to gain high grades. However, he fears that without the sorts of connections that Sean and Emily develop, classroom interactions are often useless, going "in one ear and out the other," because they are not rooted in students' pasts or tied to their futures. In other words, a Deweyan analysis tells us more about the *meaning* of students' education—how they *use* it, what they *do* with it—than it does about knowledge acquisition or training in discrete skills.

In addition to offering insights concerning students' use of the curriculum, the ways they integrate it into their lives, a Deweyan study offers a second type of information. Because Dewey highlights student motivation, his approach allows us to get a foothold on a particularly controversial aspect of the classroom, namely, moral education. We think Deweyan tools are especially valuable in this regard, as we can see from the stories of four of our five students. If we had neglected the habits they were practicing and the traits of character they were developing, we would have missed an important dimension of their education in Introduction to Philosophy.

THE DIVORCE BETWEEN LEARNING AND its use is the most serious defect of our existing education. Without the consciousness of application, learning has no motive.... [It] is separated from the actual conditions of the child's life, and a fatal split is introduced between school learning and vital experience.

— JOHN DEWEY,
"The University Elementary School, Studies and Methods" 1897: 33

Chapter Ten

A DEWEYAN PERSPECTIVE ON STUDENT PROJECTS: CONSTRUCTION AND CRITICISM, SYNTHESIS AND ANALYSIS

———————— ✦ ————————

Lucille McCarthy with Steve Fishman

In this chapter, I focus on another of the nested dualisms—construction and criticism—that Dewey says we must attend to if we hope to achieve student-curriculum integration. Construction and criticism are activities Dewey also describes as synthesis and analysis, and this is the way I will refer to them throughout this chapter. In general, as Fishman points out in Chapter 2 of this volume, Dewey views analysis as clarification of a thing's defining characteristics and synthesis as connection of a thing to other objects and events (*How* 157–59). Some of Fishman's students were able, as I will show, to use philosophy to analyze and synthesize their problems and, thus, see them in fresh ways. Put differently, these students were able to ask philosophic questions about the key actors in their dilemmas and use philosophic concepts to freshly characterize and regroup these actors. And this analytic-synthetic work helped them clarify and broaden their moral problems.

In order to show how philosophic synthesis and analysis worked for students, I focus on their term project essays. Fishman announced this assignment on the first day of the semester, describing the project as a philosophic exploration of a personal moral dilemma. He asked students to begin by discussing an ongoing conflict in their lives, one he hoped they could, in subsequent drafts, with his own and classmates' help, examine philosophically. He placed no limitations on length or topics, simply urging students to focus on "a problem that won't go away." Although Fishman offered pupils an alternative to this personal philosophic essay, a library research paper, no one in fall, 1995, chose this option. The first draft of the essay was due November 7, the final draft on December 8, the last day of the semester. (For the full written assignment, which Fishman distributed in mid-October, see Appendix D.)

In Chapter 6, Fishman describes his longstanding frustration with these projects, his inability to get more than a handful of students each semester to connect philosophic ideas and their personal conflicts. It was his ongoing disappointment in this regard which led him to his pedagogical experiments in fall, 1995. And these experiments must have worked, because a greater proportion of his Intro students than ever before—nearly half of the 25—achieved student-curriculum integration in their papers in some measure. Although there were, of course, multiple reasons for this success, I believe a particularly important factor was one of Fishman's new techniques in fall, 1995, his use of audiotaped rather than written responses to student drafts.

AUDIOTAPED RESPONSES TO STUDENTS' DRAFTS: EXPLORATIONS RATHER THAN MAPS

Audiotaped responses are an especially intriguing pedagogy because teachers' revision instructions always run the danger of being too directive and, thus, of inadvertently appropriating students' papers. My interviews with Fishman's students suggest that recorded responses—although they are indeed examples of an instructor's direct advice—are a way of reducing this danger. They seemed to minimize Fishman's appropriation of student drafts by allowing him to share with students his unrehearsed thinking—what Dewey calls the *psychology* rather than just the *logic* of discovery—that is, his pauses, his blind alleys, and the multiple possibilities he considers as he thinks through the dilemmas at the core of his students' drafts (*Child* 197–201).

Because of the significance I attach to these audiotapes, I give them a dominant role in this chapter. However, by spotlighting this pedagogy, I risk making it appear that, in regard to student essays, Fishman risked betraying his commitment to indirect teaching, his resolution to reserve explicit instruction for those situations when it was likely to encourage rather than discourage student initiative. But this appearance of betrayal is misleading: Fishman remained as determined as ever to help students use his subject matter rather than passively receive it. Therefore, my readers should keep in mind the special context in which these tapes were used. First, as we have seen in Chapters 8 and 9, students were accustomed to owning their work, having spent a good part of the semester playing teacher and student to one another and thus themselves practicing the sort of mentoring they would hear from Fishman. They understood from their own experiences that responding to someone else's work is a fallible, hermeneutic affair. Second, Fishman's tapes were only one of a series of exchanges focused on pupils' in-progress essays. Pairs of students also traded written critiques of their drafts, pinpointed course texts they thought most relevant to each others' topic, and jointly listened to Fishman's tapes in an effort to better understand and respond to them.

Fishman hoped, then, that set in this environment, his taped responses, in contrast to his written ones in previous semesters, would model and encourage, rather than dictate, the sort of philosophic thinking he wanted. That is, he hoped his recordings would allow students to listen in on his own struggles to philosophize about their moral dilemmas, the tapes functioning as "explorations," to borrow Dewey's metaphor, rather than as "maps" of completed revision routes (*Child* 197–99; *How* 73). And, by and large, this is what happened. Students reported that Fishman's audiotapes provided opportunities for them to think along with the teacher—inviting a kind of provocative eavesdropping on revision possibilities rather than receipt of rigid marching orders.

SYNTHESIS AND ANALYSIS IN THREE SUCCESSFUL STUDENT PROJECTS

In what follows, I examine the essays of three students, pupils with whom we are already familiar: Sean Wilson, Emily Parrish, and John Lucas. I find that to the degree these students successfully applied philosophic analysis and synthesis to their own problems, they displayed signs of self-clarification or reconstruction as well as enriched experience. Although I focus on cognitive and downplay noncognitive factors in my discussion of student essays in this chapter, I found that when the analytic-synthetic dualism was reconciled, it was accompanied by integration of the emotional and intellectual forces of intelligent inquiry. This was especially true in the cases of two of the three students, Sean Wilson and John Lucas.

Sean Wilson: Using Philosophic Synthesis and Analysis to Explore and Reconstruct Family Problems

Sean Wilson's Initial Draft

Sean's draft, written on November 1, vividly describes the conflict he has faced his entire life: how to deal with his mother's alcoholism. He writes that he does not hate his mother, but neither does he love or respect her. Despite numerous rehabilitation and 12-step programs, she continues to drink, and "just about the only in-depth dialogues my mother and I have ever shared have taken place while she was in a drunken stupor."

His draft is a narrative with considerable analysis and synthesis, but the implicit questions and categories are psychological rather than philosophic. After describing his problem, Sean in effect offers the reader an answer to a classic psychological question: What is my emotional state, my psychic health? He tells us he feels guilty, depressed, and enraged, often battling low self-esteem. His imagery suggests he lives in an environment which he finds emotionally dangerous and life threatening. "I consider my relationship with my mother comparable to a nude, fleet-footed flight through a deep thicket of briars and trees. From within my perpetual 'forest' of tribulations, the one tree of despair that interminably hangs its gnarled, tangled limbs in the fore-ground of my life is the disdain I feel for my mother."

It is his guilt about this disdain on which Sean focuses his draft. He then turns to a second classic psychological question: What are the sources of my guilt? His answer names three: first, his grandmother's Biblical exhortations to love and respect his mother no matter what; second, "sappy" media images depicting idyllic mother-son relationships; and, finally, his own conscience. Sean concludes his draft by asking:

> Am I heartless? Has my heart been ripped from my chest?...I am tortured by these questions relentlessly and have never been able to answer them....I feel nothing but emptiness for my mother....Sometimes I think I am the loneliest person in the world.

Fishman's Audiotaped Response to Sean's Draft

In Sean's draft, Fishman has the beginnings of the sort of project he hopes for. It is written by a student possessing what Dewey believes is the ultimate motivator: Sean "has something to say" (*How* 246). Fishman's challenge is to help Sean think about his conflict philosophically, seeing it in terms of a culturally constructed clash of values, rather than in terms of psychological categories like guilt, rage, and depression. Fishman hoped to help Sean clarify and, perhaps, reconstruct his perspective. If this led to "solace" or "relief" for Sean, so much the better; it was obviously not something Fishman could guarantee.

After reading Sean's three-page draft twice, Fishman spoke into the tape recorder. His first move was to suggest that Sean might sharpen his analysis of the key players—his family members, popular culture, and himself—by asking some philosophical questions of each position. Second, Fishman suggested that Sean should try to replace the psychological lenses or concepts at work in his first draft—notions like guilt, rage, and depression—with philosophic ones like the religious viewpoint on family relations versus a more utilitarian and contractual one. In this way, Fishman hoped, Sean would use philosophy, its special questions and concepts, to better analyze and clarify the conflicting individuals in his dilemma while synthesizing or grouping them according to the ethical positions they represented.

The audiotape begins with Fishman reminding Sean of the sorts of philosophic questions he might ask.

Hey, Sean, I've just read your draft. It's a heartfelt piece about a very difficult problem.... However, I think the paper at this point does not yet have much philosophic exploration. You present a dilemma: Should you respect your mother, or should you treat her in some other way? Your grandma and popular culture say you should respect her, but you have some doubts and may want to take a different position. You say you feel empty and angry toward your mom. You present these two positions, but you don't yet explore them as I'd like you to, looking at them with philosophic eyes.

What you want to ask—and this would give you an opportunity to do some philosophic analysis—is how would your grandmother defend her view? And what basic assumptions does she make about human life, the good life, and family, which lead her to conclude you should respect your mother no matter what?

After Fishman's reference to the questions philosophers ask about human nature and the good life (knowledge Fishman assumed he and Sean shared), he then goes on to suggest to Sean some categories he might use to group or synthesize the answers he develops for the actors in his dilemma:

> Let's say your grandma's answers are that family is a given, determined by God, indissoluble, and let's say the answers you construct for yourself are that families are contracts which may be broken when certain terms are violated. You might learn more about your grandmother's answers by placing her with religious people who would say children have unquestionable, divinely sanctioned obligations to parents. On the other hand, you might group yourself with people holding a kind of social contract theory. People in this camp would say that when a parent falls below some standard, children have the right to rebel.

Fishman concluded his audiotape by trying to convey that his suggestions were not dictates and that there might be other revision paths Sean would want to pursue. Fishman ended by summarizing his reflections and wishing Sean luck:

> There may be other alternatives you want to look at, Sean, but as I see it, one way to turn this into a philosophic essay is to focus on various perspectives on parent-child relationships—their differing assumptions about what constitutes human nature, the world, and the moral or good life. I hope I've been of some help. Please come by if you want more conversation. I wish you well with the paper, and hope you get some clarification.

Sean Wilson's Revised Term Project Essay

In rewriting his draft, Sean engaged in analytic-synthetic work that pleased Fishman. In particular, Sean was able to explore, as Fishman had suggested, alternate conceptions of parent-child relations within his family, and, in the process, "make some philosophic discoveries on his own." Sean's attempt to analyze and clarify his grandmother's position was good, in Fishman's estimate, and his newly added exploration of his father's stance was even better. And, added to these was a thoughtful examination of his own perspective: all in all, a strong effort on Sean's part, according to Fishman, to use philosophic questions and categories to gain new perspective on his moral dilemma.

Sean begins his philosophic questioning of his grandmother's position by asking about the view of the good life which lies behind her claim that children should love and respect their parents no matter what. For "Mama

Strong," Sean writes, "the Good Life leads to heaven and can only be achieved by following God's Word, and God says one should obey one's parents." Thus, he tells us, his grandmother has often instructed him to "honor thy father and thy mother that thy days may be long upon the land which the Lord thy God giveth thee." However, Sean then slides out of philosophic questioning about his grandmother's position and readopts the view that dominated his first draft. Asking psychologic questions and categorizing according to psychologic ideas, Sean writes that another reason for his grandmother's position is that she has had good relations with her own five children. She raised them single-handedly and is beloved by all. Sean concludes his discussion by grouping his grandmother with people who are limited by their own experiences: "The fact Mama Strong has been so loving may help explain why she cannot understand what I have been through."

Although Fishman was disappointed that Sean's analysis of his grandmother takes this psychologic direction, he was pleased with Sean's analysis of his father's position. In this discussion, Sean returns to philosophic questioning; specifically, to ask about the ideal of the good life motivating his father. Sean writes, "What principle could possibly possess a man so greatly that he would thanklessly endure so many years of pain and unhappiness? Why would he stick by my mother for 27 years despite her countless committals to recovery programs, despite endless verbal and mental abuse?" Because Sean and his father have never actually discussed this, the only way Sean can find out about his father's philosophic position—his views of the good life, a good husband, a good marriage—is to "to ask him outright." Sean writes,

> One night I blatantly asked my father what could make him so steadfast in his marriage to an alcoholic. All he said was, "Sean, your mother and I are married." Then he quietly went back to reading his newspaper. At that moment, I knew exactly where my dad was coming from. A flood of understanding washed over me.

Sean realizes, "from that one simple statement," that his father uses a different standard to evaluate his wife and marriage. His father sees marriage not as a contract that can be broken, but as vows he will "stick to forever… in sickness and in health." Sean then synthesizes his father's position on marriage with other aspects of his father's worldview, specifically, his beliefs that a man's word is his bond and that fidelity and protection of family are signs of male strength. His father has often told him that "blood is thicker than water" and "that a man must always take care of family." However, Sean concludes,

> What troubles me is that even though my father has been looking after family and upholding his idea of the "Good Life," he has been noticeably unhappy for most of my life. I thought living your idea of the "Good Life" was supposed to make you happy. If my father's outward appearance is the measure of his notion of "Good Life," I honestly want no part of it.

Having identified his grandmother's and father's differing assumptions about the good life—beliefs which similarly dictate maintenance of the family at all costs—Sean rejects them both. He then starts to philosophically question his own position, struggling to construct his own view of the good life and what this means for family relations. His answer seems to be that the good life involves focusing less on family or religious obligations than on individual development. Opposing his grandmother and father, Sean argues that, in fact, when the family is destructive, its members' first obligation is to themselves, and they may choose to withdraw. Aligning himself first with enlightenment individualism, Sean approvingly quotes Thomas Paine: "It is necessary to the happiness of man that he be mentally faithful to himself" (*Age of Reason*, ch. 1). Sean concludes this section: "After suffering the atrocities of growing up in an alcoholic family, I have decided that my only path to the 'Good Life' is to detach from any emotional bonds with my mother."

Sean then switches from his own answers about the good life to questions about his position on knowledge construction. Once again, his answers are at variance with his grandmother's and father's, and he has to place himself in a different tradition. Whereas his grandmother believes knowledge is constructed through listening to God, and his father sees knowledge as established by tradition, Sean argues that knowledge is developed by attending to present experience. He then aligns himself with Dewey to argue for using current information to evaluate traditional solutions, ones which may wield powerful emotional force but prove useless—even harmful—in present circumstances. Sean ends his essay with his own reconstructed view of how knowledge is developed:

> We should set aside feelings and emotions that are involved with past experiences; not depend so much on past social and moral values to render an answer.... I acknowledge that each day is a new one, and I must find new solutions to problems that arise between my mother and me. Today's approach

may not work tomorrow. The plan I present here may not be turmoil-free, but it is better than what I've tried to do until now: be guided by past ideals which have proven less than beneficial to both my mother and myself.

In Sean's philosophic analysis of himself, then, he no longer is talking about guilt, rage, and depression. Rather, he is exploring his identity in terms of a whole new set of questions and concepts. He synthesizes several traditions, grouping himself with Paine's view of the good life as focused on individual development and Dewey's view of knowledge as tradition tested against present and future experience. And in Sean's and my post-essay interview, he engaged in yet more analytic/synthetic work, explaining Alcoholics Anonymous to me in philosophic terms. Although he does not mention it in his essay, Sean told me he had had "a little experience" with Al-Anon, and that its "day-by-day" approach to alcoholism reminded him of Dewey. "Every day is a new struggle for my mother too," he commented. "That is something I have not, until now, explored or accepted." Although Fishman felt Sean might have unfairly cast Dewey in the role of totally ignoring the past or supporting an unsystematic approach to the present—a go-with-the-flow orientation—he was, nonetheless, pleased that Sean was analyzing and categorizing a movement like Al-Anon in this philosophic way.

In sum, Sean's paper provides some details about Deweyan student-curriculum integration. Sean achieves this integration by asking philosophic questions about himself, his grandmother, and his father. He then clarifies and groups his answers using philosophic concepts like individualism, traditionalism, and experimentalism in a process of mutually informing analysis and synthesis.

The Effects of Student-Curriculum Integration on Sean Wilson

We found that students' experiences of student-curriculum integration in these essay projects meant something quite different to each. In Sean's case, he felt himself less isolated and strange as a result of being able to identify with such figures as Paine and Dewey. In turn, his ability to see his grandmother and father as members of groups with whom they shared views of the good life and knowledge construction enabled him to be more charitable toward them. His philosophic work contextualized their views, making their perspectives seem less wrongheaded, less mysterious and sacrosanct, less powerful and frightening.

Interestingly, Sean's own description of what had happened to him as he wrote his paper showed, understandably, that he was still not fully at home in philosophic discourse. Fortuitously, just after his post-essay interview with me on December 8, Sean spoke with Fishman, who tape-recorded the conversation. In comparing these two conversations, I find that in speaking with me Sean fell back into the psychological language and theory that marked his first draft. He told me:

> Writing my essay was therapeutic. I stepped into my grandmother's and father's shoes, into their life experiences. . . . I wanted to get behind their opinions, the ones I had been subjected to while growing up—ones which clashed with what I was feeling and made me guilty and confused. I had all this pain, but I had never studied *why* I felt this way. It was purging.

When Sean spoke with Fishman a few minutes later, however, instead of talking about a kind of "programming" at the hands of his grandmother and father, he referred to their "viewpoints." And instead of talking about his feelings of guilt and confusion, he spoke about "making better decisions," about finding reasons for agreeing or disagreeing with their philosophic perspectives. Sean told Fishman:

> I think I'm going to be a little happier because I have learned to do this sort of thinking. I can now clarify for myself the viewpoints of others. As I gather this new sort of information about them, it helps me accept them—accept, but not necessarily agree. . . . As a result I think I can make better decisions. I'll certainly be wrong, sometimes, but even when I'm wrong, I want my mistakes based on open-minded listening and careful analysis rather than on inherited judgments about right and wrong.

In conclusion, Sean Wilson, in the process of integrating student and curriculum, moved, as Dewey would have hoped, into new areas of subject matter, using these to develop greater insight and control over his life. He employed philosophic questions as probes, making his grandmother and father give up, if you will, their "philosophic secrets." The result of his use of philosophic concepts to analyze and synthesize the answers he got to these questions was the sort of personal reconstruction—the sort of deepened, thickened, and widened experience—that Dewey sees as one of education's primary aims (*Democracy* 76; *Experience and Education* 74, 87). What Sean had felt as frustration and isolation, he began to see as inability to make himself plain to others holding alternative conceptions of family and knowledge. And what he experienced as sinfulness and self-loathing, he began to understand as nascent individualism and experimentalism.

Emily Parrish: Using Philosophic Synthesis and Analysis to Explore Conflicts with the Church

Emily Parish's essay project provides an interesting contrast to Sean's. Although Emily, a senior political science major, manages to use philosophic questions to investigate a personal dilemma, her problem or for-what is simply not as important to her as Sean's was to him. Whereas his conflict results from clashes which truly "refuse to go away," Emily's problem—the role of religion in her life—is less insistent, apparently more the result of having to complete the assignment than of needing to get relief from a pressing difficulty. In fact, Emily told me in mid-November, she wasn't really sold on her topic and was considering abandoning her draft and starting over with a new conflict. However, because she let this rewriting go until 3 days before the final due date, she had little choice but to stick with her original problem. At that time, she told me, she listened again to Fishman's response tape. "The way Dr. Fishman talked about my conflict made me realize, Yes, this is important to my life. I guess I'll stay with it."

Because Emily's dilemma is at the periphery rather than the center of her life, it does not drive her into new subject matter with the same high energy she exhibited when, earlier in the semester, she was motivated to influence classmate Warren Murray (see Chapter 9). In fact, the new subject matter or to-whats that Emily focuses on in her paper are treated summarily. That is, unlike Sean, Emily does not expand her interests or identify with figures or positions she discusses in her essay, failing almost entirely to relate her own views to theirs. Thus, the sort of clarification which comes to Sean as a result of his new associations with such figures as Thomas Paine and John Dewey appears nowhere in Emily's paper. And Emily's inability to see herself in new ways limits her ability to reconfigure her problem about religion. Her syntheses and analyses are just too weak to bring about the kind of self-reconstruction and insights we witness with Sean.

Of course, other factors besides Emily's initial low interest in her topic may have contributed to the mechanical, uninspired tone of her essay. First, her inability to make progress as she wrote, to achieve insights into herself and her dilemma, probably kept her interest and effort at a low level. Second, Fishman may have provided inadequate assistance in his response tape, failing to help Emily sufficiently with ways to analyze and synthesize her own beliefs. And, finally, Emily may also have been hindered because, unlike Sean, she did not have actual conflicting individuals in her life whom she could question, compare, and characterize. By contrast, her dilemma stemed from conflicting lifestyles that she herself had lived at different times in her history.

Emily Parrish's Initial Draft

Emily's essay project differs from Sean's, then, in its lower levels of interest and effort. It also contrasts with his in that she employs, in her first draft, implicit questions and categories which are not psychological but, rather, close kin to philosophic ones. Her questions and concepts are legalistic. That is, Emily's analysis and synthesis in her first draft—a paper focusing on a dispute in her church 7 years earlier—are organized around these legal and moral questions: Who is protected in the church? Who gets to speak and be heard? And who gets to judge? And Emily's answers to these questions are categorized in terms of her criteria of fair play.

Her conflict originated, Emily writes, when, at age 15, she saw in her church what she believed to be the mistreatment of women. This occurred when congregation leaders rendered a judgment about a male church member accused of a crime. It is about this decision that Emily asks her questions concerning church power and rights. Her categorization of her answers—which reveal church patriarchy as highly prejudiced against women—helps her clarify her own response to this incident as she synthesizes or groups it with other cases of misogyny.

The incident to which Emily applies her legal and moral questions and her idea of due process centers on "Jim," a church member and Sunday school teacher accused of child molestation. A public middle school teacher, Jim played with church children after services and attempted to fondle some of the adolescent girls, including, on one occasion, Emily herself. She was not surprised, therefore, when Jim was formally charged with molesting a 13-year-old at his school. But what did shock her was the reaction of church deacons and elders (all male) who defended Jim, deciding that his activities in the church would continue until the courts decided his case. When mothers of young children protested, Emily was further shocked to watch the elders silence—even ridicule—them. And to make matters worse, when, some months later, Jim was found guilty and sentenced to 3 to 6 years in prison, church leaders offered these women no apologies. In fact, when one woman mentioned in a subsequent church meeting that she had been deeply hurt by the way she was treated, Emily watched as "she was, once again, quietly dismissed by one of the men."

In Emily's implicit analytic/synthetic work with this incident in her initial draft, she categorizes people's answers to her questions about individual rights from the standpoint of someone who sees Jim's case as not just an instance of local prejudice but as an example of patriarchal insensitivity to women. Emily writes,

> How could I support an institution which brushed women aside so easily? What would society as a whole think of this?... The men in our church gave the women no role in shaping this situation, and they would hear no questioning of their decisions.

Thus, Emily's draft, her depiction of church leaders as misogynist, reinforces the decision she made as a 15-year-old to abandon her church.

However, after reexploring the "cruel things" she witnessed 7 years ago, Emily bridges, toward the end of her initial draft, to the current legacy of the incident regarding Jim. She writes that now, as a college senior, she feels conflicted about eschewing all religion. In fact, she admitted to me in a post-essay interview, she may have been using this event as an excuse for not bothering to attend church during college when, actually, she just did not need religion at this stage of her life. However, in her life after college, this might change, she believed, and in the final paragraph of her draft, she pinpoints her present dilemma. Despite her long absence from church, Emily still believes in God and would like to find a way to salvage some positive aspects of churchgoing. But how can she do this, she wonders, in light of her lingering disgust with church politics? In her last sentence, Emily poses the question which becomes central to her final paper: "As I leave college and begin the rest of my life, should I readopt some parts of my religion? Can I develop my own meaning for the good life?"

Fishman's Audiotaped Response to Emily's Draft

Steve Fishman's main task with Sean was to help him train philosophic, rather than psychologic, lenses on a continuing and insistent family problem. By contrast, his job with Emily was not so much to help her change the tools of her analysis and synthesis as to help her philosophically explore a dilemma which emerges only at the end of her initial draft, namely, what role religion should play in her life.

Fishman begins his audiotaped response by identifying the conflicting values he hears in Emily's new problem, a clash between religious and secular ways of life. He then reminds her of philosophic questions she might ask to clarify these alternative positions, and suggests concepts she might use to group or synthesize her answers. He starts his 5-minute taped response:

> Hello, Emily, I've just read your untitled draft. You vividly describe your disappointment with the church elders and their treatment of women. Although you certainly show how this incident led you to ask questions about the church's role in your life, it is not yet a philosophic paper. Insofar as you hint at a conflict you might explore philosophically, it is should you be religious or not? Should you go to church or not?... To get some philosophic analysis, you need to clarify your basic concepts. What is it to live a religious life? By contrast, what is it to live a secular life?

Fishman then thinks through some classic philosophic questions Emily might consider asking about these conflicting perspectives:

> Once you clarify these opposing lifestyles, Emily, the important work is to get to the basic assumptions underlying each position. How do they differ?... Philosophers would ask how members of these groups understand the world, how they view human nature, and what, for each group, constitutes the moral or good life. Do these groups differ in their views of women and patriarchy?

Finally, Fishman asks Emily to consider rereading relevant class texts which might provide a framework or context for her. "In sorting out your answers, you might get help from Elizabeth Spelman, Mary Daly, and Bertrand Russell, all of whom talk about patriarchy, its power in religion, and its effects upon the rest of a religious person's life." Fishman concludes his audiotape by advising Emily to condense the story of Jim into an introductory paragraph, "so you can pop right into the dilemma you face."

> I hope this helps, Emily, and if you need more conversation about it, don't hesitate to catch me, and we can talk further. I wish you luck with the paper, and I hope you clarify your position and learn something by doing it.

Emily Parrish's Revised Term Project Essay

Emily was able, to some degree, to profit from Fishman's tape. And yet, although Fishman believed her essay was "solid," integrating philosophy and student life better than most papers he received in previous semesters, he felt he had not done well enough by Emily. He felt her final essay lacked the sort of initiative and invention—what Dewey refers to as the quality of putting oneself into it—which marks successful constructive work ("How the Mind" 220).

Emily begins her revised essay with a brief summary of the "Jim" incident, hurrying to launch the philosophic analysis and synthesis Fishman suggested. At the end of her first paragraph, she poses her dilemma: "Is it possible to live a secular life and still hold on to some religious beliefs?" She then, in the first part of her paper, defines the secular and religious positions generally, drawing upon her own experiences with both perspectives. She characterizes the religious lifestyle as marked by devotion to church life, participation in church rituals, and display of one's beliefs to the world. By contrast, according to Emily, people who place themselves in the secular camp believe that individuals determine for themselves how to live, and, because secularists believe that life on earth is their only chance, they see living well as its own reward.

After laying out these initial definitions, Emily, in the second section of her essay, works to analyze and further clarify these alternative positions by posing classic philosophic questions. She asks, How does each group view the world? How does each conceive human nature? And what counts as the good and moral life for each? As Emily generates answers to these questions regarding religious and secular positions, she finds significant opposition. For example, in response to her first question regarding their views of the world, Emily writes that whereas the religious perspective understands the world as evil, earthly life as temporary and sin filled, by contrast, "some secularists view the world as a wonderful place." Referring to a course reading by a Native American feminist, Emily writes, "Starhawk sees the earth as a place from which she draws energy, . . . a beautiful place, and she does not look for a paradise beyond." Regarding their assumptions about human nature and the good life, Emily discovers equally strong differences between religious and secular approaches, and, predictably, she explores their perspectives on women. She finds that whereas religionists view women as naturally inferior to men—and therefore subservient to their husbands and unworthy of church leadership—by contrast, for the secularist, "women are somewhat more accepted, nowadays taking traditionally male roles in the family and the workplace."

This is the sort of clarification Emily needs in order to find out if the religious and secular worldviews are reconcilable, or if they must remain mutually exclusive, as they have seemed to her until now. Unfortunately, however, she gets little insight from her exploration of these opposing approaches because she fails to relate her own answers to these key philosophic questions to theirs. She thus misses opportunities to clarify and reconstruct her own perspective.

As Fishman read Emily's essay, he remarked that although he believed Emily had profited from his audiotape, in retrospect, he wished he had been more explicit about the importance of bringing herself into the picture. That is, he wished he had done a better job of outlining how she might use the answers she generated to her philosophic questions to categorize and clarify her own position. For example, he thought Emily's reference to Starhawk was valuable, but he regretted that she had lost an important chance for self-clarification when she failed to explore and analyze her own version of secularism and then contrast or synthesize it with Starhawk's.

Following Emily's questioning of the secular and religious positions in the second part of her essay, in her final section, she moves to her main concern: Can these apparently opposing lifestyles be reconciled? "Is it possible," Emily wonders, "to combine beliefs from both systems and live a life I will be satisfied with?" She wants to find, as she said in the last sentence of her initial draft, "my own meaning for the good life."

She begins her attempt to reconcile these perspectives on an optimistic note, quoting a class reading by Lin Yutang, who has apparently succeeded in this endeavor. A former Christian now claiming to be a "pagan who believes in God," Lin Yutang writes, according to Emily, that religion is "an individual thing, something every person must work out on his or her own." But Emily, once again—perhaps because of Fishman's lack of help—misses an opportunity to bring herself into the paper and learn more about her own views. Fishman thought Emily's reference to Lin Yutang was excellent because, he told me, she was right about Yutang's achieving the sort of reconciliation she herself was attempting. Yet Emily again lets slip away a chance to clarify her own views when she fails to synthesize or compare herself to Yutang.

When Emily ultimately does try to articulate her own hybrid spirituality, her failure to clarify and reconstruct her own position limits her success. Because she has not related her own views to the religious and secular stances of others, she is left with the same contradictory views with which she started her essay. Yet despite this obvious drift, she returns to the vague hope with which she began, ending her essay by repeating her wish "to some day live a good life that both pleases me and incorporates some religious beliefs."

In sum, as Emily integrates student and curriculum, she employs philosophic questions to explore her dilemma regarding the role of religion in her life. However, she makes only modest progress. Although her characterizations of religious and secular perspectives are developed somewhat by her questioning, she never moves far from the rough and general definitions with which she started. Given the lack of reconstruction of her starting beliefs—her failure to clarify her own position by comparing it, for example, to those of theorists like Starhawk and Lin Yutang—Emily is unable to see her own beliefs or her conflict in new ways. In the end, she avoids her essay's general upshot, that religious and secular lives are irreconcilable, concluding instead with an ill-supported hope for future rapprochement.

The Effects of Student-Curriculum Integration on Emily Parrish

Although Fishman was not fully satisfied with Emily's essay, she told me afterward that she actually found revising it "satisfying." She believed the paper had initiated an inquiry into the role of religion in her life which would be ongoing. As she put it, "I'll probably be revising my ideas about religion for a long time to come." And I learned in a follow-up interview 4 months later that she was right. Emily had indeed continued her exploration, revisiting her home church in Winston-Salem. "I'm still in my secular lifestyle," she explained, "but I continue to investigate ways to integrate religion." She believed this would in the end be possible and added that she still recalled Lin Yutang's success in this regard.

When Emily went back to her church, she told me, she had pursued her concern regarding the church's treatment of women, speaking to a woman who had been silenced by church elders 7 years earlier. Although she and this woman had never conversed about the "Jim" incident, Emily knew that this woman had, like herself, been offended enough to leave the church. Emily also knew that the woman had returned, and she wanted to know why. When Emily questioned her about how she could go back, the congregant explained that she had been able to forgive by "looking to God instead." Although Emily indicated she did not know if this would work for her, she told me she was glad she had had the conversation.

Emily's follow-up account is important because it suggests that her paper generated what Dewey would deem educationally worthy continuities (see *Democracy* 358–59; *Experience and Education* 33–44, 48). That is, writing her paper increased, if only in modest ways, Emily's curiosity, initiative, and desire for more learning about the church and its treatment of women. However, despite this evidence of positive residue for future learning, we have no proof Emily will actually succeed in developing richer ways to envision the church. It remains to be seen whether her work in Intro to Philosophy will actually lead to enriched religious experience, that is, to a relationship with the church which will harmonize with her desire to be a successful, self-determining woman.

John Lucas: Using Philosophic Synthesis and Analysis to Explore Racism

The final student whose term project I will examine, senior English major John Lucas, was different in important ways from both Sean Wilson and Emily Parrish. Whereas Emily's analytic and synthetic thinking is limited by her failure to bring her own views into play, John's work is limited for the opposite reason. Although he does a nice job of focusing on his own perspectives, he fails to use class readings to help him challenge and develop them. In sharp contrast to Sean and Emily, John had avoided the assigned texts all semester and, therefore, cannot draw upon other, well-articulated positions in the course of writing his essay. Nevertheless, by making use of Fishman's tapes, John ultimately comes to see himself in new ways. As a result, he achieves something like the growth which Sean experiences but which eludes Emily. That is, whereas Emily begins and ends her project with nearly the same set of beliefs, John moves to a new place. He seems to leave his term project with a more meaningful or enlarged self, a self more complex than the one with which he began.

What accounts for this about-face? Although John could only bring to his paper a minimal familiarity with the assigned literature, he was nevertheless able, for the first time, to engage in some of the analytic-synthetic thinking Fishman desired. For despite his resistance to reading, John liked to write, and this assignment piqued his interest. He chose a topic he cared about, used Fishman's audiotape to good advantage, and was able to make progress. And his pride and excitement at this progress fueled further effort. In fact, his growing excitement functioned as an important continuity or for-what which motivated him to write four drafts and request three teacher response tapes—more than any other student in the class.

John Lucas thus provides an interesting case: first, because of his dramatic end-of-semester improvement, a course trajectory quite different from that of either Sean or Emily, and second, because of the unusual challenge his topic presented to Fishman. As a teacher, Fishman had to decide how to respond to a student whose discourse and ideology differed sharply from his own, whose discourse was, in this case, racist. Unlike Sean and Emily, both of whom critique traditional aspects of their communities, ones they deem oppressive, John defends a longstanding tradition in his: the separation of races. Specifically, he argues that African Americans and whites should not marry. Fishman, following Dewey's principle that students cannot be handed ideas like bricks, avoids the impulse to directly criticize John's point of view or insist he adopt a more politically correct, liberal stance—one closer to Fishman's own. Rather, Fishman focuses on John's methods and works indirectly, helping him use philosophic questions and categories to expand his inquiry. Keeping in mind the hallmarks of Dewey's ideal of student responsibility and ownership, Fishman treats John with respect, urging him to conduct an "open-minded" examination of his own and alternative ideas as well as their consequences (*Democracy* 173–79; *How* 29–33). As Fishman explains in Chapter 4, Dewey is less concerned with the particular political views with which students might leave class than he is with what they take in the way of desire for further reflection, criticism, and reconstruction (see also Fishman and McCarthy "Teaching").

John Lucas's Initial Draft

In John's initial draft, as in that of Sean Wilson, the analytic-synthetic work is not yet philosophic. Rather, the questions John asks about his own position on interracial marriage, and the concepts he uses to categorize his answers, are social, psychological, and biological. John asks himself, Is it right for people of different races to marry? His answer is no, but the three reasons he offers to support his view focus more on personal hardship and negative social and genetic consequences than on moral or philosophic principles.

First, John writes, the cultural differences between African Americans and whites are so great that they present mixed couples with insuperable psychological difficulties in understanding one another. Because the races face such different "pressures and problems, . . . how can a person who is white know how life is for one who is black?" Despite these barriers, however, John acknowledges the trend toward increased acceptance of interracial marriage, and this brings him to his second reason: the fate of mixed-race children. John worries they may be outcast by both African Americans and whites, their self-identities uncertain, and this, John believes, is a situation God surely cannot want. Further, because these mixed-race children are said to be African American, if their numbers become too great, he predicts, there will be a third negative outcome, a biological one: the downfall of the white race. "Sooner or later there will be few white people left in the world. We will be wiped out." John's reasoning leads to the implicit conclusion that, on the one hand, his own group—opposing interracial marriage—cares about marital understanding and communication, the welfare of children, and the preservation of separate races, whereas those who accept mixed-race marriages are insensitive to these personal, social, and genetic concerns.

Despite these oversimple, mutually exclusive categories, John does not wrap things up as neatly as one might expect. Instead, in his last two paragraphs, he makes a puzzling appeal to authority, and this complicates things. John's appeal is to the Bible, but he finds nothing in the Scriptures to support his position. He writes, "I am a Christian and believe God's word to be true, but nowhere in the Bible does God reject interracial marriage and child-bearing. Therefore, He must approve. I struggle with this because it doesn't seem right. I ask God, 'Well, why did You split us up into all these different colors if You did not want us to stay separate?'" Perhaps emboldened by this apparent Biblical approval of interracial relations, John is willing at least to peek into opposing territory, into a world accepting of mixed-race marriages. And what he sees is not so frightening after all. John concludes his initial draft with some unexpected questions:

What would be wrong with all the people of the world being one color? Wouldn't prejudice and hate be slowed? Wouldn't there be fewer problems? What is the goal God had in mind for us? I do not know the answer to this, but I constantly struggle with it.

Fishman's Audiotaped Response to John Lucas's Draft

Steve Fishman's challenge, as with Sean and Emily, is to help John explore his question in philosophic ways. That is, he wants to help John move away from the psychological, social, and biologic questions he directs toward positions on interracial marriage to an exploration of the clashing values behind opposing views on this issue. In his audiotaped response, Fishman proceeds along familiar paths.

He begins by thinking out loud about ways in which John might clarify or analyze differing approaches to intermarriage by posing classic philosophic questions and then offers categories John might use to synthesize or group his answers, perspectives Fishman terms "traditional" and "modern." As he tape records his reflections about John's dilemma, he suggests ways John might broaden his view by situating his own position in relation to the opposing one. Although Fishman holds this opposing view, as I have said, he never announces his disagreement with John, fearing that his teacherly authority might intimidate or silence him. Instead, Fishman conducts the sort of patient, sequential, contextual thinking—the interplay of analytic, defining work and synthetic, comparative work—that Dewey calls for. He starts his audiotape:

> Hey, John, . . . You say you've got a friend who is dating someone of another race, and you list the reasons you are against interracial marriage. Now that's a start, but I'm going to ask you to consider two sides: those who would say no to intermarriage and those who would say it's fine. And I'm going to ask you to do the philosophic work of trying to get to the assumptions and values which lie behind those two different stances. To do this, a philosopher asks certain basic questions.

The philosophic questions which seem most relevant to John's concerns are, Fishman tells him, ones about the nature of knowledge and the nature of the good or moral life. Regarding the nature of knowledge, Fishman asks John,

> When you say that blacks and whites cannot understand one another, what are you assuming about knowledge and learning? Maybe your philosophic assumption is that we cannot know what is different; we can only take in what is sufficiently familiar. Maybe you're suggesting that we learn best by sticking with our own kind, with people who share our ideas and values, so we affirm one another. . . . People who share your perspective may want to avoid the unfamiliar, even viewing novelty and difference as dangerous. Therefore, they will probably want to conserve traditional beliefs and practices and avoid change. . . .
> By contrast, the other side, which says intermarriage is okay, might take the Deweyan view that says that the spirit of modernity is characterized by interest in challenge, novelty, experiment, and change. Folks in this group might say that differences are desirable. They would welcome them because they believe they are necessary for learning. In our own classroom we've seen some of this as we listen to conflicting views from people with different experiences.

Fishman suggests that after John clarifies these alternative ways of knowing and learning, he might discuss them. "What might it mean, John, when one group says, 'Look to the past, to a time when whites and blacks stuck with their own kind?' By contrast, what are the implications when the other group assumes life involves change and, therefore, we must always be trying out new things?"

The second question Fishman suggests John might use to fill out these opposing groups' "philosophic profiles" focuses on their views of the good life. Fishman explains that, naturally, people differ in their views about what life should be, its ideal purpose, our proper roles and obligations. He tells John:

> You may find that people who oppose intermarriage assume it is their obligation in life to uphold and pass on particular religious or communal traditions. These folks may believe it's hard to pass on the stories and practices of one's culture if one marries outside it.
>
> The opposing view—and I'm trying to help you out here, John, about what the other side would say—might be that our obligation is not to the past, but to the future and ourselves. One way to discover self-identity, they might say, is to leave the traditions you came from, and strike out on your own.

When Fishman finishes discussing these philosophic questions and the answers each side might provide, he concludes by suggesting that John divide his paper into three parts. First, John might defend the view that intermarriage is bad or immoral and outline its assumptions and, second, do the same thing for the opposing view. Finally, he should present his own position, describing what he finds convincing about each of these two perspectives. Fishman concludes his tape:

> Remember, John, a rich paper will be sympathetic to both sides. In fact, you want to bend over backward to be to especially sympathetic to the position you are going to reject—in your case what you may want to call the modern view. Spend a little extra time defining it, and talk about it as if you were a modern person defending it. . . .
>
> I hope this helps. What I'm asking you to do is not easy: it's a kind of reflection, not library work. . . . If you need more conversation, please come by.

Although John did not "come by" to speak to Fishman in person, he did, after revising to Fishman's taped suggestions, submit yet another draft for Fishman's response. Thus, on a last tape, 2 days before the paper was due, Fishman offered praise for what John had accomplished so far, and provided a few more minor suggestions. I turn now to John's completed essay.

John Lucas's Revised Term Project Essay
In John's eight-page revision, he tries to use Fishman's suggested questions, directing them at the pros and cons of the intermarriage issue. Although

John does not construct full "philosophic profiles" of both positions, as Fishman had hoped, and although John never alters his opposition to inter-marriage, he is, by thinking along with Fishman, able to see his dilemma in new ways. John replaces his psychological, social, and biological questions about interracial relations with philosophic ones about the good life and theories of knowledge.

With regard to the nature of the good life, John finds that those who are against interracial marriage want to preserve tradition, upholding what they already believe. They want to "stick to what they know, retaining old solutions to present problems." He labels these people conservative. Conversely, when he mentally questions supporters of interracial marriage, he finds their view of the good life focused on a world of new harmonies, "a better world" brought about by fresh solutions to old problems. John labels these people modernists. Although John's effort to this point shows little originality, the mere fact that he is willing to try out Fishman's advice and generate answers to the philosophic good-life question was an advance over his earlier work.

However, John actually moves into new territory, making progress on his own, when he asks epistemological questions of both sides of his issue. As might be expected, he sees conservative opponents of intermarriage as closed-minded and modernist proponents as open-minded. These answers, however, leave him in a significant dilemma—one which helps him clarify his view of himself. Understandably, his immediate inclination is to synthe-size or group himself with opponents of interracial marriage, but when he uses the theory-of-knowledge question to explore that position, he is not so sure. He finds himself reluctant to identify with closed-minded people because he actually thinks of himself as open-minded and is thus tempted to group himself with modernists who embrace interracial relationships. For despite John's deep-seated objection to intermarriage, he is proud of the fact he accepts gays and feminists. He writes, "The old solution for dealing with someone who is different is to try to change or even destroy them, but I've found it easier to adopt a modernist frame of mind regarding gays and women. I just accept the good of these people and ignore the bad." It was this use by John of philosophic synthesis and analysis upon himself which most pleased Fishman. It led, in the end, Fishman believed, to John's recon-structing and complexifying his self-image.

And, indeed, John's think-aloud as he revised his final draft suggests that his excitement about his newly fashioned self-image was an important stimulus for his increased effort at the close of the semester. After listening to Fishman's tape, he says,

> I know where I want go with this! I can look at both sides like Fishman wants if I label *myself* both conservative and modern. Although I am conservative on this issue, I actually *am* modern in many other ways. So I'll show the two sides of myself.

And John carries out this plan, his analysis focusing on his discomfort at realizing he is not as modern as he likes to think, that his view of himself as "open to everything" is not completely accurate. He writes: "If I think of myself as modern, why do I find it hard to accept interracial marriage when it seems to be the modern thing to do? It is the struggles between my conservative and my modern beliefs that lead me to confront this issue."

About 20 minutes into his revising session, John stops to celebrate. He finally understands, he says, "what's supposed to be going on in this class." He is delighted.

> Wow! I may be getting the hang of philosophy. I understand now that I've got to explore both sides, to get behind opposing positions—like in our class discussions and our textbooks. I feel like my essay might fit into that book with the black cover [Edwards and Pap]. I'm excited to write this now. I'll do headers for the three sections.

After exploring both modern and conservative perspectives from a neutral stance, John outlines his own position. Although he reiterates his opposition to interracial marriage, he is able to acknowledge its dark side. He admits that under the separatist banner there has been plenty of violence and conflict. However, these problems are, he argues, at least familiar. By contrast, in an effort to be fair to the other side, John writes that the modernist stance "might possibly lead to the ideal, peaceful society." However, he concludes, he is not willing to risk it. He prefers to side with the traditional perspective, the separatist stance, which "has withstood the test of time."

Given John's previous performance in this class, Fishman judged that his essay was, as I have said, a significant leap forward in terms of philosophic thinking. John had used analysis and synthesis to achieve some level of growth, an enriched and complexified view of himself. Fishman was also gratified by John's sympathetic consideration of both sides of the issue. However, he still wished John's student-curriculum integration had gone further, had taken him into new and challenging parts of the curriculum. He wished John had further explored ways to justify his being closed to interracial marriage while open to the gay and feminist movements. In other words, Fishman was sorry John missed the opportunity to explore philosophically why he believed people should be free to chose their sexual orientation and stance toward women but not their marriage partners. Had John been able, for example, to use class readings to contrast himself to someone like Dewey—someone who argues for more thoroughgoing open-mindedness—he might have made progress in understanding why he held back on this particular issue.

The Effects of Student-Curriculum Integration on John Lucas

In his term project essay, then, John was finally able to integrate student and curriculum: "The course clicked for me at last," he put it. By relying on Fishman's tapes, John was able use philosophy to explore the conflict which, he said, had "driven a wedge" between him and his best friend, Charlie. Charlie's dating of African American women had genuinely disturbed John, and, in his essay, John was able to think about this problem in new ways. Although this resulted in self-reconstruction for John, at the same time, it also, not surprisingly, left him much the same. In his post-semester interview—3 months after he graduated, and a few days before he joined the Navy—we hear both these strains.

John explained in our follow-up conversation that he now saw himself as a more complicated person. Although his essay did not cause him to alter his position on interracial marriage, he learned from writing his term project essay that his perspectives and allegiances are mixed. That is, instead of just having an opinion "and that's all there is to it," he now realized that behind his positions lay commitments which may cause him, in other situations, to align himself quite differently. "I learned in philosophy class that I'm complex," he told me, "that people have a main label, but most of us also have many sublabels."

However, despite John's new understanding of himself as a mix of sometimes contradictory perspectives, and despite his success sympathizing with the opposing position, he remained the subjective knower. That is, he continued to focus on his own views, little concerned about reading or taking in the perspectives of others. This is evidenced in his post-semester remarks about authority. John realized for the first time, in his essay, he said, that he could gain authority by constructing his own definitions of key terms. Referring to "John Lucas's meanings" for conservatism and modernism, he commented, "I didn't know you were allowed to do that." Specifying his own meanings for these terms, he told me, made him feel like "an authority," a person who could "lay things out and explain myself." Although John claims credit for his definitions, they are actually ones he borrowed from Fishman's tape. And, according to Fishman, that was all right. He was pleased John could at least apply these concepts to his own problem. Yet, once again, Fishman wished that John had recognized himself as part of an ongoing conversation, that he could have understood that his newly won authority was, as Dewey says of all learning, the result of a social process (*Experience and Education* 58).

FINDINGS ABOUT RECONCILING SYNTHESIS AND ANALYSIS

Reconciling Synthesis and Analysis Led to Student Self-Reconstruction and Enriched Experience

Looking back at the essay projects of Sean Wilson, Emily Parrish, and John Lucas, we see these students using the critical work of analysis and the constructive work of synthesis to philosophically explore personal problems. That is, we observe in these students' essays the interplay of stepping closer to something in order to clarify and define it and then stepping away in order to compare and group it with other things. And, judging from these students' experiences, I find that when the third dualism underlying student-curriculum tensions—construction and criticism (synthesis and analysis)—is successfully reconciled, it leads to integration of students' school and nonschool lives as well as to self-reconstruction.

We see this self-reconstruction most strongly in Sean, less so in Emily and John. Yet, as already noted, these sorts of changes in student self-image are crucial if we are to take seriously Dewey's educational aims. Because Sean, Emily, and John manage various levels of self-reconstructions, they understand not only themselves, but also their worlds, as more complicated, more filled with meaning and possibility. Fishman's emphasis on integrating construction and criticism, then, seems to move these students in the direction in which Fishman, following Dewey, wanted them to go. Their essays are rich experiences for them, apparently leaving them with increased capacity for rich experiences in the future.

Reconciling Synthesis and Analysis Led to Integration of Cognitive and Noncognitive Aspects of Intelligent Inquiry

In addition to promoting self-reconstruction and enriched student experience, these projects reveal the potential of synthesis and analysis to achieve another sort of reconciliation: the integration of thought's cognitive and non-cognitive factors. As Steve Fishman and I reflect on these students' term projects, what stands out for us is the excitement which colors the work of Sean and John. As they succeed with their constructive and critical thinking, they are buoyed by their progress. As noted above, this is especially surprising for John, because throughout most of the semester he had focused on grades, alternately trying to avoid finding out about them or trying to bolster them. Yet, at least for a few moments at the end of the course, John's sense of progress puts worry about grades into second place. For John, as for Sean, the philosophic essay seems to take on a life of its own, their experiences providing examples of students transforming what Dewey would call their *indirect* interest in the course into a *direct* one (*Interest* 38–41). That is, for Sean, John, and, to a lesser extent, Emily, their essays become more than just necessary requirements to pass the course; they become inherently valuable and emotionally meaningful. All three speak of their term project experiences in noncognitive terms, John calling it "inspiring," Sean "therapeutic," and Emily "important and satisfying."

These students' experiences show that integration of the emotional and intellectual dimensions of synthetic-analytic work is important for two reasons. First, they vitalize students' present experience. Second, they make these present experiences more accessible in the future, freeing them from the "watertight compartments" to which, Dewey fears, most school experiences are confined (*Experience and Education* 47–48). Thus, the reconciliation of synthesis and analysis goes hand in hand with the reconciliation of the other dualisms—continuity and interaction, interest and effort—underlying student-curriculum oppositions.

EVERY EXPERIENCE LIVES ON IN FURTHER EXPERIENCES. Hence the central problem of...education...is to select the kind of present experiences that live fruitfully and creatively in subsequent experiences.

— JOHN DEWEY,
Experience and Education 1938: 27-28

Chapter Eleven

STUDENTS' RESIDUES FOR FUTURE LEARNING

———— ✦ ————

Lucille McCarthy with Steve Fishman

I n this chapter, I focus on the residues students took from Steve Fishman's Introduction to Philosophy class, that is, their dispositions toward future learning. Evaluation of the deposit of an educational experience is crucial in any study informed by Deweyan theory, because, as we have explained, Dewey's aim for education is to provide students with rich experience which renders them capable of even richer experience (*Experience and Education* ch. 2). The test of Fishman's class, then, is its ability to generate student habits which promote enriched experience or continued learning and growth.

I base my conclusions on several sorts of data: students' end-of-term reflections, both written and oral, and, more important, their follow-up interviews the next semester. I conducted these on the telephone, conversing with each of my 12 focus students for between 30 and 90 minutes. Once again, however, I return to the five pupils I have featured in preceding chapters. These are focus students I chose in an effort to represent diversity of race, gender, major, and experiences within the course.

OPEN-MINDEDNESS AND CAREFUL LISTENING TO OPPOSING POSITIONS

Comments made by several focus students in their follow-up interviews centered on claims of increased openness and sensitivity to a variety of positions. And because open-mindedness is a hallmark of intelligent thinking for Dewey, it is also an important school residue. Dewey defines open-mindedness not as mere freedom from prejudice and partisanship, a passive stance which "hang[s] out a sign: 'Come right in; there is nobody at home.'" Rather, open-mindedness is an active "hospitality" to new ideas. It is, Dewey writes, an

> alert curiosity and spontaneous outreaching for the new.... an active desire to listen to more sides than one; to give heed to more sides than one;... to give full attention to alternative possibilities; and to recognize the possibility of error even in the beliefs that are dearest to us. (*How* 30–31)

In addition, this sort of active "outreaching for... alternative possibilities," Dewey cautions, requires an ability to tolerate doubt. He writes, "One can think reflectively only when one is willing to endure suspense and to undergo the trouble of searching" (*How* 16).

In post-semester interviews, John Lucas, Sean Wilson, and Ashley Posten all claimed that as a result of Fishman's course, they were more open-minded. John said that in writing his paper he learned to label alternative positions and sympathetically explore the strengths and weaknesses of each. And he retained an approach to the world, John later told me, that was open to complexities, to the notion that opposing positions likely have their own strong features.

Similarly, Sean Wilson described himself as developing an enhanced ability to tolerate disagreement. In an interview 3 months after Fishman's course concluded, Sean said he now looks at a problem from multiple perspectives rather than giving a simple answer. He is more accepting of difference and more prone to self-analysis. "I used to immediately judge people who disagreed with me. They were wrong, and I was right. What Philosophy class did for me was make me less impetuous, less self-righteous. I take in more information now before I decide, trying not to be so bound to my viewpoint that I block out other possible views."

When I asked Sean to provide an example of his new tolerance for difference—his willingness, in Dewey's terms, "to endure suspense and to undergo the trouble of searching" (*How* 16)—Sean illustrated with a non-school event. He had been dating, for the first time ever, a northerner, a young woman from Boston, who, he said, was altogether different from the sort of woman he was used to. She was independent and assertive, paying her own way (and sometimes his), even saying, when he interrupted her, "Please let me finish." Because Sean found that his usual "southern gentleman—man initiates everything" approach would not work in this situation, he "set [his] old ways aside." Instead of dismissing her immediately, he decided to slow down and gather more information. "I visited her family in Boston, and they were wonderful. We had nice times and good conversations. But because of our differences, I knew we had to end our relationship, so I dropped some hints, and, finally, we mutually agreed. I was more sensitive, better able to hear her, than I would have been before."

In response to Sean's comments, I found myself unable to believe a single course could make such a difference, so I pressed him. Sean assured me his new openness was indeed something he learned in Philosophy. As evidence, he reminded me that as the semester had progressed, he had not only listened better to his classmates, he had actually prodded them, insisting they articulate their viewpoints more clearly. He had played devil's advocate on a number of occasions, especially to those classmates he viewed as closed-minded or "just not thinking." He questioned them, he said, "so I could get different perspectives. I realized their views helped me understand myself." Sean concluded our post-semester interview claiming, "All in all, Philosophy class made an important deposit into my mental well-being."

In addition to John Lucas and Sean Wilson, a third student, Ashley Posten, also described a residue of open-mindedness. In her follow-up interview 4 months after the semester ended, Ashley claimed she too had learned in Intro "a new way of arguing," explaining, "I learned to critique my own position as well as see arguments for other ones." She is particularly aware of this new openness, she said, because it contrasts so sharply with the closed-mindedness she grew up with. In her small hometown in Ohio, "if anyone was different, people wrote them off. 'Ignore them,' I was always told." By contrast, Ashley explained,

> in philosophy class, people told *why* they held their view, and they also explained its shortcomings.... Our class had to learn to do that, though; we didn't start out that way. In the beginning we just argued, saying this is the way it is, and nothing is changing me. Then people began looking into the other sides, questioning more, understanding where others are coming from. We might not change our views, but we listened and saw where they were coming from.

As proof of her increased open-mindedness, Ashley offered two personal examples. First, she told me, she had observed this attitude in a recent academic situation. In her Small Group Communications class, she and three others collaborated to solve an assigned problem and then coauthored a paper describing their work. Although it was not her job to write the group's solution, she told the person who was doing that to "explain our conclusion, but be sure you also state other possibilities and the reasons for them. Admit there are problems with our solution, but that, all in all, we think it's best."

Second, Ashley saw signs of increased openness in her nonschool life, specifically in her changed attitude toward homosexuals. Recalling a heated discussion in Intro, she said a classmate's comments "really opened my mind—changed my mind basically." That classmate, a young woman named Kellie McManus, spoke about her gay friends and described their struggles against discrimination. Kellie's sympathy with their predicament contrasted starkly with sentiments Ashley herself voiced; this juxtaposition was, according to Ashley, a powerful force for reconstruction. She explained, "My exchange with Kellie made me understand that my negative feelings were the result of my social conditioning." Ashley is now, she claimed, more open to friendships with gay women, more likely to see her similarities with them rather than their differences.

SELF-DISCIPLINE AND INITIATIVE

When I urged Ashley to reflect further on how she gained this increased openness—what Dewey would call an "active desire to listen to more sides than one" (*How* 30)—she said it was by practicing it in class situations like the one above. She recalled that Fishman explicitly described this method, telling the class before the midterm, for example, that "a good essay answer will show sensitivity to both sides." But even more important was his "letting us practice it in our own way." This led, Ashley claimed, to self-discipline and the sense she controlled her own learning. She explained,

> I knew Dr. Fishman expected certain things, but I had control of what I did with those things. It was up to me to *use* what he expected. This meant I had to take a position and really understand it.... My friend recently asked me about Fishman's course, if she should take it. I told her it's more work, but it's also more interesting. You have to listen to others' arguments and try to get something from them whether you agree or disagree. It's not just cram for the test, regurgitate, and forget it. You have to be active, take responsibility for your views.

Ultimately, Ashley said, the practice she got in Intro constructing and supporting her positions gave her new confidence when confronted with texts. She realized, she told me, "I was in control of the meanings I made." In Chapter 9, we witnessed Ashley's struggle to interpret Bertrand Russell's *Marriage and Morals* in her letter exchange with Demika Braxton. This sort of analytic-synthetic work, along with frequent opportunities to compare her interpretations to her classmates, she said, "helped me understand that people relate to texts in various ways depending on their life concerns." Ashley concluded, "Literature used to scare me, like in high school where the teacher interpreted every word. I now realize I can relate to a text, I can construct my own view. This is because I could never say, in Fishman's class, 'I don't get it.' I always had to try."

Ashley's sense of control over meaning construction, her ability to develop her own position after comprehending the views of others, is another hallmark—along with open-mindedness—of what Dewey would call intelligent reflection. It is the sort of pupil self-direction, he argues, that is missing from traditional education (see *How* 17; 86–87). Ashley's comments suggest that part of the residue she has taken from Fishman's class is a sense of what that self-control and initiative feels like. It is something she recommends to her friend as a worthy experience.

Demika Braxton, the junior medical technology major who, like Ashley, played a prominent role in Chapters 8 and 9, also reported new habits of self-discipline and initiative. Demika thrived, as I have shown, with Fishman's indirect pedagogy. As she played the roles of teacher and student to her classmates, articulating her own views and listening to theirs, she experienced the joys of active learning, and her self-confidence increased significantly. Demika recalled in her follow-up interview, "I was proud when I helped others think about the reading or about their own issues." She also realized she learned more when she was "involved" in a class than when she took notes and let her mind wander. She now tries to participate in her classes, she told me, to take a hand in directing her own learning. And, she claimed, she had developed "study habits" in Fishman's class, which were helping her do this.

When I pushed Demika to provide examples of this new self-discipline, she described her experiences in an upper division English course, Mythology, in which she was currently enrolled. Because she wanted to be actively involved in that class, she read the assignments carefully. "How in the world," she asked rhetorically, "can you have a discussion if you have not read the material?" In Fishman's class, she said, she had gotten into the habit of reading because she *had* to. "In Intro," she explained,

> there was no way to hide.... In a lot of classes, you can avoid the homework, sit in the back of the class, and get away without saying a word. In Dr. Fishman's class, that was not an option, and if you tried it, you would be embarrassed. Or you'd let your classmates down. I learned I *had* to prepare for class, and I liked being able to join the discussion. And when Dr. Fishman got excited about a point I was trying to make, it pumped me up. It made me want to think better.

Because Demika prepared for Mythology and participated in class discussion, her experiences contrasted sharply with those of her friend Melissa. "Melissa doesn't do the reading, so she is very lost," Demika remarked. "She tells me she's bored, but that's because she never contributes anything. In fact, the other day she couldn't even take the quiz." By contrast, Demika was doing well on the quizzes, but, more important, she took initiative in class discussions and even, at times, a leadership role. In Mythology class, then, Demika no longer depended solely upon the teacher to tell her what to do. Building on her experiences in Fishman's course, she was finding that her academic tasks were more self-imposed.

INTELLECTUAL RESPONSIBILITY AND COURAGE

Demika's new habits of self-discipline and initiative led, as I have just shown, to an increased capacity for active learning. And this was connected to residues that I observed of two additional character traits, attitudes Dewey also wanted for students: responsibility and courage. According to Dewey, students may explore ideas, but if their inquiries are to be "intellectually responsible," they must do more than simply articulate their own and others' views. They must also be willing to consider the consequences of their positions and adopt these consequences "when they follow reasonably" (*How* 32). That is, responsible students ask about "the *meaning* of what they learn, in the sense of what difference it makes to the rest of their beliefs and to their actions" (*How* 33). Both Demika and Emily Parrish, to whom I turn next, demonstrate intellectual responsibility as well as the courage it sometimes requires.

As Demika interacted with her classmates in Intro to Philosophy, this shy, African American newcomer to UNCC became increasingly self-confident. By semester's end, she could successfully articulate and defend her positions—even when they were unpopular. In fact, she said she enjoyed doing so. She recalled: "Dr. Fishman and the others always made it seem like the points I was making were good ones. They encouraged me. Now I'm not afraid to say my view and stick to my guns, even if it means I stand alone." I questioned Demika about this claim, pressing her for evidence, for incidents in which she had actually stood up for her beliefs and carried though on them in ways Dewey would deem responsible. She offered two examples, one from outside school, and another from inside, once again from her Mythology class.

The first incident occurred in her gospel choir, a singing and Bible study group, in which interpersonal conflicts had recently made cooperation difficult. Choir members agreed to a "rap session" to clear the air, but, according to Demika, people were reluctant to speak. She, however, summoned her courage and spoke about Christian ideals and choir members' behavior, which, at the moment, were at odds. Everyone agreed, she said, and her willingness to speak up initiated additional conversations.

But speaking up in choir was easy, Demika assured me, compared to the courage it took in Mythology. Prior to her experiences in Intro to Philosophy, she would never have disagreed with a teacher and especially not about religion. "I would have been afraid I was wrong or that I'd offend someone. Philosophy made me realize that people do disagree, but that's okay." So when Demika's Mythology teacher said that much of religion is story or myth, Demika felt compelled to raise her hand. "I told her I disagreed, that I believe that some things in the Bible actually did happen, like Moses and the Flood. But nobody knows who wrote it, so it comes down to faith." Although Demika's teacher continued to maintain that "all religions are stories," she listened to Demika and "respected" her point of view. And once again, Demika reported, others followed her lead and joined the discussion, some supporting her position, some not.

Demika Braxton was not the only student whose residue pointed to increased intellectual responsibility and courage. We also hear it in the post-semester interview of senior political science major, Emily Parrish. Emily too said she was more self-confident as a result of her experiences in Intro to Philosophy, and this translated, she claimed, into speaking and acting in accord with her beliefs. Not surprisingly, one arena in which Emily demonstrated this integrity was women's issues. In nonschool situations, she commented, "I seem to hear more discussions about women than I used to, and when people make derogatory comments, I'm more vocal. I tell them 'That's not fair.'" By confronting sexist comments, Emily was acting upon her beliefs in ways Dewey would deem intellectually responsible. That is, she was cognizant of "the *meaning* of what [she had] learned," its logical consequences for "the rest of [her] beliefs and...actions" (*How* 33).

In school situations as well, Emily reported new habits of self-confidence and courage that resembled Demika's. Emily too had blossomed in the welcoming climate of Intro to Philosophy, becoming increasingly "comfortable" speaking up. Contributing to class discussion prepared her, she said, for the senior course in political science which she was taking that semester. Although it was taught by an "intimidating" professor, Emily found herself "less nervous...and able to come forward" when the teacher invited participation. She concluded our post-semester interview by saying, "I wish I had more classes where I could talk." Although Emily did not use these terms, she seemed to appreciate the opportunity to be self-directing and intellectually responsible. She appeared to value the person she was becoming.

In this chapter, I have focused on student progress with regard to personal attitudes and moral traits of character, dispositions Dewey believes are crucial to intelligent thinking and students' ongoing education. Given his assumption that our world is constantly changing, Dewey is—as he indicates with the title of his widely read methods book for teachers, *How We Think*—more concerned about *how* students think than about *what* they think. Although students' personal character traits are not easy to chart, and although we obviously cannot predict with certainty the development of these traits for any of Steve Fishman's students, we agree with Dewey that these "collateral" aspects of learning are of utmost importance (*Experience and Education* 48). And the fact that students' follow-up assessments of

Fishman's class generally focused on habits and attitudes rather than on specific information suggests they are important to students as well.

This does not mean that Dewey ignored pupils' need to become familiar with the knowledge and values of their culture (see *Democracy* 1–9). In fact, as Fishman discusses in Part I of this book, Dewey's efforts to integrate student and curriculum are aimed at helping students use and, as a result, master new "facts and principles" as well as "new fields of subject-matter" (*Way* 31). However, the purpose for Dewey of such mastery is preparation for future adjustment, and this means continual attention to the habits of good thinking, habits which are as much emotional, moral, and practical, in his view, as they are cognitive and theoretical.

As if to underline the moral and practical aspects of these habits, Dewey frequently uses the term intelligent *inquiry* rather than intelligent *thinking* (see *How* 12–16). He does this to suggest that successful reflection involves action rather than simply armchair speculation. Dewey, very much in the pragmatic tradition, holds that the meaning of an idea is its impact upon behavior. And this is why habits of open-mindedness, self-discipline, responsibility, and courage are so important for his vision of inquiry. Thus, to the extent Fishman's students left his class having practiced these habits, Intro to Philosophy helped them deepen traits of character Dewey hopes all school situations will promote.

IN A WORLD THAT HAS SO LARGELY ENGAGED in a mad and often brutally harsh race for material gain by means of ruthless competition, it behooves the school to make ceaseless and intelligently organized effort to develop above all else the will for co-operation and the spirit which sees in every other individual one who has an equal right to share in the cultural and material fruits of collective human invention. . . .

— JOHN DEWEY,
"The Need for a Philosophy of Education" 1934: 13

CONCLUSION

DEWEY'S RELEVANCE
TO CONTEMPORARY
EDUCATION

———————— ✧ ————————

Steve Fishman and Lucille McCarthy

I n this closing section, we circle back to our opening question, Why Dewey now? Our study points to a three-part answer. First, Dewey's ideas are relevant to contemporary criticisms leveled at public education. Second, his ideas are feasible as well as effective in promoting teacher development, and, third, they are feasible and effective in promoting student learning.

THE PRESENT EDUCATIONAL CLIMATE

We live in a time of extraordinary attention to teacher performance, a scrutiny coming from both within and without our educational institutions.

Although America's public, locally controlled schools have been the focus of considerable citizen debate ever since their inception in the 1860s, they enjoyed general support from the turn of the century through the World War II period. Since that time, however, they have been the object of a growing chorus of criticism. At best we now see them as helping individuals get a piece of the "success pie" and, at worst, as mirroring our culture's deterioration, its inability to stem the rise of poverty and despair.

This chorus of pessimism comes from across the political spectrum. On the Right, numerous conservatives argue that public school teachers do too much. As long as they stick to the three Rs, these conservatives claim, teachers are fine, but once they attempt to speak about morally or politically sensitive issues, they cannot be trusted. By contrast, liberal theorists on the Left frequently argue that insofar as teachers encourage mastery of standard English or academic prose, they do too little. These theorists claim that in failing to show students how to resist the dominant language and practices of our culture, teachers simply reproduce its repressive ways.

RESTORING A CONCERN FOR COMMUNITY

In this climate of widespread disappointment in American education, John Dewey's philosophy offers a reasonable starting point for reconstruction. He provides what we consider a more balanced and, therefore, badly needed alternative to conservative and liberal approaches. For despite their differences, spokespeople on the Right and Left often share the same vision of schooling's mission, namely, to prepare students for professional and commercial competition. That is, they frequently have a common conception of human nature and individual liberty, both ends of the political spectrum seeing freedom as "freedom from." Many conservatives want freedom from government interference with economic competition, and many liberals want freedom from racial, ethnic, and gender prejudices which unjustly restrict such competition. Yet despite their different views of what constitutes a fair playing field or marketplace, these conservatives and liberals are alike in stressing individual independence and personal striving, supporting the dominant "don't-tread-on-me" ethos of our time. Naturally, this same ethos is reflected in our schools. For the most part, students compete for individual grades and honors while doing their homework alone in their homes and their classwork alone at school.

Although Dewey grants the importance of personal liberty, he also recognizes the need to balance this emphasis with concern for community.

In his view, historians and philosophers have described the rise of individual liberty in narrow and misleading ways. According to Dewey, Enlightenment reformers could successfully fight for personal rights because they themselves lived in a world with strong family, religious, and occupational ties. In an effort to change the existing order, reformers stressed the idea of individual independence but conveniently ignored their own reliance on communal cooperation. This led to a view of human nature as self-sufficient, a view which, Dewey claims, is more fiction than reality. Insofar as subsequent generations have taken this fiction too seriously, they have fostered an exaggerated notion of personal independence.

We see Dewey's resistance to these claims about personal independence as a possible first step out of our present educational morass. As numerous conservatives struggle to protect their piece of the pie, and as many liberals struggle to help the disadvantaged gain theirs, both groups only reinforce our dominant individualistic creed. They both favor competition at the cost of cooperation, independence at the cost of dependence, and professional mobility at the cost of communal allegiance. In strong opposition, Dewey works to balance these dualisms, unwilling to sacrifice either component. Although he certainly takes individual rights seriously, wanting schools to stress personal initiative and creativity, he also believes schools have an obligation to help students develop what he considers their natural ability to cooperate with one another. He would argue that the world for which many conservatives and liberals want to prepare students no longer exists, that although their notion of individuality may have been appropriate for a frontier America, it is inappropriate for a highly technologic and interdependent America.

Behind Dewey's ideology and his approach to education is a view of human nature starkly different from the one often shared by both right- and left-wing theorists. Whereas for the latter two, individuals are primarily self-interested, rational agents, always acting to maximize personal advantage, Dewey, by contrast, believes we have a natural tendency to connect with others, "to give out, to do, and to serve" ("Ethical" 119; *Experience and Education* 55). This leads him to take a different approach to education, one which stresses the importance of learning to get along with others, not just as part of a do-gooder's hope for some distant utopian democracy, but because cooperation actually satisfies a deep-seated human need. This, we believe, accounts for Dewey's confidence that schools more focused on the habits of cooperative living will, in the long run, and with proper teacher training and development, be successful.

PROMOTING TEACHER DEVELOPMENT THROUGH CLASSROOM RESEARCH

When we look closely at our study, we believe it provides support, not only for Dewey's relevance to contemporary education's problems, but also for the feasibility of his recommendations about teacher research. First, we conduct the sort of qualitative investigation which Dewey believes most appropriate for classrooms, given their multiple and ever shifting variables. Second, as Dewey would also have wanted, our work is designed, carried out, and assessed with the classroom teacher involved at every stage. Finally, our study provides evidence of Dewey's claim that teacher research is effective in promoting teacher empowerment and development. As we have seen, Steve Fishman's classroom research energizes his teaching. He finds it makes his classes more of a two-way street. He is now able to give his students more energy, and, because of their cooperation with his classroom inquiries, students give him more energy in return. Our study also shows that Fishman has become, as Dewey would have wanted, a more astute observer and judge in his own classroom as well as a practitioner more sensitive to educational theory. And just as important in Dewey's terms, Fishman's classroom inquiries have given him community with other researchers with whom he can share as well as test the results of his investigations.

We believe Fishman's case is instructive because when, in 1983, he began examining his classroom more seriously, he was in a situation typical for many teachers across the grades. As he recounts in Chapter 6, after more than 15 years working in the same institution, he was bored and frustrated. And like many school practitioners, he had had no training in classroom research. Yet once initiated into teacher research, Fishman—although still at the same university and still teaching many of the same courses—began to approach his classroom with new purpose.

This emphasis by Dewey on promoting teacher development through classroom research is, we believe, an overlooked aspect of his educational strategy. And given our culture's exaggerated emphasis on independence, it is particularly timely. The world of instruction can be isolating, and thus, for Dewey, shared teacher research helps overcome our culture's stress on independence, an overemphasis Dewey calls "an unnamed form of insanity" (*Democracy* 44). But not only does shared teacher research help us overcome our isolation, it also affords us the opportunity to experience the very sort of cooperative, intelligent inquiry which Dewey urges us to teach our students. After all, how can we wholeheartedly encourage our students to work together on conjoint projects if, in a highly competitive and individualistic world, we ourselves have never experienced the benefits of such work?

Dewey's stress on teacher inquiry is an attempt not only to dissolve barriers separating teacher from teacher, but also to break down what Dewey considers a false dualism between educational theory and educational practice. And this barrier is as big an impediment to teacher empowerment and development today as it was in Dewey's time. As we compose this conclusion, we note in the *Chronicle of Higher Education* a call for just this sort of separation at the university level. In a well-intentioned piece, the author suggests we meet new demands for teaching competency by separating American institutions of higher education into those which teach and those which do research (Atwell). From a Deweyan perspective, this would be a disaster, promoting the sort of either-or distinctions he most abhorred. In this case, it would reproduce the ill effects of a similar rupture at lower levels—where principals and superintendents dictate research-based curricula and pedagogy to faculty from whom they solicit little input or advice. And because such watertight compartments diminish both research and practice, Dewey consistently urges that teachers do both.

Despite Dewey's (and our own) commitment to teacher research, however, we want to avoid overly large claims. That is, we have little ground for arguing that if teachers join with peers to share their research they will, by themselves, save America's public schools. We recognize that state legislators, politically appointed superintendents, local school boards, and parents' organizations wield enormous influence. We also acknowledge that since the establishment of free public education in America, countless reform movements have come and gone. Nevertheless, teachers have always been a crucial part of the educational equation, and we think it reasonable to expect that teachers actively engaged in classroom research would present a more informed and respected voice in ongoing debates about our nation's schools.

PROMOTING STUDENT LEARNING THROUGH INDIRECT PEDAGOGY

As we remarked in the Introduction to this book, the practicability of Dewey's educational vision has been questioned ever since the founding of his Laboratory School at the end of the 19th century. Our study reveals, however, that Fishman was able to enact not only a Deweyan approach to teacher research but also a Deweyan approach to teacher practice in an ordinary public classroom. Specifically, our study demonstrates the feasibility of integrating student and curriculum in Dewey's indirect fashion. As we saw, Fishman succeeded in helping at least some of his students use the curriculum to clarify their own problems and reach personally significant goals. In addition, our study shows the feasibility of setting classroom conditions in which a teacher can promote the moral traits of character Dewey thought just as essential to student learning as cognitive skills.

Student-Curriculum Integration

Fishman found that Dewey's pedagogical principles were more effective in achieving student-curriculum integration than anything he had previously tried. His indirect approach enabled both Sean Wilson and Emily Parrish, for example, to see the curriculum as a means for achieving personal ends. Sean was able to use philosophic texts, questions, and categories to see a vitally important personal problem—his mother's alcoholism—in new ways. He reconstructed himself and other family members in a fashion which enriched his experience of them, affording him new opportunities for reconciliation. Emily Parrish worked in similar ways in her correspondence with Warren Murray, using class texts to explore what she considered unfair treatment and stereotypes of women. And both students then took the next step, the one Dewey hopes for. Sean and Emily were able to turn their *indirect* interest in the curriculum—their view of it as merely an instrument to achieve their own goals—to what Dewey calls a *direct* interest. That is, Sean developed a desire to learn about Dewey's philosophy and Emily became interested in reading more about feminist issues.

Moral Traits of Character

In addition to promoting student-curriculum integration, Fishman's use of Dewey's indirect pedagogy was also effective in encouraging Deweyan moral traits of character. Although we grant it is hard to measure traits like whole-heartedness, cooperativeness, and responsibility, our data show these are detectable, manifest in both student work and behavior. For example, in letters exchanged by Demika Braxton and Ashley Posten we saw the sort of student cooperation Dewey highly values. Both Demika and Ashley worked hard, devoting extraordinary attention to their cooperative effort to clarify a difficult text. These students' cooperation offered them, in Dewey's view, an important counterbalance to America's overemphasis on competition and independence. Demika's and Ashley's experience with cooperative inquiry, moreover, was not just a flash in the pan. As their follow-up interviews indicate, they took with them a residue from the course which continues to influence the sorts of students they are, the sorts of persons they are becoming.

In conclusion, we believe Dewey's persistent refusal to accept either-or choices makes his philosophy a timely and potentially effective one in the present educational climate. His insistence on reconciliation—of individual and community, research and teaching, student and curriculum, as well as cognitive skills and moral traits of character—makes his approach a worthy centerpiece for the slow, piecemeal work of educational reconstruction. If our study makes a small contribution to this large, necessary, and ongoing enterprise, we will have achieved our purpose.

APPENDIX A

Introduction to Philosophy "Class Reflection Log"

❖

CRL Questions

Fishman handed a question to students at the end of most class periods, asking them to answer at home. He collected their responses three times during the semester, reading and commenting on them, giving credit but no grade. There was no length requirement.

CRL #1
In reflecting on today's class (our first class meeting, Thursday, August 24, 1995), which classmate's comments had the most weight for you? What was it about his or her comments which gave them this weight?

Also reflecting on today's class, did you learn anything as you listened to your classmates' remarks? If so, what did you learn and from whom?

CRL #2
What must happen in Philosophy 2101 for you to call the class a success? In other words, ideally, this coming December, as you look back on our class, what would you hope has transpired for you?

What about Fishman? What do you think he hopes will happen in 2101?

CRL #3
Please describe and evaluate your letter exchange experience during our second week of class.

Which aspects were difficult? Did you learn more about Plato's two dialogues than you might have if you had just read the two dialogues and taken your own notes? Any suggestions about how such letter exchanges might be improved?

CRL #4

Compare the letter exchange and study questions. Which helped you learn more about the assigned texts? Please provide some details.

(For those who added late and did not participate in the letter exchange, please comment on the effectiveness of the study questions as aids to your reading.)

CRL #5

What have you learned in the class so far, and how have you learned it?

CRL#6

Please comment on today's work in your small group. Were people cooperative? Did anyone help you? In turn, did you help anyone else? Please give an example of a challenge your group faced and how your group dealt with it.

In your view, should this small-group work continue? Why or why not?

CRL #7 and #8

With regard to the assigned readings in 2101, how much time do you estimate you spend each week in completing the readings? Is there any one place where you do these readings? If so, please describe it.

Do you take notes? Specifically, do you use a highlighter or make an outline while reading? Do you summarize after completing a reading or use any other techniques to help you with your reading?

Do you read just enough to answer study questions and complete letter exchanges, or do you read the entire text through before beginning the written work called for by the assignment?

Have you read any of the texts more than once? If so, which ones and why?

Finally, how successful has your reading of the assigned texts been? Which texts have you understood best? Which texts have you understood least? What might you do to improve your reading compehension in the future?

CRL #9

Reflect on the last two class periods, when we discussed Carol Christ and Starhawk.
    a) What was said about women during these classes which you particularly
       remember or found striking?
    b) Did anything that was said lead you to understand or see women a
       little differently?

CRL #10

    (a) As you complete your preparation and writing for your first philosophy
        exam, and as you finish our first unit dealing with the soul/body and
        God/Goddess distinctions, do you feel part of the classroom group? In
        which ways yes? In which ways no?
    (b) At this time do you feel common ties with those philosophers who have
        come before you—Plato, Spelman, Holmes, Darrow, Christ, etc.? That

is, do you feel any common bond with those who ask about the nature of men and women, the structure of the world, the essence of knowledge and the good life? In which ways yes? In which ways no?

CRL#11
Please reflect on our recent in-class exam.
   a) What sort of questions did you expect; that is, did the exam questions surprise you in anyway?
   b) How much time did you spend preparing for the exam? What helped you most in your exam preparation? Do you feel you learned anything by getting ready for the exam? Please explain.
   c) What, if anything, did you learn by taking the exam?
   d) How do you feel about your exam grade?

CRL # 12
   a) What responses from the teacher to your recitations in class or to your writing do you particularly remember? What effect did these have on you?
   b) What responses from your peers to your oral or written communications do you particularly remember? What were their effects on you?

CRL # 13
   a) Please choose another class you are taking this semester and compare it to Philosophy 2101 in terms of teaching style, interaction with classmates and teacher, reading, and writing.
   b) Compare the two classes in terms of how you figured out how to do well. Please be specific about the things which have helped you figure it out in each class.

CRL # 14
   (a) Describe the characteristics of your ideal of femininity.
   (b) Describe the characteristics of your ideal of masculinity.
   (c) Which person or persons—someone you know or someone you've never met (fictional, historical, popular culture, etc.)—best approximates the ideal of femininity you describe above in (a).
   (d) Which person or persons—someone you know or someone you have not met—best approximates the ideal of masculinity you describe above in (b).
   (e) From our class discussions, how do your views of femininity and masculinity seem to compare with the views of your classmates?

CRL # 15
(*Please answer this CRL in the next few days. Otherwise I will not get an accurate sense of your thinking at this point.*)

The first draft of your term paper is due one week from today. What are the biggest challenges you face at this point in the writing process?

CRL # 16
a) What is the highest level of education of your parents, and what do they do in life?
b) If your parents were to sit in on our philosophy class discussions, what do you think their reactions would be?

CRL # 17
a) Fishman gives daily assignments and has a strict attendance policy. In which ways have these helped you? In which ways have they not been helpful?
b) Are these requirements typical or not in your other college classes?
c) What do you think Fishman's motives are in running the class this way?
d) How would the class be different if he simply required a midterm exam, a final exam, and a term paper?

CRL #18
This past Tuesday (Nov. 7) we did a freewrite in which you related a philosophy text with your partner's rough draft for their term paper.
a) What, if anything, did you learn from that freewrite and the subsequent class discussion?
b) Will this past Tuesday's class help you be a better respondent to your term paper partner when you meet this coming Tuesday (Nov. 14)?

CRL #19
In this class, Fishman has often asked you to discuss and share answers to response questions, freewrites, letters, and drafts with other students. Please describe how this has worked for you. Please describe one or two interactions you particularly remember.

CRL #20
How has this class affected your self-confidence as a learner? What elements in the class—teacher, classmates, texts, writing assignments, and so on—have influenced this?

CRL #21
Pick one text or class discussion or writing assignment you feel you are most likely to remember a year from now. Please describe it and tell why it has meaning for you.

CRL #22
(a) Has this class caused you to alter or see in new ways any of your views?
(b) Has this class caused you to become more open-minded in any way?

APPENDIX B

McCarthy's Memo to Focus Students About Think-Alouds

✦

Lucille McCarthy

To: Fellow Researchers
From: Dr. McCarthy
Re: Tape-Recording Your Writing and Reflections in Philosophy
Date: September 7, 1995

Thank you for agreeing to join me in studying your experiences in philosophy this semester. I'll summarize here what I mentioned to you on the phone, but please feel free to call me collect if you have questions.

When to Turn on the Tape Recorder and What to Say
1. When you are writing anything for this class (study questions, questions for group, CRL's, drafts of paper, notes on reading, classnotes, etc.) Please try to speak aloud during writing, tracking your decision making, describing where you get stuck, how you get out of trouble, how you decide to structure the piece, and so forth. In addition to your *thinking*, I am also interested in your *feelings* (frustration, boredom, mind wandering, excitement, understanding, etc.) Please talk also about your *social* situation when relevant (where you write, TV on, interruptions by phone, kids, roommates, getting up to get a snack, etc.) In other words, I am interested in a *movie of your mind and body* during writing. Please be detailed and honest.

2. During and after reading. Please tell me about your reading of various texts during or soon after you finish. As with your composing, describe your think-

ing, feeling, and social situation and interactions. Again, I'm interested in your problems and challenges as well as your successes. Please be detailed and honest.

3. Please also turn on the tape to reflect for a few minutes on what you particularly remember from the previous class. What struck you? What did you learn and why (or fail to learn?) What helped you (or failed to help?): other students, the teacher, some reading or writing you or someone else did, and so on? What frustrated, angered, pleased, excited, embarrassed you? Again, there are no right answers here; my goal is to experience the class from your point of view. Please be detailed and honest.

Each time you speak into the tape, please begin by telling me the date and assignment that you are working on. If you are reflecting on a class, please tell me the date of that class. In other words, be sure I know what you are composing, reading, or commenting on.

Taping Log
Please keep a log where you note the date and subject of each taping so I also have a visual record of what is on your tapes.

My Meetings with You
I will meet with you on each of my visits to UNCC this fall in order to talk further with you about your experiences in Introduction to Philosophy. I will collect your tapes and logs at the end of the semester. Please keep receipts of anything you spend for this work, and I will reimburse you. Again, thanks a million.

APPENDIX C

Fishman's Final Letter Exchange Assignment

Steve Fishman

Each of the semester's four letter exchanges took two class days. On the first, students traded letters with a randomly assigned classmate in which they posed a question about the assigned text. On the second, they brought a response to their partner's question. Fishman assigned these letters on the longer course readings—Plato's *Apology* and *Crito*, Bertrand Russell's *Marriage and Morals*, and Dewey's *Reconstruction in Philosophy*, chapter 1 and chapter 2—believing this 2-day exchange provided students a larger arena in which to explore their confusions. And he used them as the basis for class discussion. On December 5, for example, he began by asking students to read a neighbor's question letter about *Reconstruction*, chapter 1 and compare it with their own in a 10-minute freewrite. Class discussion then drew upon students' reports of the differences and similarities they identified. The December 7 discussion, which we describe in Chapter 8 of this volume, also centered around an initial freewrite. Because students were required to type their letters and, therefore, could not compose them in class, they could retain and refer to them until the end of the period. At the close of class students handed their letters to one another with a copy to Fishman.

The final letter exchange on December 5 and 7, 1995, focused on chapter 1 of Dewey's *Reconstruction in Philosophy*. (Students had worked with chapter 2 in the previous letter exchange five weeks earlier.) The assignment Fishman handed to his students on Thursday, November 30, read as follows:

ASSIGNMENTS 20 AND 21 – EXCHANGE LETTERS

All exchange letters are to be typed. Two copies of your letters are due on Tuesday, December 5 and Thursday, December 7.

Your Question Letter: Please read chapter 1 of Dewey's *Reconstruction in Philosophy* and write a one- to two-page letter to a classmate describing some aspect of this chapter that you have are having trouble understanding—a specific area you are having difficulty interpreting or fully comprehending. Please refer to specific passages in Dewey's text. Indicate what you do understand and what you do not understand. In other words, you should provide a context so your reader can see your difficulties and thereby give you some assistance.

This final reading of the semester brings us full circle to questions we faced at the beginning of the term when we read Plato's account of Socrates' trial. In chapter 1, Dewey provides an historical account of the trial and concludes with a discussion of his own definition of philosophy, its method and subject matter.

Your Response Letter: For Thursday, December 7, write a one- to two-page letter in response to the inquiry you received from a classmate on Tuesday. Please suggest possible answers to your classmate's question and raise any other issues which you believe are relevant to her or his questions.

Fishman marked the letters, as he did all the homework assignments (22 in total), with *high pass*, *low pass*, and *pass*, often commenting briefly in the margins and at the top. Because his goal for the letter assignment was to get students to probe difficult and unfamiliar texts, he gave high passes to those students he believed had actually struggled with them, as evidenced by good questions or helpful answers for their correspondent.

APPENDIX D

Fishman's Instructions Regarding the Term Project Essay

❖

Steve Fishman

October 19, 1995

Dear 2101 Students,

What follows are some ideas and suggestions about the term paper, the draft of which is due for class on Thursday, November 2. Please remember to bring *two* typed copies of your draft to class that day, one for your partner, one for me. Also, please keep in mind that prior to November 9, you will need to put a properly labeled *audiocasette tape* in your folder so I can respond to your draft over the weekend of November 11–12.

As I indicate on this semester's syllabus, your term paper should be about a conflict you care about. But it should not be a trivial conflict, like what to eat for dinner or whether to pay your rent, but a conflict about which you can see various "sides" or points of view. To make your paper philosophic, to engage in what Hallman refers to as "meditative" thinking, you will need to explore those different sides or points of view by examining their different assumptions. That is, as you look at different ways of seeing the conflict you care about, you want to ask what different assumptions lie behind these different points of view. Specifically, what different assumptions do they make about the world, about human nature, about the ideal life, about what we know or the limits of knowledge?

For example, in the Edwards and Pap text, we see that Bishop William Paley and Clarence Darrow come to very different conclusions about the existence of God. A philosophic way to look at their conflict is to ask, What different basic assumptions stand behind their different conclusions and points of view? We might note that Darrow acknowledges that the world has regularity (such as in the law of gravity) but denies that the world has a creator's design or purpose. Paley also recognizes regularity. In fact, he thinks the world is quite wondrous as a mechanically sophisticated sort of machine. But Paley finds a creator's design, whereas Darrow does not. Why do they come to such different conclusions?

We might explore the idea that Darrow believes that regularity can come about from random forces. He accepts evolution and believes that if it goes on long enough, a variety of adjustments will take place. Paley conceives of evolution quite differently. He assumes the world is much younger than does Darrow, and so Paley looks for failed evolutionary experiments and, finding none, concludes that evolution must be a false doctrine. There must be a creator.

In addition, Paley and Darrow seem to have different assumptions about human nature. Paley seems to believe that without God and the possibility of an afterlife, earthly life would have no meaning. It would seem like thin soup, too transient, perhaps, with too little to show for it. By contrast, Darrow assumes that people can supply their own meaning for life, that earthly life has meaning in itself even if it isn't a *means* to another sort of (spiritual) existence. Developing the contrast between Paley and Darrow in a philosophic way (as opposed to a more historical or psychological or religious studies sort of way) would mean pursuing the differences in their assumptions and trying to back up our speculations about their assumptions by appealing to their texts.

I offer these comments about Paley and Darrow only to illustrate what I see as meditative thinking (to borrow Hallman's phrase) or philosophic inquiry. Rather than urging you to work on the conflict between thinkers like Paley and Darrow, I much prefer that you explore a conflict which is important in your life and which you care about. As an aid, I offer some suggestions drawing upon student papers from past semesters.

1. A few years ago, a young woman from Charlotte wrote about her parents, who were drug dealers. Her conflict had to do with whether she should turn them over to the police. She considered the pros and cons of yes and no answers, examining the assumptions behind them. She decided that the issue had to do with how to rank order her different responsibilities—to her family and to her society. She saw analogies between her dilemma and Socrates'— should Socrates worry about his family or should he put his community first? She also realized that there were different assumptions she could make about what it means to respect her parents. The Ten Commandments say we should respect our parents. But how should she interpret this? Would it be more respectful to ignore what they were doing (and in this way respect their wishes since they obviously did not want to go to jail)? Or would it be more respectful to honor them by taking their lives seriously and trying to reform them, even if it took sending them to prison?

2. A number of students in past years have written about conflicts over career choices. In such cases, I have urged them to examine the different

assumptions behind these possible choices. What sorts of views of the good life stand behind choosing business over teaching or choosing the ministry over professional sports? What sorts of assumptions about human nature and the purpose of career lie behind these different possible choices? If some careers promise considerable travel or financial compensation, what do these choices say about the importance of money and glamor versus staying home with family or between pleasing ourselves versus bettering society or helping those less fortunate?

3. Three or four semesters ago, an Intro student, Ginny, wrote about the conflict she felt about angry stares she received when she dated her African American friend. She said white men had made nasty comments in a small restaurant just outside Winston-Salem, and black women had been hostile to her at a craft fair in Durham. In her paper, she tried to examine the different assumptions that she was making as opposed to the assumptions made by those who disapproved of her relationship with her boyfriend from high school. She explored whether the white men would have been just as disturbed if it had been an African American woman with a white male, and she analyzed what people assume who argue that one race is superior to another or that different races should be respectful but kept separate from one another.

4. I've had a number of students who wrote about their unhappiness at college, who really didn't want to attend but were going through the motions for their parents or grandparents. In such cases, I've suggested that students examine alternate ways of looking at parent-child relations, different assumptions behind different views of the obligations parents owe children and vice versa. I've also suggested they consider different ways of looking at the purpose of college—to establish a career, to save one's soul, to learn about one's culture, to play sports, to find a mate, to enjoy social life—and the assumptions about human nature and the good life that lie behind these different approaches to college.

Although I would like you to philosophically explore a conflict you care about, if this doesn't seem attractive, another alternative is to do a more traditional philosophic paper. For example, you could compare some articles we've read (like Bishop Paley's and Darrow's) or you could consider some traditional philosophic issues like capital punishment, abortion, premarital sex, just war, and so on. My only caution is that if you choose a more traditional sort of topic—since the "conversations" about them are so long and rich—you will need to do some library research so that you do not simply stay at the surface of the issue or repeat arguments which are by now well worn or overly familiar.

Please see this as an opportunity as well as a challenge!

Sincerely,

Steve Fishman

WORKS CITED

———————— ✦ ————————

In listing Dewey's writings, we use a code for citations found in *The Collected Works of John Dewey*. After giving the original publication date of the cited piece, we use letters and numbers to indicate its location in *The Collected Works*. We first identify the relevant volume as *Early, Middle,* or *Later Works* and then provide its number, the referenced pages, and the copyright date. All 34 volumes in *The Collected Works* are edited by Jo Ann Boydston and published by Southern Illinois University Press at Carbondale. They are divided as follows:

EW	*The Early Works, 1882-1898*
MW	*The Middle Works, 1899-1924*
LW	*The Later Works, 1925-1953*

Adler, Mortimer. *Reforming Education: The Schooling of a People and Their Education beyond Schooling*. Boulder: Westview, 1977.

Anselm, St. "There Exists Something than Which a Greater Cannot Be Thought." 1077–1078. *A Modern Introduction to Philosophy*. Ed. Paul Edwards and Arthur Pap. 3rd ed. New York: Free, 1973. 403–07.

Anson, Chris. "In Our Own Voices: Using Recorded Commentary to Respond to Writing." *Writing to Learn: Strategies for Assigning and Responding to Student Writing across the Disciplines*. Ed. Mary Dean Sorcinelli and Peter Elbow. San Francisco: Jossey-Bass, 1997. 105–114.

Applebee, Arthur. *Contexts for Learning to Write: Studies of Secondary School Instruction*. Norwood, NJ: Ablex, 1984.

Aquinas, St. Thomas. "The Five Ways." *A Modern Introduction to Philosophy*. Ed. Paul Edwards and Arthur Pap. 3rd ed. New York: Free, 1973. 408–10.

Atwell, Robert. "Doctoral Education Must Match the Nation's Needs and the Realities of the Marketplace." *Chronicle of Higher Education*. 29 Nov. 1996: B4–5.

Ayer, A. J. *Language, Truth, and Logic*. 1936. New York: Dover, 1952.

Belenky, Mary, Blythe Clinchy, Nancy Goldberger, and Jill Tarule. *Women's Ways of Knowing: The Development of Self, Voice, and Mind*. New York: Basic, 1986.

Bell, Daniel. *The Reforming of General Education: The Columbia College Experience in Its National Setting*. Garden City: Doubleday, 1968.

Berkenkotter, Carol. "Paradigm Debates, Turf Wars, and the Conduct of Sociocognitive Inquiry in Composition." *College Composition and Communication* 42.3 (May 1991): 151–169.

———. "A 'Rhetoric for Naturalistic Inquiry' and the Question of Genre." *Research in the Teaching of English* 27.3 (Oct. 1993): 293–304.

Berlin, Isaiah. *Four Concepts of Liberty*. New York: Oxford UP, 1970.

Berliner, David, and Bruce Biddle. *The Manufactured Crisis: Myths, Fraud, and the Attack on America's Public Schools*. New York: Addison-Wesley, 1995.

Bernstein, Richard. *John Dewey*. New York: Washington Square, 1967.

Bestor, Arthur. *Educational Wastelands: The Retreat from Learning in Our Public Schools*. Urbana: U of Illinois P, 1953.

Britton, James, Tony Burgess, Nancy Martin, Alex McLeod, and Harold Rosen. *The Development of Writing Abilities: 11–18*. London: Macmillan, 1975.

Brookfield, Stephen. *Becoming a Critically Reflective Teacher*. San Francisco: Jossey-Bass, 1995.

Brubacher, John. "Ten Misunderstandings of Dewey's Educational Philosophy." *Bulletin of the School of Education*. Indiana U 35 (1960): 27–42.

Buchler, Justus. *Charles Peirce's Empiricism*. New York: Harcourt, 1939.

———. "Reconstruction in the Liberal Arts." *Columbia College on Morningside*. Ed. Dwight Miner. New York: Columbia UP, 1954. 48–135.

Burnett, Joe. "What Ever Happened to John Dewey?" *Teachers College Record* 81 (1979): 192–210.

Carroll, Pamela: "John Dewey for Today's Whole Language Middle School." *Middle School Journal* 26 (Jan. 1995): 62–68.

Christ, Carol. "Why Women Need the Goddess: Phenomenological, Psychological, and Political Reflections." *Expanding Philosophical Horizons: A Nontraditional Philosophy Reader*. Ed. Max Hallman. Belmont: Wadsworth, 1995. 268–78.

Clifford, James. "On Ethnographic Authority." *Representations* 1.2 (1983): 118–46.

Clifford, James, and George Marcus, ed. *Writing Culture: The Poetics and Politics of Ethnography*. Berkeley: U of California P, 1986.

Cochran-Smith, Marilyn, and Susan Lytle. *Inside Outside: Teacher Research and Knowledge*. New York: Teachers College, 1993.

Cremin, Lawrence. *The Transformation of the School*. New York: Vintage, 1964.

Daiker, Donald, and Max Morenberg. *The Writing Teacher as Researcher: Essays in the Theory and Practice of Class-Based Research*. Portsmouth: Boynton/Cook-Heinemann, 1990.

Daly, Mary. "Transvaluation of Values: The End of Phallic Morality." *Expanding Philosophical Horizons: A Nontraditional Philosophy Reader*. Ed. Max Hallman. Belmont: Wadsworth. 159–71.

Darrow, Clarence. "The Myth of Immortality." 1928. *A Modern Introduction to Philosophy*. Ed. Paul Edwards and Arthur Pap. 3rd ed. NY: Free, 1973. 261–69.

Davis, Matthew. "Democratic Schooling: Toward a Renewed End-in-View." *Education and Culture* 13.2 (fall 1996): 29–35.

De Lima, Agnes. *Our Enemy, the Child*. 1926. New York: Arno, 1969.

Denzin, Norman. *Sociological Methods*. New York: McGraw, 1978.

Depencier, Ida. *The History of the Laboratory Schools: The University of Chicago, 1896–1957*. Chicago: U of Chicago P, 1960.

Descartes, Rene. *Discourse On Method and The Meditations*. Trans. F. E. Sutcliffe. Middlesex, UK: Penguin, 1983.

Dewey, John.

———. "Are the Schools Doing What the People Want Them to Do?" *Educational Review* 21 (May 1901): 459–74.

———. *Art As Experience*. 1934. New York: Capricorn, 1958.

———. "Attention." 1902. Brigham Young Educational Lectures. *LW*17: 269–83, 1990.

———. "Authority and Social Change." 1936. *LW*11: 130–45, 1991.

———. *The Child and the Curriculum*. 1902. *The School and Society. The Child and the Curriculum*. Introd. Philip Jackson. Chicago: U of Chicago P, 1990.

———. *A Common Faith*. 1934. New Haven: Yale UP, 1962.

———. "Construction and Criticism." 1930. *LW*5: 127–43, 1988.

———. "Creative Democracy: The Task before Us." *The Philosopher of The Common Man: Essays in Honor of John Dewey to Celebrate His Eightieth Birthday*. Ed. Sidney Ratner. New York: Putnam, 1940. 220–28.

———. *Democracy and Education*. 1916. New York: Free, 1967.

———. "The Democratic Faith and Education." 1944. *Problems of Men*. New York: Philosophical Library, 1946. 23–45.

———. "Does Human Nature Change?" 1938. *Problems of Men*. New York: Philosophical Library, 1946. 184–92.

———. "Education and Social Change." 1937. *Intelligence in the Modern World*. Ed. Joseph Ratner. New York: Random, 1939. 691–96.

———. "Education as Engineering." 1922. *MW*13: 323–28, 1983.

———. "Education as Politics." 1922. *MW*13: 329–34, 1983.

———. "The Educational Situation: As Concerns Secondary Education." 1902. *John Dewey on Education*. Ed. Reginald Archambault. Chicago: U of Chicago P, 1964. 404–21.

——. "Ethical Principles Underlying Education." 1897. *John Dewey on Education*. Ed. Reginald Archambault. Chicago: U of Chicago P, 1964. 108–38.

——. Ethics. 1932. *LW7*, 1989.

——. *Experience and Education*. 1938. New York: Collier, 1963.

——. *Experience and Nature*. 1st ed. 1925, 2nd ed. 1929. LaSalle: Open Court, 1989.

——. "Experience, Knowledge, and Value." *The Philosophy of John Dewey*. Ed. Paul Schilpp. Evanston: Northwestern UP, 1939. 517–608.

——. "From Absolutism to Experimentalism." 1930. *LW5*: 147–60, 1988.

——. "How Much Freedom in New Schools?" 1930. *LW5*: 319–25, 1988.

——. "How the Mind Learns." 1902. Brigham Young Educational Lectures. *LW17*: 213–25, 1990.

——. *How We Think*. Rev. ed. 1933. Lexington: Heath, 1960.

——. *Human Nature and Conduct*. 1922. New York: Modern Library, 1930.

——. *Individualism Old and New*. 1929. New York: Capricorn, 1962.

——. *Interest and Effort in Education*. 1913. Carbondale: Southern Illinois UP, 1975.

——. "Interest in Relation to Training of the Will." 1896. *John Dewey on Education*. Ed. Reginald Archambault. Chicago: U of Chicago P, 1964. 260–85.

——. "Introduction to Elsie Ripley Clapp's The Use of Resources in Education." *Dewey on Education: Selections*. Ed. Martin Dworkin. New York: Teachers College, 1959. 127–34.

——. *Liberalism and Social Action*. 1935. New York: Capricorn, 1963.

——. *Moral Principles in Education*. 1909. New York: Philosophical Library, 1959.

——. "The Need for a Philosophy of Education." 1934. *John Dewey on Education*. Ed. Reginald Archambault. Chicago: U of Chicago P, 1964. 1–14.

——. "The Need for Orientation." 1935. *Problems of Men*. New York: Philosophical Library. 1946. 88–92.

——. "The Period of Technic." 1902. Brigham Young Educational Lectures. *LW17*: 284–97, 1990.

——. "Philosophy and Civilization." 1927. *LW3*: 3–10, 1984.

——. "Philosophy and Democracy." 1919. *MW11*: 41–53, 1982.

——. "Philosophy and Education." 1930. *LW5*: 289–98, 1988.

——. *The Problems of Men*. New York: Philosophical Library, 1946.

——. "Progressive Education and the Science of Education." 1928. *Dewey on Education: Selections*. Ed. Martin Dworkin. New York: Teachers College, 1959. 113–26.

——. *Psychology. EW2*, 1887.

——. "The Psychology of the Elementary Curriculum." *The Elementary School Record* 1 (Dec. 1900): 221–32.

——. *The Public and Its Problems*. 1927. Athens: Swallow, 1988.

——. "Qualitative Thought." 1930. *LW5*: 243–62, 1988.

——. *The Quest for Certainty*. New York: Milton Balch, 1929.

——. *Reconstruction in Philosophy*. 1920. Boston: Beacon, 1962.

———. "The Relation of Theory to Practice in Education." 1904. *John Dewey on Education*. Ed. Reginald Archambault. Chicago: U of Chicago P, 1964. 313–38.

———. "Religion, Science, and Philosophy." 1936. *LW*11: 454–63, 1987.

———. *The School and Society*. 1900. *The Child and the Curriculum. The School and Society*. Intro. Philip Jackson. Chicago: U of Chicago P, 1990.

———. "Significance of the School of Education." *The Elementary School Teacher* 4 (Mar. 1904): 441–53.

———. "Social Aspects of Education." 1902. Brigham Young Educational Lectures. *LW*17: 226–42, 1990.

———. "Social Value of Courses." 1902. Brigham Young Educational Lectures. *LW*17: 310–22, 1990.

———. "Some Elements of Character." 1902. Brigham Young Educational Lectures. *LW*17: 336–47, 1990.

———. "Sources of a Science of Education." 1929. *LW*5: 3-40, 1988.

———. "Teaching Ethics in the High Schools." 1893. *EW*4: 54–61, 1967.

———. "The Theory of the Chicago Experiment." *The Dewey School: The Laboratory School of the University of Chicago, 1896–1903*. Katherine Camp Mayhew and Anna Camp Edwards. New York: Appleton–Century, 1936. 463–77.

———. "The Theory of Emotion." 1894. *EW*4: 152–69, 1971.

———. *Theory of Valuation*. Chicago: U of Chicago P, 1939.

———. "Three Years of the University Elementary School." 1899. Stenographic record. *The School and Society. The Child and the Curriculum*. Introd. by Philip Jackson. Chicago: U of Chicago P, 1990. 163–78.

———. "The University Elementary School." 1900. *MW*1: 317–20, 1976.

———. "The University Elementary School, Studies and Methods." *University Record* 21 May 1897. *The Dewey School: The Laboratory School of the University of Chicago, 1896–1903*. Katherine Camp Mayhew and Anna Camp Edwards. New York: Appleton-Century, 1936. 24–36.

———. *The Way Out of Educational Confusion*. Cambridge: Harvard UP, 1931.

Doheny-Farina, Stephen, and Lee Odell. "Ethnographic Research on Writing: Assumptions and Methodology." *Writing in Nonacademic Settings*. Ed. Lee Odell and Dixie Goswami. New York: Guilford, 1985. 503–35.

Edman, Irwin. *Philosopher's Holiday*. New York: Viking, 1938.

Edwards, Paul, and Arthur Pap. *A Modern Introduction to Philosophy*. 3rd ed. NY: Free, 1973.

Elbow, Peter. "Embracing Contraries in the Teaching Process." *Embracing Contraries*. New York: Oxford UP, 1986. 142–59.

———. "The Uses of Binary Thinking." *Journal of Advanced Composition* 12.1 (1993): 51–78.

———. *Writing Without Teachers*. New York: Oxford UP, 1973.

Emig, Janet. "The Tacit Tradition: The Inevitability of a Multi-Disciplinary Approach to Writing Research." *The Web of Meaning: Essays on Writing, Teaching, Learning, and Thinking.* Upper Montclair: Boynton/Cook, 1983. 146–56.

Featherstone, Joseph. "John Dewey and David Reisman: From the Lost Individual to the Lonely Crowd." *On the Making of Americans: Essays in Honor of David Riesman.* Ed. Herber Gans, Nathan Glazer, Joseph Gusfield, and Christopher Jencks. Philadelphia: U of Pennsylvania P, 1979. 3–39.

Feinberg, Walter. "Progressive Education and Social Planning." *Teachers College Record* 73 (1972): 485–505.

Fishman, Stephen M. "Explicating Our Tacit Tradition: John Dewey and Composition Studies." *College Composition and Communication* 44 (1993): 315–30.

Fishman, Stephen, and Lucille McCarthy. "Community in the Expressivist Classroom: Juggling Liberal and Communitarian Visions." *College English* 57 (Jan. 1995): 62–81.

———. "Is Expressivism Dead? Reconsidering Its Romantic Roots and Its Relation to Social Constructionism." *College English* 54 (Oct. 1992): 647–61.

———. "Teaching for Student Change: A Deweyan Alternative to Radical Pedagogy." *College Composition and Communication* 47:3 (Oct. 1996): 342–66.

Fleischer, Cathy. *Composing Teacher-Research: A Prosaic History.* Albany: State U of New York P, 1995.

Flesch, Rudolf. *Why Johnnie Can't Read.* 1955. New York: Harper, 1986.

———. *Why Johnnie Still Can't Read: A New Look at the Scandal of Our Schools.* New York: Harper, 1981.

Florio-Ruane, Susan, and Julie deTar. "Conflict and Consensus in Teacher Candidates' Discussion of Ethnic Autobiography." *English Education* 27.1 (Feb. 1995): 11–39.

Frankena, William. "The Naturalistic Fallacy." *Mind* 48 (1939). Rpt. in *Readings in Ethical Theory.* Ed. Wilfrid Sellars and John Hospers. New York: Appleton-Century-Crofts, 1970. 54–62.

———. *Three Historical Philosophies of Education.* Chicago: Scott, Foresman, 1965.

Fraser, Nancy, and Linda Nicholson. "Social Criticism without Philosophy: An Encounter between Feminism and Postmodernism." *Feminism/Postmodernism.* Ed. Linda Nicholson. New York: Routledge, 1990. 19–38.

Frazer, Elizabeth, and Nicola Lacey. *The Politics of Community: A Feminist Critique of the Liberal-Communitarian Debate.* Toronto: U of Toronto P, 1993.

Freedman, Sarah. *Response to Student Writing.* National Council of Teachers of English Research Report no. 23. Urbana: National Council of Teachers of English, 1987.

Fulwiler, Toby, and Art Young. *Programs That Work.* Portsmouth: Boynton/Cook, 1990.

Geertz, Clifford. *The Interpretation of Cultures*. New York: Basic, 1973.

——. *Works and Lives: The Anthropologist as Author*. Stanford: Stanford UP, 1988.

Gergen, Mary. "Toward a Feminist Metatheory and Methodology in the Social Sciences." *Feminist Thought and the Structure of Knowledge*. Ed. Mary Gergen. New York: New York UP, 1988. 87–104.

Gilmore, Perry, and Allan Glatthorn. *Children In the Out of Schools*: Washington, DC: Center for Applied Linguistics, 1982.

Goswami, Dixie, and Peter Stillman, ed. *Reclaiming the Classroom: Teacher Research as an Agency for Change*. Upper Montclair: Boynton/Cook, 1987.

Graves, Donald. *Writing: Teachers and Children at Work*. Portsmouth: Heinemann, 1983.

Greene, Maxine. "Dewey and American Education, 1894–1920." *John Dewey: Master Educator*. Ed. Willaim Brickman and Stanley Lehrer. Westport: Greenwood, 1975. 75–92.

Hallman, Max. *Expanding Philosophical Horizons, A Nontraditional Philosophy Reader*. Belmont: Wadsworth Publishing, 1995.

Harding, Sandra. "Feminism, Science, and the Anti-Enlightenment Critiques." *Feminism/Postmodernism*. Ed. Linda Nicholson. New York: Routledge, 1990. 83–106.

——. "Introduction: Is There a Feminist Method?" *Feminism and Methodology*. Ed. Sandra Harding. Bloomington: Indiana UP, 1987. 1–14.

——. *Whose Science? Whose Knowledge?: Thinking from Women's Lives*. Ithaca NY: Cornell UP, 1991.

Hartsock, Nancy. "Foucault on Power: A Theory for Women?" *Feminism/Postmodernism*. Ed. Linda Nicholson. New York: Routledge, 1990. 157–75.

Heath, Shirley Brice. "Ethnography in Education: Defining the Essentials." *Children In and Out of School: Ethnography and Education*. Ed. Perry Gilmore and Alan Glatthorn. Washington, DC: Center for Applied Linguistics, 1982. 33–55.

Herndl, Carl. "Writing Ethnography: Representation, Rhetoric, and Institutional Practices." *College English* 53.3 (March 1991): 320–32.

Hlebowitsh, Peter. "Critical Theory Versus Curriculum Theory: Reconsidering the Dialogue on Dewey." *Educational Theory* 42 (winter 1992): 69–82.

——. "The Forgotten Hidden Curriculum." *Journal of Curriculum and Supervision* 9.4 (summer 1994): 339–349.

Hofstadter, Richard. *Anti-Intellectualism in America*. New York: Vintage, 1963.

Holder, John. "An Epistemological Foundation for Thinking: A Deweyan Approach." *The New Scholarship on Dewey*. Ed. Jim Garrison. Dordrecht, Neth.: Kluwer, 1995. 7–24.

Holmes, John H. "Ten Reasons for Believing in Immortality." 1929. *A Modern Introduction to Philosophy*. Ed. Paul Edwards and Arthur Pap. 3rd ed. New York: Free, 1973. 250–60.

Hook, Sidney. *John Dewey: An Intellectual Portrait*. New York: John Day, 1939.

———. "John Dewey: His Philosophy of Education and Its Critics." *John Dewey on Education: Appraisals*. Ed. Reginald Archambault. New York: Random, 1966. 127–60.

———. *Out of Step*. New York: Harper, 1987.

Hubbard, Ruth S., and Brenda M. Power. *The Art of Classroom Inquiry: A Handbook for Teacher-Researchers*. Portsmouth: Heinemann, 1993.

Hutchins, Robert. *The Conflict in Education*. 1953. Westport: Greenwood, 1972.

Itzkoff, Seymour. *Cultural Pluralism and American Education*. Scranton: International Textbook, 1969.

Jackson, Philip. "Introduction." *The School and Society. The Child and the Curriculum*. John Dewey. Chicago: U of Chicago P, 1990. ix–xxxvii.

Jones, Donald. "Beyond the Postmodern Impasse of Agency: The Resounding Relevance of John Dewey's Tacit Tradition." *Journal of Advanced Composition* 16 (1996): 81–102.

Kirk, Russell. *The Conservative Mind: From Burke to Santayana*. Chicago: Henry Regnery, 1953.

Kirsch, Gesa, and Joy Ritchie. "Beyond the Personal: Theorizing a Politics of Location in Composition Research." *College Composition and Communication* 46.1 (Feb. 1995): 7–29.

Kliebard, Herbert. "The Question of Dewey's Impact on Curriculum Practice." *Teachers College Record* 89.1 (fall 1987): 139–41.

Lamont, Corliss, ed. *Dialogue on John Dewey*. New York: Horizon, 1959.

Larrabee, Harold. "John Dewey As Teacher." *John Dewey: Master Educator*. Ed. William Brickman and Stanley Lehrer. Westport: Greenwood, 1975. 93–100.

Lasch, Christopher. *The New Radicalism in America*. New York: Knopf, 1965.

Latour, Bruno, and Steve Woolgar. *Laboratory Life: The Construction of Scientific Facts*. Princeton: Princeton UP, 1979.

Lincoln, Yvonna. "The Making of a Constructivist: A Remembrance of Transformations Past." *The Paradigm Dialog*. Ed. Egon Guba. Newbury Park: Sage, 1990. 67–87.

Lincoln, Yvonna, and Egon Guba. *Naturalistic Inquiry*. Beverly Hills: Sage, 1985.

Locke, John. *Two Treatises of Government*. 1690. Ed. Thomas Cook. New York: Hafner, 1947.

MacIntyre, Alasdair. *After Virtue: A Study in Moral Theory*. Notre Dame: U of Notre Dame P, 1981.

Mathison, Sandra. "Why Triangulate?" *Educational Researcher* 17 (Mar. 1988): 13–17.

Mayhew, Katherine Camp, and Anna Camp Edwards. *The Dewey School: The Laboratory School of the University of Chicago, 1896–1903*. New York: Appleton-Century, 1936.

McCarthy, Lucille. "A Stranger in Strange Lands: A College Student Writing across the Curriculum." *Research in the Teaching of English* 21.3 (Oct. 1987): 233–65.

McCarthy, Lucille, and Stephen M. Fishman. "Boundary Conversations: Conflicting Ways of Knowing in Philosophy and Interdisciplinary Research." *Research in the Teaching of English.* 25.4 (Dec. 1991): 419–68.

———. "A Text For Many Voices: Representing Diversity in Reports of Naturalistic Research." *Ethics and Representation in Qualitative Studies of Literacy.* Ed. Peter Mortensen and Gesa Kirsch. Urbana: National Council of Teachers of English, 1996. 155–76.

McCarthy, Lucille, and Barbara Walvoord. "Models for Collaborative Research in Writing Across the Curriculum." *Strengthening Programs for Writing Across the Curriculum.* Ed. Susan McLeod. San Francisco: Jossey-Bass, 1988. 77–90.

McCaul, Robert. "Dewey, Harper, and the University of Chicago: September, 1903–June, 1904." *John Dewey: Master Educator.* Ed. Willam Brickman and Stanley Lehrer. Westport: Greenwood, 1975. 62–74.

Miles, Matthew, and A. Michael Huberman. *Qualitative Data Analysis.* Beverly Hill: Sage Publications, 1984.

Mill, John Stuart, and Harriet Taylor Mill. *Essays On Sex Equality.* Ed. Alice Rossi. Chicago: U of Chicago P, 1970.

Mills, C. Wright. *Sociology and Pragmatism: The Higher Learning In America.* 1943. Ed. Irving Horowitz. New York: Oxford U P, 1966.

Mohr, Marian, and Marion MacLean. *Working Together: A Guide for Teacher Researchers.* Urbana, IL: National Council of Teachers of English, 1987.

Mulhall, Stephen, and Adam Swift. *Liberals and Communitarians.* Oxford, Eng.: Blackwell, 1992.

Mumford, Lewis. *The Golden Day: A Study in American Experience and Culture.* New York: Boni and Liveright, 1926.

Murray, Donald. *A Writer Teaches Writing.* Boston: Houghton, 1968.

Myers, Greg. "Reality, Consensus, and Reform in the Rhetoric of Composition Teaching." *College Composition and Communication.* 48.2 (1986): 154–71.

National Commission on Excellence in Education. *A Nation at Risk: The Imperative for Educational Reform.* Washington, DC: GPO, 1983.

Newkirk, Thomas. *More than Stories.* Portsmouth: Heinemann, 1989.

Novack, George. *Pragmatism Versus Marxism.* New York: Pathfinder, 1975.

Odell, Lee, Dixie Goswami, and Anne Herrington. "The Discourse-Based Interview: A Procedure for Exploring the Tacit Knowledge of Writers in Nonacademic Settings." *Research on Writing: Principles and Methods.* Ed. Peter Mosenthal, Lynne Tamor, and Sean Walmsley. New York: Longman, 1983. 221–36.

Paine, Thomas. *Age of Reason.* Indianapolis: Bobbs-Merrill, 1957.

Paley, William. "The Watch and the Human Eye." 1802. *A Modern Introduction to Philosophy*. Ed. Paul Edwards and Arthur Pap. 3rd ed. New York: Free, 1973. 419–34.

Perkinson, Henry. *Two Hundred Years of American Educational Thought*. New York: McKay, 1976.

Peters, R.S. "John Dewey's Philosophy of Education." *John Dewey Reconsidered*. Ed. R.S. Peters. London: Routledge, 1977. 102–23.

Plato. *The Last Days of Socrates. Euthyphro. The Apology. Crito. Phaedo*. Trans. Hugh Tredennick. London: Penguin, 1969.

Polanyi, Michael. *The Tacit Dimension*. New York: Doubleday, 1966.

Pratt, Mary Louise. "Arts of The Contact Zone." *Profession* 91 (1991): 33–40.

Pritchard, Ruie Jane. "Effects on Student Writing of Teacher Training in the National Writing Project Model." *Written Communication* 4.1 (Jan. 1987): 51–67.

Randall, John Herman, Jr. "The Department of Philosophy." *A History of The Faculty of Philosophy, Columbia University*. Ed. Jacques Barzun. New York: Columbia UP, 1957. 102–45.

——. "John Dewey, 1859–1952." *The Journal of Philosophy*. 50.1 (1953): 5–13.

——. "The Religion of Shared Experience." *Philosophy after Darwin: Chapters for the Career of Philosophy*. Vol. 3. Ed. Beth Singer. New York: Columbia UP, 1977. 241–67.

Ratner, Joseph. "Dewey's Conception of Philosophy." *The Philosophy of John Dewey*. Ed. Paul Schilpp. Evanston: Northwestern UP, 1939. 49–73.

Ravitch, Diane. *The Troubled Crusade*. New York: Basic, 1983.

Ray, Ruth. *The Practice of Theory: Teacher Research in Composition*. Urbana, IL: National Council of Teachers of English, 1993.

Robertson, Emily. "Is Dewey's Educational Vision Still Viable?" *Review of Research in Education* 18 (1992): 335–67.

Rockefeller, Steven. *John Dewey: Religious Faith and Democratic Humanism*. New York: Columbia UP, 1991.

Rorty, Richard. *The Consequences of Pragmatism*. Minneapolis: U of Minnesota P, 1982.

Ruddock, Jean, and David Hopkins, eds. *Research as a Basis for Teaching: Readings from the Work of Lawrence Stenhouse*. London: Heinemann, 1985.

Rugg, Harold. *Foundations for American Education*. New York: World Book, 1947.

Rugg, Harold, and Anne Shumaker. *The Child-Centered School: An Appraisal of the New Education*. 1928. New York: Arno, 1969.

Russell, Bertrand. *Marriage and Morals*. 1929. New York: Liveright, 1970.

——. *Religion and Science*. 1935. London: Oxford UP, 1961.

Ryan, Alan. *John Dewey and the High Tide of American Liberalism*. New York: Norton, 1995.

Santayana, George. *Scepticism and Animal Faith*. 1923. New York: Dover, 1955.

Sarason, Seymour. *The Case for Change: Rethinking the Preparation of Educators*. San Francisco: Jossey-Bass, 1993.

Scheffler, Israel. *Four Pragmatists.* New York: Humanities P, 1974.

Schilpp, Paul, ed. *The Philosophy of John Dewey.* Evanston, IL: Northwestern UP, 1939.

Schniedewind, Nancy. "Cooperatively Structured Learning: Implications for Feminist Pedagogy." *Journal of Thought* 20.3–4 (fall 1985): 74–87.

Sheils, Merrill. "Why Johnny Can't Write." *Newsweek* (December 8, 1975): 58–65.

Shrewsbury, Carolyn. "What is Feminist Pedagogy?" *Women's Studies Quarterly.* 21.3–4 (fall/winter 1993): 8–16.

Slater, Philip. *The Pursuit of Loneliness.* 1970. Boston: Beacon, 1990.

Sleeper, Ralph. *The Necessity of Pragmatism: John Dewey's Conception of Philosophy.* New Haven: Yale UP, 1986.

Spelman, Elizabeth. "Woman as Body: Ancient and Contemporary Views." *Expanding Philosophical Horizons: A Nontraditional Philosophy Reader.* Ed. Max Hallman. Belmont, CA: Wadsworth, 1995. 32–44.

Spindler, George. *Doing the Enthnography of Schooling: Educational Anthropology in Action.* New York: Holt, 1982.

Spradley, James. *The Enthnographic Interview.* New York: Holt, 1979.

——. *Participant Observation.* New York: Holt, 1980.

Starhawk. "Witchcraft and Women's Culture." *Expanding Philosophical Horizons: An Nontraditional Philosophy Reader.* Ed. Max Hallman. Belmont: Wadsworth, 1995. 279–85.

Stedman, Lawrence. "An Assessment of Literacy Trends, Past and Present." *Research in the Teaching of English* 30.3 (Oct. 1996): 283–302.

Tedlock, Barbara. "From Participant Observation to the Observation of Participation: The Emergence of Narrative Ethnography." *Journal of Anthropological Research* 47.1 (spring, 1991): 69–94.

Trimbur, John. "Consensus and Difference in Collaborative Learning." *College English* 51.6 (Oct, 1989): 602–616.

Vygotsky, L.S. *Mind in Society: The Development of Higher Psychological Processes.* Ed. Michael Cole, Vera John-Steiner, Sylvia Scribner, and Ellen Souberman. Cambridge: Harvard UP, 1978.

Walvoord, Barbara, Linda Lawrence Hunt, H. Fil Dowling, Jr., and Joan D. McMahon. *In the Long Run: A Study of Faculty in Three Writing-Across-the Curriculum Programs.* Urbana: National Council of Teachers of English, 1997.

Walvoord, Barbara, and Lucille McCarthy. *Thinking and Writing in College: A Naturalistic Study of Students in Four Disciplines.* Urbana: National Council of Teachers of English, 1990.

Westbrook, Robert. *John Dewey and American Democracy.* Ithaca : Cornell UP, 1991.

White, Alan. "Dewey's Theory of Interest." *John Dewey Reconsidered.* Ed. R. S. Peters. London: Routledge 1977. 35–55.

Williams, Robert, ed. *John Dewey: Recollections.* Washington, DC: UP of America, 1982.

Wirth, Arthur. *John Dewey as Educator*. New York: Wiley, 1966.

Wissot, Jay. "Two Treatments of Cultural Difference: Dewey on Nationalism and Kallen on Pluralism." *Journal of the Midwest History of Education Society* 4 (1976): 49–59.

Young, Art. "Mentoring, Modeling, Monitoring, Motivating: Response to Students' Ungraded Writing as Academic Conversation." *Writing to Learn: Strategies for Assigning and Responding to Writing Across the Disciplines*. Ed. Mary Dean Sorcinelli and Peter Elbow. San Francisco: Jossey:Bass, 1997. 27–40.

Yutang, Lin. "Why I Am a Pagan." *Expanding Philosophical Horizons: A Nontraditional Philosophy Reader*. Ed. Max Hallman. Belmont: Wadsworth, 1995. 286–92.

Zeller, N.C. *A Rhetoric for Naturalistic Inquiry*. Diss. Indiana U, 1987.

Zilversmit, Arthur. *Changing Schools: Progressive Education Theory and Practice, 1930–1960*. Chicago: U of Chicago P, 1993.

INDEX

About the

Authors

———————— ✠ ————————

STEPHEN M. FISHMAN teaches philosophy at the University of North Carolina Charlotte. Since attending his first Writing Across the Curriculum workshop in 1983, he has been studying student writing and learning in his classes. He is an alumnus of Camp Rising Sun, Rhinebeck, New York.

LUCILLE MCCARTHY teaches composition and literature at the University of Maryland Baltimore County. She is the coauthor of two other books: *Thinking and Writing in College* with Barbara Walvoord (1990) and *The Psychiatry of Handicapped Children and Adolescents* with Joan Gerring (1988).

Together, Fishman and McCarthy have previously published a number of classroom studies. These have appeared in *College English, Research in the Teaching of English,* and *College Composition and Communication.*